100 THINGS
FLYERS FANS
SHOULD KNOW & DO
BEFORE THEY DIE

Adam Kimelman

TRIUMPH
B O O K S

Triumph Books and colophon are registered trademarks of Random House, Inc.

Library of Congress Cataloging-in-Publication Data

Kimelman, Adam, 1975-
  100 things Flyers fans should know & do before they die / Adam Kimelman.
    p. cm.
  ISBN 978-1-60078-396-8
  1. Philadelphia Flyers (Hockey team)—History. I. Title. II. Title: One hundred things Flyers fans should know & do before they die.
  GV848.P48K52 2010
  796.962'640974811—dc22
                                        2010013357

This book is available in quantity at special discounts for your group or organization. For further information, contact:
  Triumph Books
  542 South Dearborn Street
  Suite 750
  Chicago, Illinois 60605
  (312) 939–3330
  Fax (312) 663–3557
  www.triumphbooks.com

Printed in U.S.A.
ISBN: 978–1–60078–396–8
Design by Patricia Frey
All photos courtesy of AP Images unless otherwise indicated

For Flyers fans everywhere.

Contents

Foreword

Like every kid growing up in Quebec in the 1970s and '80s, I loved the Montreal Canadiens and hated the Philadelphia Flyers and their Broad Street Bullies reputation. I always felt like my favorite team never played well at the Spectrum, and I never understood why until many years later when I had to go into Philadelphia as a visiting player and realized just how tough it was there, especially in the playoffs.

As I became a professional hockey player and learned my way around the league, I saw just what kind of an organization the Flyers really were. And when I became a free agent in 2007, I knew Philadelphia was the place for me. But in the spirit of this book, *100 Things Every Flyers Fan Should Know & Do Before They Die*, you should know just how I came to pick the Flyers—and while the contract was nice, it was far from the only reason.

Goalie Marty Biron was here at the time, and playing with him again was a selling point, as was the chance to play with Simon Gagne. The travel being among the easiest in the NHL was a big deal. There was a chance to play with a group of young players like Mike Richards, Jeff Carter, Scottie Upshall, Joffrey Lupul, and Braydon Coburn, as well as older veterans like Mike Knuble, Scott Hartnell, Jason Smith, and Kimmo Timonen. And the chance to be a part of the Flyers family was impossible to pass up; it's no secret that Mr. Snider is one of the best and classiest owners in all of sports.

My time in Philadelphia has been very special, culminating in this past spring's amazing playoff run. Actually, it started Saturday morning, the day before the final game of the season. Not too many people knew that Coach Peter Laviolette made Richards, Gagne, Claude Giroux, Carter, and myself watch video of Rangers goalie Henrik Lundqvist on breakaways, and after Saturday's practice that he made the five of us practice our shootout moves at the end of the workout. I guess it worked, because without us winning that shootout the next day, we never would have made the playoffs.

Here's something else I'll let you know now—I never doubted we'd come back against Boston, even being down 3–0 in the series, until Game 7. Falling behind 3–0 in the first period, I'll admit now, had me a bit scared. But after James van Riemsdyk scored late in the first period, we could see Boston get scared, and we grabbed the momentum and won the game and the series.

Those are just some of the things that maybe you didn't know about me and my time with the Flyers. There's a lot more here, and I'm curious to learn some of the history of this great organization. I hope you'll have as much fun reading about it as I will.

—Danny Briere

1 Bob Clarke

There's no statue of Bob Clarke anywhere in the Delaware Valley. No schools named after him. No giant billboards with his picture along I–95 or any other highway. No radio show or TV commercials. No tell-all autobiography chronicling his life on and off the ice.

And that's exactly how Clarke likes it.

"I guess I'm not real comfortable having the attention directed at me," Clarke said. "Even though I know I played on a great team, was a decent player, and a lot of attention has come my way, I never enjoyed going out of my way to get more attention."

In the pantheon of Philadelphia sports, there might not be any more influential or important sports figure than Bob Clarke. From winning two Stanley Cups as a blood-and-guts leader on and off the ice to becoming an executive who built teams that went to the Stanley Cup Final three times, the conference finals seven times, and were in the playoffs 16 times in 17 full seasons (not counting the 2004–05 lockout or his aborted 2006–07 season), Clarke has earned his spot on the Mount Rushmore of Philadelphia sports.

It's Clarke who helped turn Philadelphia into a full-fledged hockey town and make the Flyers one of the NHL's benchmark franchises. No one outside of Ed Snider has been more dedicated to the orange and black.

"Bob Clarke, more than any other person…is responsible for the success the Flyers have had through the years," Snider said.

Clarke arrived in Philadelphia in 1969, and for more than 40 years, he's never really left. Even when he did leave, he was never

The teams that passed on Bobby Clarke in the 1969 draft because he was a diabetic passed on a two-time Stanley Cup champion, three-time MVP, and Hockey Hall of Famer. (AP Photo)

really gone—Clarke always maintained a house in South Jersey while he worked for the Minnesota North Stars and Florida Panthers.

It wasn't supposed to be this way. Clarke didn't possess impressive size, overwhelming speed, or a blistering shot. He came from a town that was remote even for western Canada—the mining town of Flin Flon, Manitoba, hard on the Saskatchewan border, a 12-hour drive north from Winnipeg.

Oh, and he was a diabetic. In the late 1960s, not much was known about the disease—only that it made you too sick to play pro hockey. "As long as I looked after myself, the diabetes wouldn't affect my game," Clarke said. "I was playing in Flin Flon, and I guarantee you the travel and the hockey life up there was a lot tougher than the hockey life in Philadelphia. And the [NHL] travel was a lot easier than it was in Flin Flon. So if I could play junior in Flin Flon and if I was good enough to play in the NHL, it was a lot easier to play in the NHL than it was up there."

The Flyers took him in the second round of the 1969 draft with the 17th pick, and within five seasons the Flyers won the first of back-to-back Stanley Cups. In 15 seasons, he had 358 goals, 852 assists, and 1,210 points. He's the club's all-time leading scorer, was league MVP three times, played in eight All-Star games, and was elected to the Hockey Hall of Fame in 1987.

"He never gave up," teammate Gary Dornhoefer said. "The fights for the puck, aggressiveness in the corner. He did whatever he had to do to win a hockey game. His attitude and how he played rubbed off on everyone else."

His run of success continued when he moved into the GM office in 1984. Things always seemed more interesting with Clarke in charge, and whether he was changing coaches, feuding with Eric Lindros, or eternally searching for that final piece to a Stanley Cup puzzle, Clarke always had winning in mind.

Why No Clarke? "We Already Have a Center"

There was little agreement among the Flyers' staff at the 1969 NHL Draft. Against his scouts' advice, GM Bud Poile took Cornwall Royals center Bob Currier with the sixth overall pick.

Top scout Gerry Melnyk stormed out of the room, and owner Ed Snider sent assistant GM Keith Allen to find out what the problem was. Allen reported Melnyk wanted to pick a center from Flin Flon, Manitoba, named Bobby Clarke. Melnyk believed Clarke would be the best player on the team the minute he arrived in Philadelphia.

Poile believed Currier was a can't-miss prospect. What about Clarke, Snider asked. "[Poile] said we already have a center, I don't need another center," was the response Snider received.

Snider had heard enough.

"I'm the kind of guy who lets executives make their own decisions, but I went over to Keith and I said, 'Look, if Clarke is there in the second round, I want you to tell Poile to take him,'" Snider said. "And Keith says I can't do that, I work for him. 'Just tell him that I want him, I want to take him.' Poile got very upset, but he took him."

"Through most of it, we were always competitive, we were always good, we were always trying to do the right things to try and win the Cup," Clarke said.

And when he decided to leave in 2006, he did it because he thought it was for the best of the club.

"He himself decided that he had done a poor job," Snider said the day Clarke quit as GM. "I think that's the measure of a man. I didn't ask him to leave; he decided to leave the position."

Bob Clarke remains a fixture in the Delaware Valley and a fixture with the Flyers as a senior vice president. He's a sounding board for GM Paul Holmgren, does some scouting, and occasionally works with the players on the ice. There have been job offers from other teams that would allow him to run a team again, but he's quite content in his current position.

"I've been here 40 years," Clarke said. "The few years that I was away I always had a home here.... This is home for me now.

"This is where they'll bury me, I suppose."

2 Walking Together Forever

They were eight words. Eight words that changed a hockey team and sparked them to a championship. And the players who saw those words firsthand still live them today:

Win together today and we walk together forever.

"The significance of it probably never hit home for 10 years," Bob Clarke said. "For me, anyway. Now, 35 years later, you still remember the players, you remember them with a fondness. You consider them a friend even if you haven't seen them in 10 years. It made a special bond among the men on that team. Like he said it would."

The words were scrawled on a chalkboard in the Flyers' locker room at the Spectrum by coach Fred Shero hours before they were to take the ice for the biggest game of their lives—Game 6 of the 1974 Stanley Cup Final against the Boston Bruins. The Flyers, in just their seventh year of existence, were about to do what was believed to be impossible. They were on the precipice of becoming the first expansion team, the first of the Second Six, to win the Holy Grail of hockey.

Shero's memorable words that May 19 afternoon are memorable and fitting. Shero, like his players, was overlooked and underestimated. Many saw the Flyers as the Broad Street Bullies, bloodthirsty animals who did little more than punch the puck into the net. They overlooked the four 30-goal scorers. They looked past Bernie Parent's 1.89 goals-against average and 12 shutouts.

The same goes for Shero. People remember him as The Fog and for his corny sayings. They missed the fact that the man was a visionary.

"He was one of the first to have an assistant coach and the video, breaking things down, doing some studying in Europe," Bill Barber said. "He was a man before his times."

Through his days coaching in the minor leagues, Shero learned how to get inside his players' heads and motivate them to be the best they could be—or better, perhaps, than they thought they could be.

It was Shero who convinced his team that giving the puck to Bobby Orr in the 1974 Finals would work. It was Shero who told his Flyers they could beat the Russians in 1976. And it was Shero who took equal parts brutality and finesse and created a championship equation.

"Freddy Shero was the perfect guy for this bunch of characters," said Keith Allen in Jim Jackson's *Walking Together Forever*. "He wasn't one of these guys who told them what they could and couldn't do at every turn. Instead, he let them develop their own personality as a team. As a result, the players developed a great deal of respect for him. He was loved by those guys."

Loved, but not always understood. That had to do with the frequent notes that appeared either on the locker room blackboard or in their locker stalls.

Some memorable Shero-isms:

"When you have bacon and eggs for breakfast, the chicken makes a contribution, but the pig makes a commitment."

"Success is not the result of spontaneous combustion. You must first set yourself on fire."

"There are no heroic tales without heroic tails."

And then there was his most memorable one, on that long-ago blackboard in the bowels of the Spectrum—"Win together today and we walk together forever."

"No truer words were ever said," Bob Kelly said.

3 Please Hurt 'Em, Hammer

What do Terry Carkner, Luke Richardson, Keith Acton, Behn Wilson, and Bob Dailey all have in common?

All pulled on an orange and black sweater more times than Dave Schultz.

In just 297 games—one game as a rookie in 1971–72, then four full seasons, 1972–76—no player in any town in any sport more defines a team than Dave "The Hammer" Schultz defines the Philadelphia Flyers.

"Davey is the player who gave the Broad Street Bullies their personality that the organization carried long after Davey was gone," said Bob Clarke in an interview on the Flyers' website. "We had good players, but that personality was a big part of our organization."

"When they talk about the Flyers winning back-to-back Stanley Cups, they talk about Bob Clarke, Bernie Parent, and I'm right there with them.... It's usually Clarke, Parent, and Schultz," Schultz said.

Schultz may have played just four seasons in Philadelphia, but what a memorable four seasons they were. The Flyers won a pair of

No player defined the Broad Street Bullies better than Dave Schultz. "When they talk about the Flyers winning back to back Stanley Cups," Schultz said, "it's usually Clarke, Parent, and Schultz." (AP Photo/Rusty Kennedy)

Stanley Cups, went to the Final three straight seasons, and memorably beat the Russian Central Red Army team in 1976.

He led the NHL in penalty minutes three times, including a league single-season record of 472 in 1974–75. His 1,386 penalty minutes rank him fifth on the club's all-time list.

Schultz had 51 goals and 115 points, but he's best remembered for bringing pugilistic excellence to a new level. Schultz made his mark by twice pummeling Chicago's Keith Magnuson, considered the NHL's top tough guy at the time. And some credit his beating of the Rangers' Dale Rolfe in Game 7 of the 1974 semifinals as the spark that pushed the Flyers to the Stanley Cup.

"That took something out of New York," Coach Fred Shero said that night. "They didn't do as much hitting after that."

Schultz did more than pummel the opposition. He hit double-figures in goals twice, including a career-best 20 in 1973–74. He had the primary assist on Bob Clarke's memorable overtime goal to beat the Bruins in Game 2 of the 1974 Stanley Cup Final, and he had two goals against the Sabres in Game 5 of the '75 Final.

But what Schultz will be most remembered for are the brawls. It was Schultz more than anyone else who epitomized the toughness of the Broad Street Bullies.

"It wasn't like we invented [fighting]," Schultz said. "We were trying to protect ourselves from the big, bad Bruins and the St. Louis Blues. We didn't invent it."

But thanks to Schultz, they mastered it. The master, though, didn't come to his craft until well into his hockey career.

When the native of Waldheim, Saskatchewan, was growing up playing junior hockey, "I had two fights in three years," he said. Instead, he was a scorer, producing 35 goals in 59 games with the Swift Current Broncos of the Western Canadian Junior Hockey League when he was 18. The Flyers selected him in the fifth round of the 1969 draft and sent him to the Salem Rebels of the Eastern Hockey League. That's when things started to change.

"Got in a fight in my first game, got in a fight my second game, did well in both games," Schultz said. "Never fought until I was 20 years old [but] three years in the minor leagues was a great training ground for me."

This Hammer Can Sing

Dave Schultz was used to knocking out players on the ice. But in the 1970s, he knocked them out on the charts.

Schultz's agents, looking to capitalize on his popularity, hooked him up with a songwriter, and the result was a love song called "Penalty Box." Some of the lyrics: "Love is like an ice hockey game, sometimes it can be rough/You got me checking and holding and hooking and then you blow the whistle on me."

Despite Schultz's far-from-*American Idol* vocal abilities and lame lyrics, the song was a big hit on Philadelphia Top 40 AM radio and flew off record store shelves.

That first year in Salem, Schultz finished with 32 goals and 356 penalty minutes. The following season, he had 14 goals and 382 penalty minutes with the Quebec Aces of the American Hockey League. Then in 1971–72, he had 18 goals and 392 penalty minutes with the AHL Richmond Robins. The following season, he brought his unique style of play to the NHL.

Schultz's time in Philadelphia ended following the 1976 play-offs, when he was dealt to the Los Angeles Kings.

He may have been gone, but the Hammer never will be forgotten. He's lived in the Delaware Valley since 1982, and he's been active at charity events for decades with the Flyers' alumni association. He received the ultimate honor from the club on November 16, 2009, when he was inducted into the team's Hall of Fame.

"Dave Schultz helped define Philadelphia Flyers hockey," Ed Snider said. "He played with a high level of intensity, always proudly defending the orange and black and making it difficult for our opponents. He never backed down and he fought hard every night, wearing his heart on his sleeve. While his temporary home was in the penalty box, we're glad that he will have a permanent home in the Philadelphia Flyers Hall of Fame."

Eric Lindros—The Good, the Bad, and the Ugly

In the 40-plus year history of the Philadelphia Flyers, no player ever has generated more headlines than Eric Lindros. From his sea-changing arrival to his acrimonious departure, through all the rumors and innuendos, concussions and contract holdouts, every day on the Flyers' beat seemed like another day on Lindros watch.

There was a great deal of good accomplished during Lindros' eight seasons in Philadelphia. He had 290 goals and 369 assists for 659 points in 486 games. He won the 1995 Hart Trophy and finished second in the 1994–95 NHL scoring race with 70 points in just 46 games. He scored at least 40 goals four times and had personal bests of 47 goals and 115 points in 1995–96.

"He came to practice every day, and he was one of the hardest-working players on the ice every day in practice," said Terry Murray, who coached Lindros from 1994–97.

"I always got along great with Eric," said Rod Brind'Amour, a teammate for eight seasons. "I thought he cared, I thought he played hard, and I always supported him."

Lindros' run in the middle of the Legion of Doom line with John LeClair and Mikael Renberg was the high-water mark for his career, as that group led the Flyers to the Eastern Conference Finals in 1995 and the Stanley Cup Final in 1997.

But there always seemed to be off-ice issues swirling around Lindros, like rain clouds in South Florida, that could burst at any time. Whether it was injuries, contract squabbles, or other issues, there always seemed to be some dark cloud following the franchise and its star player.

"The big interference came from his mom and dad," Murray said. "When they came into town and were staying with him for

No player in Flyers history generated more headlines—good and bad—than Eric Lindros. (AP Photo/Michael Caulfield)

several days at a time, you could always see a different Eric coming to the rink every day. He had different questions, he had a lot of concerns on his mind, and he was a little more distracted. When everybody was away and he was there and just playing hockey, he was a real good player."

Lindros was only 24 when the '97 playoffs ended. But that Cup Final series was as good as it would get during the Lindros Era in Philadelphia.

On March 8, 1998, Lindros suffered the first diagnosed concussion of his NHL career, when Pittsburgh's Darius Kasparaitis caught him with a big hit to the head, an injury that sidelined him for five weeks. Eight months later came concussion No. 2, and while he missed just a few games in the 1998–99 season, that campaign is best remembered for Lindros' near-fatal collapsed lung suffered in Nashville on April 1, 1999.

The 1999–2000 season featured a bizarre six-month span that saw No. 88 suffer four concussions, publicly rip the team and its medical and training staff, and be stripped of the captaincy.

Lindros made two final appearances for the Flyers in Games 6 and 7 of the 2000 Eastern Conference Finals against New Jersey. Lindros was the Flyers' best player in a Game 6 loss, and had a special cheering section.

"I sat there in the press box for Game 6 right next to [GM Bob] Clarke," Gormley said. "I never saw Clarke root harder for somebody than for Lindros that night. He was just, 'Come on Eric, come on Eric.'"

The Flyers lost Game 6 and then lost Lindros early in Game 7 on the now-famous seismic hit by Devils defenseman Scott Stevens. "Once that happened," Gormley said, "everyone knew his career was over. I thought his career as a Flyer was over the second that hit happened."

Gormley was right, as all the bad feelings spilled out in public as Lindros sat out the 2000–01 season while demanding a trade.

Lindros first said the only team he would play for was the Toronto Maple Leafs, but Clarke was adamant in saying he would make the best trade for the Flyers.

The saga finally came to an end August 20, 2001, as the Flyers dealt Lindros to the Rangers for defenseman Kim Johnsson, forwards Jan Hlavac and Pavel Brendl, and a draft pick.

Nearly a decade later, Clarke still doesn't understand how things went so wrong.

"Through most of all the messes that went on, I liked Eric, I liked his dad," Clarke said. "I wish it had worked differently.... I don't know or understand so much that went on. Everybody had the right intent, the results were different."

5 Cup-Winning Goal by MacLeish

For Ed Snider, it's no surprise that Rick MacLeish scored the biggest goal in franchise history. "Only Rick could have done what he did," Snider said. "He had such great hand-eye coordination."

MacLeish didn't always hear those kinds of platitudes from his boss or the fickle Philadelphia fans.

MacLeish, a high scorer in junior hockey who the Boston Bruins took with the fourth pick of the 1970 draft, came to Philadelphia as part of the three-way trade in 1971 that sent Bernie Parent to the Maple Leafs. He had just two goals in 26 games after the trade and one goal in 17 games the following season. That earned him a ticket to the minor leagues, which allowed him to escape the ever-growing Spectrum boo-birds.

"Rick is a victim of his own good success in juniors," said GM Keith Allen at the time. "He was so good at Peterborough in his last year he didn't have to bear down to get results. When he came here, he played at the same tempo—too casual. He wasn't explosive. He didn't seem to realize that even the stars have to work hard up here."

MacLeish came back the next season, and motivated by competition with rookie Bill Clement for the second-line center job, he was the team's best player in training camp in 1972. His play carried on all season long, as he became the first Flyer ever to score 50 goals.

In 1973–74, he had 32 goals and became the club's best player in the postseason.

"He was the best player we had in every one of our playoff series," linemate Ross Lonsberry said in Jim Jackson's *Walking Together Forever*. "Part of that may have been because so much attention was paid to the Clarke line. However, Ricky was bigger and faster, and he scored so many big goals for us in the playoffs. He was so important to our success."

Never was he more important than on May 19, 1974.

In the first period of Game 6 of the Stanley Cup Final, MacLeish redirected a Moose Dupont shot past Bruins goalie Gilles Gilbert for the only goal in the 1–0 Cup-clinching victory.

"It was a simple play, really," MacLeish told Jackson. "I won the draw and went to the net. Moose took a regular wrist shot and I tried to tip it down just to change it up a bit, and wouldn't you know, it went in. It's something we practiced hundreds of times. In truth, it was a lucky goal."

The goal came at 14:48 of the first period. That left the Flyers more than 45 minutes to hold on to the lead against the highest-scoring team in the league. No way that stands up, right?

"I never in a million years thought one goal would stand up as the game-winner," MacLeish told Jackson. "Not against the Boston Bruins."

But with MacLeish, Lonsberry, and Gary Dornhoefer on the checking line and Parent in goal, the Flyers held on. To Bob Clarke, it was a victory for team play against individuals.

"Not letting the Bruins score is pretty hard to do," Clarke said. "We were a much more determined team than they were. We were a team; they were a lot of individual stars. Espo [Phil Esposito] was taking three-minute shifts and stuff through the whole series, and we were using three lines, rotating against him. I'd start against him, and then [Orest] Kindrachuk would play against him, MacLeish might play against him. They're taking those long shifts, eventually you run out of gas."

MacLeish and the Flyers never did, however, and now a player who was ridiculed as lazy and uninterested early in his career holds a revered place in team history.

6 Somerdale Elementary School and the Wall of Sorrow

Pulling into the parking lot of the former Somerdale Elementary School has the feel of driving onto an abandoned graveyard. The school has long since closed down, with boards on the windows and No Trespassing signs all around.

The wall that frames the school looks like it's dying a slow death, as well. The 4-foot high cement structure is dirty and dilapidated, with the paint chipping off in many spots.

But there's more than that. The wall is cold—far colder than the usual concrete wall. It's not the feeling of death, but the ground near where the wall meets the steps that marks the front of the school is littered with busted car parts—red and orange and white plastic that used to be headlights and turn signals.

There's no saying if one of them came off a turbo-charged 1983 Porsche 930 around 5:45 AM on Sunday, November 10, 1985. But you have to think if those broken pieces of plastic could

Lindbergh's Final Saves

Pelle Lindbergh was taken off life support on November 12, 1985. The only reason he had been left on for so long was to harvest his organs for transplant—in all reality, Lindbergh was dead the moment his Porsche slammed into the concrete wall outside Somerdale Elementary School.

Lindbergh's corneas helped a pair of patients regain their sight, one of them a 6-year-old girl. His liver saved another man, while another patient received both of Lindbergh's kidneys. His heart went to a 52-year-old man named John Keeler—coincidentally, a Flyers' season-ticket holder.

talk, maybe one of them could tell a story. A story about how the premier goalie of his generation, months removed from guiding his team to a Stanley Cup Final and winning a Vezina Trophy, could have ended up here.

Lindbergh loved his Porsche. He had bought it new in Germany for $52,000 and immediately had another $41,000 of upgrades done to make it faster. The speedometer went to 190 mph, and Lindbergh told friends he got it up to 150 on the Autobahn.

"He scared me," Bob Clarke said in *Full Spectrum*. "We told Pelle he had to slow down."

Clarke wasn't the only one.

"I had stopped driving with him about a month before," said Al Morganti, who covered the team for the *Philadelphia Inquirer* and counted Lindbergh as his closest friend in or out of hockey. "I'd go to Atlantic City with him, and I'd be there before we left. We all told him to slow down."

In the end, though, Lindbergh didn't listen. According to the Lindbergh biography, *Behind the White Mask*, a heavily impaired Lindbergh, driving upwards of 80 mph, didn't hit the brakes until he was about 10 feet away from the wall. Too little, too late.

The driver's side bore the greatest brunt of the accident. The entire front end was pushed back into the passenger cabin. The windshield took off like a cannon-shot, landing about 40 feet away.

Lindbergh had two passengers in his car—a friend, Ed Parvin, who Pelle was driving home, and Kathy McNeal, a friend of teammate Rick Tocchet. Both survived but suffered long-lasting injuries.

The news rattled the entire Delaware Valley, not to mention the entire NHL. Other Philadelphia athletes were grief-stricken. "The news has shaken all of Philadelphia," the Sixers' Julius Erving said. "What happened is extremely sad. Now we're all thinking about Pelle, his family, and the Flyers."

Morganti still carries a Lindbergh jersey with him when he talks to school groups and high school hockey teams about the dangers of drinking and driving.

"It's the only jersey I own of anybody's," he said. "I've used him to help other people." He also brings along three pictures—a photo of a smiling Lindbergh, a photo of the wrecked Porsche, and a photo of the memorial at the Spectrum. And there's a message with the photos—"It just takes one time to ruin a life."

Sit in that spot on the wall today and you can see cars coming down Somerdale Road, right at you, until about 50 or 60 feet before their grille is on top of yours, and then the road curves sharply to the right.

It's easy to see how a drunk driver—even one with the superior reflexes that allowed him to stop a small piece of vulcanized rubber moving upwards of 90 mph—racing 80 mph down a two-lane residential street could lose control.

In that moment, the breeze blows a little colder, the sun ducks behind a cloud, and you get that not-so-good feeling in the pit of your stomach. Something very bad happened on this spot.

It's a tough place for any Flyers fan to visit, even 25 years after the accident that claimed the life of Pelle Lindbergh. But it's a pilgrimage worth making if for no other reason than the chance to say a sort of farewell and have a bit of hope that this is the only site of its kind you'll ever have to visit.

7 Only the Lord Saved More Than Bernie Parent

Hockey may be the ultimate team game, but when it comes to winning a Stanley Cup, teams don't win unless their goaltender plays at the top of his game. It was as true in 1925 as it was in 1975, and as true as it'll be in 2075.

And there's no way the Flyers would have won their two Stanley Cups without Bernie Parent in net.

"He's the only guy on the team that we couldn't have won without," Bob Clarke said. "We could have taken anybody out, taken any other player off the team and still would have won. Take Bernie off—we wouldn't have."

There's no arguing that statement.

Not much was known about Parent when the Flyers made him the second goalie chosen in the 1967 expansion draft. Parent had been playing with the Boston Bruins farm team in Oklahoma City—about as far off the hockey map as you can get. But it didn't take long to see Parent had a wealth of talent.

In his first full NHL season, he led the Flyers to the Western Division title. Parent guided the Flyers into the playoffs twice in their first three seasons, but in 1970–71, owner Ed Snider and GM Keith Allen came to a painful realization—the Flyers' best chance of winning a Stanley Cup would be with the bounty they could get by trading Parent.

In the two seasons the Flyers won the Stanley Cup, there was no more important player than Bernie Parent. (AP Photo/Brian Horton)

"I cried when he left," Snider said of the January 31, 1971, deal that sent Parent to Toronto. That the Flyers got Rick MacLeish from Boston in the three-way deal was little salve. "I put my arms around him because the guy did everything right. He was a great guy, great player, but we didn't have any assets to build with…. We would never win the Cup in Parent's lifetime if we didn't make some moves."

Parent spent part of two seasons with the Maple Leafs, where he partnered with his idol, Jacques Plante. "Spending two years with him took me from a raw goalie talent, and he helped me become a better goalie," Parent said.

The Flyers continued to build, and when they needed one last piece to go over the top—a top-flight goaltender—they brought Parent back. "It was a great feeling," Parent said of returning on May 15, 1973. "I knew the team, the team had gotten a lot better, and I knew the team had a chance to do something. I was going back to a team that was ready to explode."

"That was the great move," Snider said. "That was the greatest moment. To get him back was such a coup."

In his first season back, 1973–74, Parent had possibly the greatest season of any goaltender in the history of the league. He won an NHL-record 47 games, played a league-high 73 games (in a 78-game season), led the NHL with a 1.89 goals-against average and 12 shutouts, and won the Vezina Trophy as the league's best goaltender.

In the playoffs he allowed just 35 goals in 17 games, had a pair of shutouts—including 1–0 in the Cup-clinching Game 6—and won the Conn Smythe Trophy as playoff MVP. It was just the fourth time ever a team has won the greatest trophy in sports by the slimmest of margins, and it hasn't happened since.

"Parent in that particular game played the best game any player's ever played for the franchise," Clarke said.

For an encore the next season, Parent led the league with 44 wins, a 2.03 GAA, and 12 shutouts. He won another Vezina Trophy, and in the playoffs he was better than the previous season. He allowed just 29 goals in 15 games, had four shutouts, again turned in a shutout in the Cup-clinching game, and won his second straight Conn Smythe Trophy.

A series of injuries conspired to derail Parent's strong play, culminating with his career-ending eye injury in 1979.

Still, what Parent accomplished from 1973–75 stands as a benchmark for not just the franchise but for goaltenders everywhere.

"With a different goalie we would have won a lot of games but probably not the Cup," Clarke said.

8 Eric Lindros and How a Trade Is Made

The Eric Lindros Era in Philadelphia is best remembered for what might have been. Controversy and turmoil always seemed to surround Lindros.

"Everything with Eric was always chaos with him," said longtime hockey writer and Philadelphia media member Al Morganti. "Nothing was clean."

There was advanced warning of what was to come on the day the Flyers traded for him.

Lindros was taken first in the 1991 NHL Draft by the Quebec Nordiques even after the Lindros camp had informed anyone who would listen that Eric wouldn't play for the team. Sticking to his word, Lindros instead played for his junior team, the Oshawa

Generals, and then for Canada at the World Junior Championships and the 1992 Winter Olympics.

Worried Lindros would hold true to his vow to sit out two seasons and re-enter the draft, the Nordiques went to the 1992 draft with the intent of holding their own version of "Let's Make A Deal," with Lindros the prize.

Flyers GM Russ Farwell knew what Quebec wanted and saw very few teams being able to meet owner Marcel Aubut's demands—which included a non-negotiable $15 million cash payment.

"They would always talk whatever the cash was going to be in addition [to the players]," Farwell said. "We had a number of meetings, and we met with [team president] Jay [Snider] and his dad [owner Ed Snider] one time, and we kind of worked it out and there were very few teams that could meet what Quebec was looking for. We were down, we were motivated, and yet we had a little more depth than other teams in the market. And teams that had players couldn't satisfy them from a cash standpoint. We thought at the end of the day we would be one of the only one or two available contenders."

Nordiques GM Pierre Page asked for Mark Recchi and Rod Brind'Amour, but Farwell said those were the only two players on the roster off limits. After a marathon negotiating session, Jay Snider got a knock on his hotel room door after 1:00 AM. It was Aubut, and he had names written on a sheet of paper. According to Tim Wharnsby's story in the *Toronto Globe and Mail*, Aubut tossed the sheet of paper at Snider and said, "Give us these players and conditions, and you have got yourself Eric Lindros."

The names on the paper: Forward Mike Ricci, defensemen Steve Duchesne and Kerry Huffman, goaltender Ron Hextall, the rights to Swedish prospect Peter Forsberg, first-round picks in 1992 and '93, and $15 million.

Lindros Deal Changed the Game

Prior to the Eric Lindros trade, NHL deals would be worked out over cocktails and written down on napkins, and then someone would get around to calling NHL Central Registry during normal business hours.

"The Lindros deal changed how deals were made," said Russ Farwell, who was the Flyers' GM when the Lindros trade happened. "Every deal was a handshake or a napkin, and you just worked it out. But that deal went sideways, and now it wasn't a deal until everything was on paper and a league person saw it."

The next morning Snider agreed to Aubut's demands and wanted to speak to Lindros. Aubut gave them Lindros' phone number—a key element, because the Nords said no one would be allowed to speak to Lindros until a deal was done.

Less than two hours later, though, chaos broke loose. After accepting the Flyers' deal at 10:30 AM, Aubut met with Rangers president Stanley Jaffe and GM Neil Smith and traded Lindros to the Rangers, reportedly for forwards Doug Weight, Tony Amonte, and Alexei Kovalev, defenseman James Patrick, goalie John Vanbiesbrouck, three first-round picks, and $12 million.

Aubut called Jay Snider to inform him of the change in plans. Snider responded by filing a grievance with NHL president John Ziegler. Toronto lawyer Larry Bertuzzi was hired to arbitrate the dispute. Ten days later, on June 30, 1992, Bertuzzi made his decision.

"It was the natural thought that the NHL is going to take care of the Rangers because they're New York," recalled longtime Philadelphia sports radio personality Howard Eskin. "[Philadelphia fans] always have that defeatist attitude that thinks New York gets everything. [Fans] were waiting, but the only thought they had was, it's New York and there was no way the Flyers would get him."

But the Flyers did get him.

Bertuzzi ruled that the late-night meeting between Aubut and Jay Snider, and the Flyers' subsequent acceptance of the deal, made for an oral contract and a valid trade agreement. And when he factored in how the Flyers had been given permission to speak with Lindros, Bertuzzi awarded the future star to the Flyers.

9 Clarkie's Greatest Hits

There's really no questioning who the greatest player in Flyers history is. He wore No. 16, won three NHL MVPs, captained the team to a pair of Stanley Cups, and earned a rightful place in the Hockey Hall of Fame after he retired.

But good luck to anyone who wants to get Bob Clarke talking about how great Bobby Clarke was as a player. There are desk drawers with bigger egos.

"I know I played on a great team, was a decent player," Clarke said. And he's not being modest when he says these things. Clarke really doesn't judge himself by the goals he scored or points he totaled.

When asked what the most memorable moments were of a career overflowing with them, his response was perfect Clarke. "Mostly the two Cups, the 35-game [unbeaten] streak," he said. No mention of the memorable overtime goal he scored in Boston in Game 2 of the 1974 Stanley Cup Final. No mention of how that score in Boston Garden—a house of horrors for the Flyers for most of their existence—gave a young team the confidence it needed to win its first championship.

No, Clarke soft-sells that goal like he does the other 358 goals and 1,210 points he racked up during his 15 NHL seasons, all with the Flyers. Clarke completely glosses over the fact that he ranks as the franchise's all-time leader in assists (852), points, games played (1,144), and shorthanded goals (32), or that he's in the top-five all-time for the franchise in goals (fourth, 358), penalty minutes (fourth, 1,453), and power-play goals (fifth, 99). Or that he's one of four players in NHL history to have a plus–.500 rating.

He's also the club's all-time leading playoff performer, holding the marks for games played (136), assists (77), and points (119). His 42 goals are fifth, and his seven game-winning goals are tied for fourth. But none of that really rings his bell.

The only time Clarke cops to any individual achievement standing out in his mind comes from 1982–83, his second-to-last season when at age 33 he won the Frank Selke Trophy as the league's best defensive forward.

"I thought that was pretty impressive," Clarke said. "Winning the Selke [Trophy] was pretty important to me. After having a fair amount of offensive success and MVPs and stuff, late in my career being the best defensive forward in the game…I think it completed my circle, that I could play forward, I could play defense—I could play hockey, that I knew both ends of the rink and could play both ends of the rink and was willing to play both ends of the rink."

To a man who defines himself by team, it's easier to let his teammates talk about him.

"Bob was a great individual," Bernie Parent said. "He cared about the players, cared about the team. It's a prime example of what leadership does for a team. I played with a lot of players in 15 years, and Bob without any doubt in my mind was one of the best leaders who ever played the game."

"He was as hard-working a player as there's ever been in sports," Dave Schultz said. "He was just dedicated to the game and to his team. It was great playing with him. He just did it all. He never stopped. I can take a couple shifts off, can't play phenomenal every shift, but he played well very consistently and he made everyone else step it up.

"He wanted to win so bad. I guess all players do, but some can't get there. To handle the pressure and to play as much as he did, it takes a phenomenal athlete."

"The team was the ultimate and he was the ultimate captain," Joe Watson said. "I don't think there was a better captain in professional sports than Clarke was."

10 Building the Bullies

Ed Snider never played hockey, but even he could see what was happening to his team in its first two seasons, which ended in first-round playoff losses to the St. Louis Blues.

His players were getting their tails kicked.

"We played St. Louis, and they had the Plager brothers [Barclay and Bob] and [Noel] Picard, and these guys were tough fighters," Snider said. "We had all these little French guys."

Those little French guys helped the Flyers make the playoffs their first two seasons, but that wasn't going to be good enough when teams like St. Louis could just bludgeon them.

"Teams had in those days what they called a policeman," Snider said. "When [Toronto's] John Ferguson takes on Simon Nolet, Simon Nolet didn't do bad in that fight, but he should have gotten the hell beat out of him. He was so scared. But when I see those kinds of things, I think, who said there can only be one policeman?"

Snider didn't just go out and get his own policeman—he got a whole precinct.

"We might not be able to skate with these guys, we may not have the talent the Original 6 [teams] have, but we'll build our team with one thing—we can be as tough as anybody else," Snider recalled. "Let's just go out and get tough guys, and nobody is going to intimidate or beat up our players ever again."

Snider started his plan at the 1969 NHL Draft. In the second round, Philadelphia chose Bob Clarke, a dynamic center from Flin Flon, Manitoba, who had three straight seasons of 50 goals, 130 points, and 120 penalty minutes.

In the fifth round, they picked a 6'1", 190-pound winger from Waldheim, Saskatchewan, named Dave Schultz; one round later, they took another rough-and-tumble winger, Don Saleski.

Keith Allen replaced Bud Poile as GM in 1970 and set out to add professionalism and toughness to the defense. Allen knew of a defenseman toiling with the Hershey Bears, the Bruins' minor-league affiliate. Barry Ashbee, who had missed the 1966–67 season following back surgery, was buried in the Bruins' organization. Allen, in his second trade as GM, sent Darryl Edestrand and Larry McKillop to Boston for Ashbee.

Ashbee's willingness to play through a debilitating list of injuries rubbed off on his younger teammates and inspired them to push aside their own aches and pains. "He was the strongest guy mentally that I've ever seen," Clarke said in *Walking Together Forever*.

In the 1970 draft, Bill Clement was taken in the second round and Bob "The Hound" Kelly in the third.

In 1971, Allen acquired Rick MacLeish from the Boston Bruins, but the cost was high—goaltender Bernie Parent. "I cried when he left," Snider said of the January 31, 1971, deal. "He was a great guy, great player, but we didn't have any assets to build with…. We would never win the Cup in Parent's lifetime if we didn't make some moves."

Allen continued to tinker during 1972, adding Cowboy Bill Flett and Ross Lonsberry in a seven-player trade with Los Angeles in January; drafting Bill Barber, Tom Bladon, and Jimmy Watson in the first three rounds of the 1972 draft; and trading for Andre "Moose" Dupont in December.

Leading the Flyers was a relatively unknown coach hired out of the New York Rangers organization named Fred Shero. "I didn't know Freddie well, but I had followed his career and he had won everywhere," Allen said in *Full Spectrum*. "The only thing that made me wonder was why [Rangers GM] Emile Francis had given other guys a chance [to coach the Rangers] and never given one to Freddie. But his record was so good, and I'd never heard anyone say a bad word about him."

Shero melded the attacking style of the 1970s Russians with a physical, take-no-prisoners approach. It was something that hadn't been seen before in the NHL. Clarke, Barber, and MacLeish scored the goals, and Schultz, Kelly, Saleski, and Dupont supplied the intimidation.

The biggest piece of the puzzle, though, was still to come.

Parent had left Toronto for the World Hockey Association for the 1972–73 season, but he quit playing when his paychecks stopped coming. He wanted back into the NHL but not with the Leafs, who maintained his NHL rights. He wanted to come back to the Flyers, and Allen made it happen by sending the Maple Leafs goalie Doug Favell and a first-round pick.

"That was the great move," Snider said of the May 15, 1973, deal. "That was the greatest moment. To get him back was such a coup."

One year and four days later, Clarke, Parent, and the rest of the Flyers were Stanley Cup champions.

11 Ron Hextall, Hockey Pioneer

Ron Hextall was unlike anything anyone had ever seen in hockey. Whether it was scoring goals or starting brawls, his size (6'3", 192 pounds), skill, and temperament set him apart from anyone who ever played the position.

Hextall was just 22 when he started in net for the Flyers on opening night of the 1986–87 season, and he didn't waste time making an impression. On opening night, Edmonton's Wayne Gretzky came down on a breakaway. Hextall dragged a pad to make the save, and as Gretzky started back up the ice he yelled at Hextall, "Who the hell are you?"

Hextall shot back, "Who the hell are you?"

Hextall had that attitude every minute he was on the ice. And it didn't seem to matter if it was a game against the defending Stanley Cup champions or a mid-week, mid-season practice.

"Brian Propp after shots [in practice] would go by the net and put pucks in the net, he was just that way," Rick Tocchet said. "It would bug Hexy and Hexy would go after him."

"Sitting in between periods [of games], he was so intense, he would sit and rock the whole intermission," Kjell Samuelsson recalled. "Then he would put his gear on and go out. It's like every period he walked into a fight. That was his thing. Every time he stepped on the ice, he was full out."

In his first season, Hextall won the Vezina Trophy and back-stopped the Flyers to the 1987 Stanley Cup Final.

"For a full 80-game schedule, that was the best goaltending I've ever seen," Mark Howe said. "Especially in the Final, as good as we played and as close as we came, we wouldn't have been that close without Ron Hextall—there's no doubt about it."

Whether he was starting fights or scoring goals, Ron Hextall did things in goal no one ever had done before. (AP Photo/Rusty Kennedy)

Hextall guarded his net with the ferocity of a rabid pit bull. He finished his career with 584 penalty minutes, the most ever by a goaltender. He famously slashed the Oilers' Kent Nilsson during the 1987 Stanley Cup Final, and chased down Montreal's Chris

Chelios, pounded him, and chucked his blocker at him in the 1989 Wales Conference Finals.

Now the assistant GM for the Los Angeles Kings, Hextall says he regrets nothing.

"The only thing I can say was when I was on the ice, I had a job to do, and I took my job very seriously," he said. "I'm opposite that off the ice, but on the ice I had a job to do, and I tried to do it to the best of my ability and sometimes my emotions got the best of me."

The emotions almost overshadow Hextall's game-altering puck-handling skills. He is the only goalie in NHL history to shoot and score a goal twice. On December 8, 1987, he scored into an empty net against the Boston Bruins. And in the 1989 playoffs, he repeated the feat against the Washington Capitals.

Persistent groin injuries limited Hextall to eight games in 1989–90, and then he was traded to Quebec in the Eric Lindros deal. He returned to the Flyers in 1994, but by then he was 30 years old, and time had dulled most of Hextall's raw edges.

The Next Generation

The Hextalls are fast becoming one of the more famed hockey families. Bryan Sr. led the NHL in scoring in the 1941–42 season; sons Bryan Jr. and Dennis played in the league in the 1970s; Bryan Jr.'s son, Ron, became the first third-generation NHL star; and soon Ron's son, Brett, could make it to the big show. Brett Hextall was a 2008 sixth-round pick of the Phoenix Coyotes.

Brett is a center at the University of North Dakota. He plays a different position than his father, but the on-ice temperament is the same.

"His son and my son are the same age, and I saw him when he was 15, 16 years old back at Cushing Academy," Coyotes GM Don Maloney told NHL.com. "I remember him because he always played mean and ignorant at 14, 15—he was one of those guys you just hated."

He retired following the 1998–99 season and holds a number of club records. He's the all-time leader in games played by a goalie (489) and wins (240), and he remains atop the franchise's list for playoff games (84) and playoff wins (45).

He also embodied all that Philadelphia hockey stood for.

"He was not a lunatic," Dave Brown said. "He was extremely competitive. He was extremely serious about winning games. He was the kind of guy you wanted on your side, because no matter what you think of him, he competed every night and he was there for you and he gave you everything he had every night."

12 They Just Couldn't Lose

If you looked at the roster of the 1979–80 Flyers and didn't know how the season went, would you guess that team could go unbeaten for 35 games?

It was an odd mix. There were a few players left over from the Broad Street Bullies days—Bobby Clarke, Reggie Leach, and Bill Barber among them. There were a few talented youngsters, like Brian Propp and Ken Linseman. The defense was highly underwhelming, featuring the likes of Behn Wilson, Mike Busniuk, Bob Dailey, and Frank Bathe. And in goal was the two-headed monster of Pete Peeters and Phil Myre.

"We probably were not the most talented team in the league," Barber said, "but we played better than all the other teams as a team."

They certainly didn't look that way to start the season. They beat the New York Islanders opening night 5–2, but then they got stomped by the Flames in Atlanta 9–2. Coach Pat Quinn couldn't explain how his team could look so good against the high-flying

Islanders one game and so bad against the bottom-dwelling Flames the next.

"You beat the best team in the league one night and [the next game pucks are] going into your net like we don't have a team out there," Quinn said.

One of the people questioning Quinn was Al Morganti, in his first year on the Flyers beat for the *Philadelphia Inquirer*. "I was brought in to be a little rough on them," Morganti said. "They said, 'Al, we need a little more critical coverage.' But I got to cover one loss, then it's like, how am I going to criticize this?"

"This" started October 14, 1979, against the Toronto Maple Leafs at the Spectrum. Paul Holmgren, Leach, and Propp scored in the first period, and Bob Kelly scored late in the third as the Flyers won 4–3. Four nights later they beat Atlanta 6–2, then went to Detroit to whip the Red Wings 7–3. They returned home the next night and held on for a 6–6 tie with the Canadiens. That was as close as the Flyers came to a loss for nine straight games, by which time they hadn't lost in more than a month.

November became December, and the Flyers still hadn't lost— 19 in a row. It was about this time that people outside Philadelphia began taking notice; the 1977–78 Canadiens NHL-record 28-game unbeaten streak became a frequent talking point.

"It was around 18 or 19 games into it [that] we started getting more and more press," Propp said. "When we hit 18 or 19 games, everyone was out to beat us. But it was just fun."

They had some real fun December 6, when they spotted the Kings a 3–0 first-period lead at the Spectrum, then scored nine in a row in a 9–4 victory. Two games later they let the Quebec Nordiques take a 3–1 lead in the third period, then scored four straight to win 6–4 as the streak reached 25.

"They can put on the tap when they want to," Quebec coach Jacques Demers told reporters.

They tied the Canadiens record with a 1–1 tie at home against Pittsburgh on December 20, and two days later the Flyers won in Boston 5–2 to break it. The Boston Garden fans gave the Flyers a standing ovation.

"There's a tremendous feeling of relief," Clarke told reporters. "Nobody can say we came in the back door. We set the record against one of the top teams, and we did it in their building."

The next milepost was the all-sports record of 33 straight games without a loss, set by the NBA's Los Angeles Lakers in 1971–72, and that mark fell January 4, 1980, in a 5–3 win at the Rangers.

The record run was at 35 when they arrived in Minnesota on January 7. Barber scored 3:49 into the game, but the North Stars scored the next seven goals, and the streak came to a crashing halt in a 7–1 defeat—the team's first loss in 83 days.

The final numbers for the streak are mind-boggling. They went 25–0–10; they won six one-goal games and 11 two-goal games; they rallied from a two-goal deficit eight times and a three-goal hole once; and they came from behind in the third period to prolong the streak six times.

"It was a magical ride," Quinn recalled in *Full Spectrum*. "With that team, with that defense, there was no reason to think we could even put a 10-game streak together."

Keith the Thief

Most of the credit for the Flyers' success during the 1970s goes— and correctly so—to the players and Coach Fred Shero.

But one man often gets overlooked—Keith Allen. "I think Keith never got nearly the credit for what he did that he should have," Bob Clarke said.

Allen was the first coach in Flyers history, but owner Ed Snider soon realized just how smart Allen was. He was promoted to assistant GM in 1968, and when Snider fired GM Bud Poile in December 1969, Allen replaced him.

The Flyers missed the playoffs in two of Allen's first three seasons, but they were in the postseason the next 11, won a pair of Stanley Cups, and went to the Finals four times. And players he drafted were at the core of teams that went to the Finals in 1985 and '87.

Along the way, Allen picked up the nickname "Keith the Thief" for moves that looked nondescript at first but ended up paying major dividends.

His second-ever trade foreshadowed a successful future. Allen looked at his team following the 1969–70 season and saw a need for professionalism and blue-line toughness. He saw those traits in 31-year-old Barry Ashbee, who was floundering with the Hershey Bears, the Boston Bruins' American Hockey League affiliate. Ashbee had missed out on expansion when back surgery caused him to miss the 1966–67 season, and the Bruins had given up on him as an NHL prospect. To get Ashbee, all it cost was Darryl Edestrand and Larry McKillop.

That trade was an easy one for Allen to make. Others wouldn't be as simple.

In January 1971, Allen knew he had to get more assets for a growing team, and used the best trade chip he had—goaltender Bernie Parent. In a three-team deal, Parent went to the Maple Leafs, while the Flyers got a young center from the Bruins they had been high on—Rick MacLeish.

"We could have gone ahead and kept trying to build this team by adding a player here and a player there," Allen told reporters, "or we could make this deal and try to strike it rich, and live or die with kids."

MacLeish was sent to the minors in his second season with the Flyers but grew into a staple on the second line, scoring the Stanley Cup–winning goal in 1974.

Before that happened, however, Allen continued to tinker. In January 1972, he pulled off a seven-player swap with the Kings that landed the Flyers "Cowboy" Bill Flett and Ross Lonsberry. In December 1972, he added Moose Dupont from St. Louis for Brent Hughes and Pierre Plante, and in March 1973 he sent Jean Potvin to the Islanders for Terry Crisp.

His biggest accomplishment, however, came May 11, 1973, when Allen re-acquired Parent from the Maple Leafs for goaltender Doug Favell and a first-round draft pick.

Not wanting to rest on his laurels after the first Cup, Allen made a trade that almost assured a second championship, sending Larry Wright, Al MacAdam, and a first-round pick to the California Golden Seals for an old junior teammate of Clarke's— Reggie Leach. Leach's best season in five previous NHL campaigns had been 23 goals, but Allen thought he would be the perfect complement to Clarke and Bill Barber.

"[Leach] has never played with a good team or a good centerman as a pro," Allen said in making the deal. "He has a chance to be a star."

All Leach did was score 306 goals in eight seasons—seventh on the club's all-time list.

Allen stole another Flyers all-timer in 1982 when he sent Ken Linseman, Greg Adams, and a pair of draft picks to the Hartford Whalers for a player lodged in the club's doghouse—Mark Howe. Howe became the best defensemen in club history, and from 1985–87 he was a remarkable plus–193 as the team went to a pair of Stanley Cup Finals.

Allen's drafts brought the club Bill Clement, Bob Kelly, Barber, Tom Bladon, Jimmy Watson, Brian Propp, Pelle Lindbergh, Ron Hextall, and Rick Tocchet, and in free agency he found Orest Kindrachuk, Tim Kerr, Ilkka Sinisalo, and Dave Poulin.

Allen hired Fred Shero to coach the Broad Street Bullies and gave Pat Quinn his first coaching job, which led to the 35-game unbeaten streak in 1979–80.

He retired following the 1982–83 season, and was enshrined in the Hockey Hall of Fame in 1992.

When asked about Allen's overlooked place in Flyers history, Clarke smiled. "Don't worry, we're all aware of it," he said.

14 Listen to the Greatest Duet in Hockey

When the Spectrum was the centerpiece of the Philadelphia winter sports scene, the old building was surrounded by statues—one of Gary Dornhoefer scoring his magical goal against the North Stars in the 1973 playoffs, one of Julius Erving soaring for a dunk, and the Rocky statue before it was moved to the Philadelphia Art Museum.

And then there's the one of a chubby woman in a flowing dress with a bright smile on her face. That would be Kate Smith, and while she never skated a shift—or even put on skates, for all anyone knows—she was one of the most important people in the club's history.

On December 11, 1969, Lou Scheinfeld was a club vice-president who decided that night to switch from a recording of the "Star Spangled Banner" to Smith's version of "God Bless America." It was an incredibly controversial move at the time; the fact the Flyers beat Toronto that night, though, made it fine by owner Ed Snider.

"I thought I'd do something to shake things up," Scheinfeld said in *Full Spectrum*. "I listened to tapes and records of various patriotic songs, tested them over the PA system in an empty Spectrum, and decided on Kate."

Smith became a lucky charm of sorts, with the Flyers going 19–1–1 in the first three years of Scheinfeld playing the song, which he saved for big games.

Smith, who was born in Virginia, learned what was going on from an uncle who lived in West Philadelphia and had been sending her newspaper clippings chronicling her effect on the team. She performed the song live at the Spectrum for the first time on opening night of the 1973–74 season.

"The cheers went right through me," Smith said that night. "I've played before larger crowds, but I've never had a bigger ovation. It was fantastic, and I'm sorry that is such a mediocre word."

The biggest moment, though, came May 19, 1974. Smith was sneaked into town to sing "God Bless America" prior to Game 6 of the Stanley Cup Final against the Bruins.

"It was chilling [seeing her live]," Bob Clarke recalled. "You're standing here, just about shivering. This is so enthralling, to see this lady sing that particular song with such passion. Of course the crowd was just screaming, the whole roof is coming off the building."

Bobby Orr and Phil Esposito skated over to Smith before she sang to present her with a bouquet of flowers, but they couldn't bribe the hockey gods. Hours later, the Flyers won their first Stanley Cup.

Smith played other times at the Spectrum—before Game 7 of the 1975 semifinals against the Islanders and January 11, 1976, prior to the Flyers game against the Russian Central Red Army team.

After years of declining health, Smith died in 1986. Her legacy, however, lives on.

Lauren Hart—daughter of Hall of Fame broadcaster Gene Hart—has been the Flyers' anthem singer since 1997 and is renowned for being the best National Anthem singer in the NHL.

And while there's nothing like playoff hockey, attending a Flyers home game has taken on a can't-miss feeling over the years because of a simple pregame song. Hart usually sings the National Anthem by herself, but when the postseason starts, she switches to "God Bless America" and gets a little help in the form of a taped version of Smith singing her version.

It's a goosebump-inducing experience no matter how many times you witness it. Hart starts, and after the first verse, her eyes turn up toward the scoreboard. And the ghostly, grainy image evokes a roar from 20,000-plus fans that rattles the Wachovia Center to its core. Two generations of fans might not have any idea who the woman in the garish green dress, brown hair, and glasses is, but they cheer and scream and sing along with her. It unites a town and a fan base, and it is as stimulating and exciting an experience as any hit or goal.

"I still get the chills," Clarke said. "It's the neatest thing ever."

"It's stirring," said Lou Nolan, the Flyers' longtime public-address announcer. "You just say, 'Wow.'"

15 Trading for Doom

Entering the 1994–95 season, the Flyers were seen as a team on the rise, and led by Eric Lindros, Mark Recchi, and Rod Brind'Amour, it seemed like a five-year playoff drought was nearing its end.

Owner Ed Snider had returned from a sojourn in California to take a more active hand in running the team, Bob Clarke had been

When the Flyers traded for John LeClair in 1995 and put him on a line with Eric Lindros and Mikael Renberg, it created an unstoppable trio that powered the club to two conference finals and the 1997 Stanley Cup Final. (AP Photo/ Chris Pizzello)

brought back to be president and GM, and Terry Murray was hired as coach.

The season started January 21, 1995, following a work stoppage that trimmed the schedule to 48 games. The Flyers lost their first three games and were 3–6–1 after 10.

"[Teams] kept throwing their biggest people out there against Eric [Lindros]," Clarke said in *Full Spectrum*. "Because we had

[6'2", 235-pound Mikael] Renberg, we could spot smaller players with the two of them for a while. But they usually would get handled by the big players on the other team. So we needed a big winger and a defenseman who could work the power play, do a lot of the penalty killing, and take the first and last shift of a period."

Clarke knew the Montreal Canadiens were in need of scoring, so when he phoned Canadiens GM Serge Savard, he gauged his interest in Mark Recchi. It's not that Clarke wanted to trade Recchi, who had 93 goals the previous two seasons; it was that Recchi was his best trade chip.

Clarke first eyed a 6'3", 233-pound forward who had taken up residence in the Montreal dog house. John LeClair had scored a pair of game-winning goals for the Canadiens in the 1993 Stanley Cup Final, but his development had stagnated and he was flip-flopping between center, left wing, and the bench.

"We thought we could try him with Lindros," Clarke said in *Full Spectrum*.

Clarke next turned his attention to defense, asking for Mathieu Schneider. Savard countered with another young blueliner.

"Serge didn't want to trade Schneider, so he brought up Eric Desjardins," Clarke said in *Full Spectrum*. "We figured either one. Desjardins wasn't quite at Schneider's level offensively, but he was steadier, more solid."

On February 9, the Flyers sent Recchi and a 1995 third-round pick to Montreal for LeClair, Desjardins, and Gilbert Dionne.

"Clarkie called and at that point I was getting flipped between center and left wing, and he mentioned about putting me on a line with Eric, which was very exciting for me," LeClair said.

"That trade changed the whole atmosphere and confidence level of our entire organization," Clarke said in a 2005 interview on the Flyers' website. "Desjardins was an All-Star, and LeClair was about to turn into one. We had no idea that LeClair was going to be that good. But that deal turned out pretty good."

That's certainly an understatement. LeClair, Lindros, and Renberg combined to form the Legion of Doom—three players with skill, speed, goal-scoring ability, and the size and strength to go anywhere they wanted on the ice.

"Nobody could get the puck off them," said Chuck Gormley, the longtime Flyers' beat writer for the *Courier-Post*. "Once they dumped the puck into the corner, regardless of which corner it was, no defenseman was strong enough to stop that line…. Even if you had a big, tough defenseman, there was only one of them out there, and there were three of these guys."

LeClair had 25 goals in 37 games as the Flyers advanced to the 1995 Eastern Conference Finals. He scored more than 50 during each of the next three seasons, and then had two more seasons with at least 40 as the Flyers went to the Stanley Cup Final in 1997 and the conference finals again in 2000.

Desjardins was just as important. He won the Barry Ashbee Trophy as the team's best defenseman five straight times starting that first season, and seven times in 11 seasons. His 93 goals, 303 assists, and 396 points are second all-time among the club's defensemen, and his mark of 738 games is eighth in franchise history.

16 The Flyers Family

Some clubs talk about their history and their great players. The Philadelphia Flyers revel in it. And it isn't just the superstar players—anyone who's ever worn the sweater is treated with respect.

"They've always said the Flyers are like family," said former Flyers coach and defenseman John Stevens. "Some places try to say that, but here it truly is."

The list of front office employees reads like an all-time roster—GM Paul Holmgren; assistant GM John Paddock; senior VP Bob Clarke; director of player personnel Dave Brown; assistant coaches Craig Berube and Kevin McCarthy; amateur scouts Dennis Patterson, Ilkka Sinisalo, Mark Greig, Neil Little, and Simon Nolet; pro scouts Al Hill and Ross Fitzpatrick; scouting consultant Bill Barber; and player development coach Derian Hatcher all played for the team; Nolet was on the original Flyers team in 1966–67.

Former players don't just slide into those traditional jobs or go into broadcasting like TV analysts Keith Jones and Bill Clement, or radio analyst Chris Therien. Gary Dornhoefer, Bob Kelly, and Bernie Parent work in community relations, and Joe Watson is a senior account executive, selling tickets not just for the Flyers, but for all events at the Wachovia Center.

"I have a special affection for most players," team chairman Ed Snider said. "Hockey is a rough sport. If I have the opportunity to give back, then I will."

He doesn't do handouts, however; as many former players work for the team now, he's overseen the firing of just as many. "These guys earn their living," Snider said. "They do a good job, they work hard. There's not one guy that we've given a job to that we don't feel has done the job."

"Organization-wise, the way the Sniders run the Flyers, it's absolutely first class," Tim Kerr said. "The loyalty has always gone both ways. You're always treated first class, [and] players give that back. It's got to be one of the greatest organizations in sports. They were always there for the players and their families. I don't think there's a better organization to play for than the Flyers."

That feeling makes its way around the league and is a big selling point for free agents.

"They're just known for their class," Danny Briere said. "I've talked to some of the players, and everybody who had a chance to play here had good things to say. Not one guy had a bad thing to say. Even guys that had tougher experiences here, they only had good things to say about the organization, about ownership, all the way down to the trainers, to the players, everybody in the organization. It was just a place that people were saying, 'It's a class organization. They'll treat you right.'"

"Every year they spend as much money as they can to go and win, try to get the better player that fits best on the team," Ian Laperriere added. "It's very attractive to a guy like me who's never won the Cup. When they called, this was the only place I wanted to come."

The tradition was started by Snider and pushed along by Clarke during his 17 seasons as GM.

"I'm grateful for what he did for me," Kjell Samuelsson said. The defenseman spent nine seasons in two different stints with the Flyers and has spent the last 10 years as a minor-league coach for the organization. "He traded for me from New York [Rangers], and that's the best thing that happened to me in my hockey career. I went to Pittsburgh for three years, and he signed me again as a free agent. Then he brought me back to work in the organization as a coach."

It wasn't just big-league guys Clarke took care of, either. Stevens, when he played for and coached the AHL Philadelphia Phantoms, saw it firsthand. "We had older players in the minors who had severe injuries in the last years of their contracts, and he's extended them based on character, maybe knowing they might have a tough time getting another job right away," he said. "But because their service was strong here, I think he puts a lot of onus on the character and loyalty of the players and he rewards that.

"They think beyond the hockey. They treat people like people here, players like people. I think that's why they're so well respected, and that's why people love playing here."

17 Classic Memories

The Flyers rivalry with the Bruins has been one of the most memorable in club history. They've played games at classic locations like the Spectrum and Boston Garden. But they've also played in some pretty far-flung locations, like Maple Leaf Gardens in 1968, when the Spectrum was under repair, and at the Met Center in St. Paul, Minnesota, the season after the North Stars moved to Dallas.

But nothing beats where they played January 1, 2010—Fenway Park. The Flyers got to play the very welcome visitor in the NHL's yearly outdoor hockey fiesta at the famed home of the Boston Red Sox. That they lost a 2–1 overtime classic to the Bruins, however, did little to dampen the fun and memories the players and staff took with them.

"Just the general atmosphere was perfect," Flyers president Peter Luukko said. "Thirty-five degrees, there was a lot of hitting. It was a good, quality game. Our fans out-cheering the Bruins fans when it was their home game, I think that was a real special moment. I know the players identified that, too."

Luukko said the game was the culmination of a build-up that started in July, when the team learned from the NHL it would be playing in the game. "It hit us somewhat by surprise," Luukko said. "We had wanted to be involved in a game. We had talked about maybe Penn State or somewhere. We got a call about a week before the press conference. We had heard it was largely because of our tradition in the [TV] ratings we get and the following we have, which made us feel pretty good."

The fans were just as excited, and despite being allotted just 5,000 tickets—of which only a few were available for lucky season-ticket holders—that didn't change the fact that the crowd was close to evenly split between Flyers and Bruins fans.

"We only received about 5,000 tickets, and there had to be 12,000 or 15,000 Flyers fans," Luukko said. "I don't know where they got them, but it was great."

The Flyers arrived in Boston late on December 30 and got their first taste of the outdoor spectacle December 31, going through a short practice, and then enjoying the rest of the afternoon at a family skate that saw wives, girlfriends, parents, and children frolic on the Fenway Park ice.

"The practice day was just amazing," Danny Briere said. "That's what I'm going to remember the most, having the chance to be on the ice with my kids, my parents, a couple of my friends [who] came down. The day was just perfect with the snow coming down. It was magical."

"I think when we got off the bus and went into the locker room and then walked out onto the field on the 31st, it was like, 'Wow, this is something,'" Luukko said. "I know a lot of us—management, the players—we all stuck our heads out of the dugout, and then everybody was excited to get out there for the practice and the family skate. The players stayed out, had their families there. It was a big, huge family event for us as a team. That was really special."

A Fighting First for Flyers

There had been 137 fights in the long, violent history between the Flyers and Bruins, so it's only fitting that the first fight at an NHL Winter Classic happen between these teams. When the Flyers' Daniel Carcillo and Boston's Shawn Thornton dropped the gloves 12:01 into the 2010 outdoor extravaganza, they made history.

"Thornton and I were kind of laughing and smiling at each other during warm-ups a little bit, and I kind of figured it would happen," Carcillo said. "I mean, he fights. I asked [Steve] Begin first and he said no, so.... He [Thornton] came up to me and said, 'Let's do it.' So, why not do it?"

Game day started with Bob Clarke skating to center ice for the ceremonial faceoff with Bruins legend Bobby Orr, but that was just the beginning of a fabulous day.

"The stealth bomber flying over was an unbelievable sight," GM Paul Holmgren said. "Just the aura of being in that historic ballpark."

The Flyers took the lead in the second period on Danny Syvret's goal—not a bad way to score your first NHL goal, eh?—but Mark Recchi tied it late in the third, and then Marco Sturm's overtime goal won it for the Bruins.

Nothing, however, could spoil the day.

"To tell you the truth, I didn't think it was going to be that special until I got there and saw the rink," Mike Richards said. "The whole experience was cool. The way they had it laid out, right in the middle of the park, you could see the Green Monster in the background. That was pretty neat."

"The experience is once-in-a-lifetime," said Flyers coach Peter Laviolette, who grew up in nearby Franklin, Massachusetts. "It's not just being a cliché. Fenway Park, Bruins, Flyers, 40,000 people on a perfect day—you couldn't ask for anything better for the game of hockey."

18 Barry Ashbee—The Definition of Tough

Keith Allen's first season as GM saw the Flyers lose their last six games and miss the 1970 playoffs. Wanting to add some toughness and professionalism, he set his sights on a 31-year-old defenseman languishing in the Boston Bruins organization.

Barry Ashbee's toughness and professionalism were among the biggest factors in the Flyers' development into Stanley Cup champions. (AP Photo)

Barry Ashbee was good enough to have been taken in the 1967 expansion draft, but back surgery sidelined him for the entire 1966–67 season, and none of the six new teams selected him. Instead, Ashbee spent the next three seasons with the AHL Hershey Bears, the Bruins' farm team.

On May 22, 1970, Allen sent Darryl Edestrand and Larry McKillop to the Bruins for Ashbee, and he immediately made an impact on and off the ice. "I have always said that he taught the younger players on our team about what it took to win," Allen said in *Walking Together Forever.*

The first lesson came prior to the 1972–73 season, when Ashbee learned some players had missed curfew during training camp. Ashbee told Allen he was too old to deal with that kind of garbage and was quitting. Allen convinced him to stay, and the decision proved beneficial to both player and team.

Ashbee's skill, desire, and professionalism helped the Flyers reach the league semifinals in 1973, and go even further the following season.

By then, however, Ashbee was held together by little more than string and tape. His back was a mess, as were both knees. Nerve damage in his neck from a chipped vertebrae sent searing pain down his arm to his hand, but he taped his arm to his body, jammed his stick into his glove, and played on. He finished the season with 17 points and a plus–52 rating, and was a second-team NHL All-Star.

"He was independently masculine," Bob Clarke said. "A very strong, independent man who was the perfect team player. Self-motivated. He overcame so many injures…. He was a guy you looked to and listened to and wanted to hang around with because there was so much strength in him as a man but so much knowledge of team play in the game and stuff. Standing up for each other and sacrificing for each other—doing it the right way."

"I sat next to him in the [locker] room," Tom Bladon recalled in *Walking Together Forever*. "I would pat him on the back as we got ready for a game or a period, forgetting about his cracked vertebrae, and he would collapse to the floor on his knees in pain. The next period, he would be out there knocking people around into the boards. He was something."

Ashbee's career came to a sudden end in the 1974 playoffs. Game 4 of the conference semifinal against the Rangers went to overtime tied 1–1. At 1:27 of the extra period, Ashbee tried to block a point shot by the Rangers' Dale Rolfe, but the shot rose faster than Ashbee expected and the puck slammed into his face,

Ashbee the Team Player

Bob Clarke was just 21 when Barry Ashbee came to Philadelphia. It didn't take him long to see just what kind of team-first presence Ashbee had.

"One time Freddie [Shero] lined us up to skate on the blue line," Clarke recalled. "He used to line guys up on the goal line, skate us up and down the ice. I was playing a lot and he goes, 'Clarke, you can go in. Ashbee you can go in.' Ash goes, '[Screw] you Freddie, as long as my teammates are skating, I'm skating.'"

A stunned Clarke stayed and skated with his teammates.

"It's a hell of a lesson for me right off the bat," Clarke said. "As long as my teammates are skating, I'm skating."

inches above his right eye. "It was like a softball was stuck in my eye, and then there was just a big red ball of fire," Ashbee later told reporters.

Ashbee's sight returned, but the damage to his retina cost him almost all of his depth perception, ending his career. "Don't write me up as the great tragic figure," Ashbee said after the team won the Stanley Cup without him. "I'm just happy I was able to get my name on the Stanley Cup. These things happen and you have to accept them."

Ashbee spent the next three seasons as an assistant coach, and Allen began thinking of him as a potential successor to Fred Shero. That all changed in April 1977. That's when Ashbee was diagnosed with leukemia; a month later, he was dead.

"It took an incurable blood disorder to quell a spirit that the loss of sight in one eye, a spinal fusion, torn ligaments in his knee, and a pinched nerve in his neck could not dampen," Clarke said in his eulogy. "Barry never gave in to the luxury of exhaustion or pain. He always played the hand the way it was dealt."

Ashbee's No. 4 hangs from the Wachovia Center rafters, and the trophy awarded annually to the club's best defenseman is named in his honor. "He was a character player who played through a lot of different elements as far as health goes," Bill Barber said. "I'm very fortunate to have played with him.... He was a brave man that any team would love to have on their roster."

Ashbee's legacy also lives on through the annual Flyers' Wives Fight for Lives Carnival. The largest chunk of money raised goes to the Barry Ashbee Research Laboratory at Hahnemann University Hospital.

The best summation of Ashbee's Flyers legacy was written by Bill Meltzer in a story on the Flyers' website, "Barry Ashbee's retired number hangs in the rafters because he was the epitome of the type of hockey player that every team needs to win. He wasn't the most talented guy around, but no one was more dedicated to winning or persevered more tenaciously."

19 Leave Leon Alone

Leon Stickle was a linesman for nearly 2,000 regular-season games and another 200 Stanley Cup playoff games. Did he make mistakes during that time? Absolutely. Did he cost the Flyers the 1980 Stanley Cup? Absolutely not.

The Flyers entered the 1980 Final still in the glow of their record 35-game unbeaten streak. That win streak, though, didn't mask the fact that they weren't really a great team.

"I pull the picture of that team out and look at it and say, 'How did we do that?'" said Pat Quinn, who coached the 1979–80 team. "With that team, with that defense, there was no reason to think we could even put a 10-game streak together."

In the Stanley Cup Final they met the dynasty-in-the-making New York Islanders. The Flyers trailed the series 3–2 going into Game 6 on May 24, 1980, at Nassau Coliseum. The Flyers took a 1–0 lead in the first period on a Reggie Leach power-play goal, but the Islanders tied it minutes later on a Denis Potvin score.

Because of what happened later, the controversy surrounding the Potvin goal often goes overlooked. Mike Bossy's shot was stopped by goalie Pete Peeters, and Potvin knocked the rebound out of the air and into the net. The Flyers screamed that Potvin's stick was above the crossbar, which should have negated the goal.

The players weren't the only ones yelling.

"It shouldn't have happened," Ed Snider said. "The supervisor of officials, Frank Udvari, said the officials felt the puck, when he [Potvin] hit it, hit our player first before it went in. I said it's still a high stick, and the whistle should have blown. He said our player touched it and we had control and then it went in. The film showed that didn't happen, and the officials changed their tune. They said it wasn't a high stick—when he made contact it was below the crossbar. That's bullshit. It was pure BS. We didn't have the technology in those days. Every time a guy raised his stick and hit the puck it was a high stick. There was no technology, there was no replay. Anytime a player had his stick up there and smacked the puck, nobody tried to gauge where he hit it, it was a high stick."

Snider would have more to complain about soon after.

Moments after the non-call on the Potvin goal, there was another missing whistle. Clark Gillies skated the puck into the Flyers' zone and dropped a pass that went about 2 feet beyond the blue line and into the neutral zone. Butch Goring, following the play, grabbed the pass and skated into the Flyers' end. With Gillies still in the zone, the play should have been blown dead for the obvious offside. That's what Moose Dupont and Brian Propp thought, which is why they let up on backchecking instead of keeping up with Duane Sutter. That allowed Goring to find an open Sutter, and his goal just 2:12 after Potvin's put the Islanders ahead 2–1.

The Flyers were incredulous and looked to Stickle, the linesman, thinking maybe the din of the crowd had drowned out his whistle. It hadn't.

"I guess I blew it," Stickle said then. "Maybe I was too close to the play. Maybe there was tape on the stick and it confused me."

Whatever the reason, here's how much that call hurt the Flyers—4:30 after Sutter's goal, Propp scored to tie the game. It was 2–2 after one period and then went to overtime. Bob Nystrom won it for the Islanders at 7:17 of the extra session.

That night, Snider, GM Keith Allen, and Quinn put the loss solely on the officiating. And time hasn't dulled Snider's edge. "We got screwed out of two goals in that game," he said in a 2007 interview. "And that team would have won the Cup."

That's a possibility. But even if those goals had been waved off, would the Flyers have won? The Islanders clearly were the better team on the precipice of a dynasty with a roster stocked with Hall of Famers. Even with that, the Flyers had 40 minutes, plus overtime, to win the game on their own. Blaming it on referee Bob Myers, linesmen Stickle and Ron Finn, or anyone else is a cop out.

20 Founding the Franchise

Ed Snider wasn't the biggest hockey fan when he saw his first game, but the passion on the ice stirred something within him, and a few years later, when he learned of the NHL's plan to expand from six to 12 teams, he saw an opportunity.

Snider was an executive with the Philadelphia Eagles at the time, and one of his jobs was securing financing for a new stadium on the south end of Broad Street, near JFK Stadium.

Ike Richman, the owner of the NBA's Philadelphia 76ers, had approached Snider to see if Eagles owner Jerry Wolman, a successful real-estate developer, would help him build a new home for his team so he could move them out of Convention Hall.

Snider said Wolman wasn't interested, but with an expansion hockey team needing a place to play and the 76ers signing on as a co-tenant, Snider told Wolman they should build an arena and bid for an NHL franchise. Wolman agreed.

"With his reputation as a developer and entrepreneur and my ideas," Snider said in *Full Spectrum*, "we went forward. It became my project."

Rangers president Bill Jennings, who was heading the expansion committee, told Snider what he would need—a $10,000 application fee; an arena with a seating capacity of at least 12,500; and all the applicants would have to make a presentation to the NHL Board of Governors, outlining why the NHL would work in their area. And there was a $2 million franchise fee.

Snider signed on but had one caveat—his had to be the only bid coming out of Philadelphia. Jennings agreed, and Snider went about constructing an organization.

His first stop was the office of Philadelphia City Council President Paul D'Ortona to pitch him on the idea of building a 15,000-seat arena on city-owned land situated between the prospective new home of the Eagles—a building later named Veterans Stadium—and JFK. Snider said the city would own the land, and the arena would be privately financed. Those were golden words to D'Ortona and Philadelphia mayor James Tate.

Snider also shored up the investment group. He, Wolman, and Jerry Schiff, Snider's brother-in-law, each would own 22 percent of the team, while Bill Putnam—the banker who first tipped off

Congratulations, You're Fired

While Ed Snider was pushing forward with the birth of the Flyers, he still was an executive with the Philadelphia Eagles. After buying Eagles owner Jerry Wolman's original investment in the hockey club, however, the relationship became frosty.

On the night of the Flyers' first game, October 19, 1967, Wolman fired Snider from his Eagles job.

While no real reason was ever given, today Snider says, "It was a blessing in disguise."

Snider about the NHL expanding—would own 25 percent and be named club president. Friends of Snider and Wolman bought the remaining nine percent.

A five-page pamphlet was prepared for a February 8, 1966, presentation to the NHL Board of Governors at the St. Regis Hotel in New York. The next day Putnam received a two-word call from Jennings—"You're in."

The new hockey team secured office space and started hiring staff, including GM Bud Poile and coach Keith Allen, and uniforms and a logo were designed. The arena, called the Spectrum, was completed in 16 months and opened on September 30, 1967.

The biggest hurdle, though, became the $2 million franchise fee. Fidelity Bank had agreed to loan them half, and Wolman had pledged the other million. Wolman, however, was running into money trouble and suggested selling the franchise; Snider balked and bought out Wolman and Schiff.

"I had never wanted to own more than 22 percent of the team," Snider said in *Full Spectrum*. "I didn't think I could afford it."

He couldn't, and when Wolman didn't come up with his money, Snider and Putnam scrambled. They came up with $500,000, but two days before the NHL's June 3 deadline, they remained $500,000 short.

Snider convinced Bill Fishman, president of ARA Services (now known as Aramark), which had bought food service rights for the Spectrum, to loan them the remaining $500,000. Fishman agreed, and using his company stock as collateral, he signed over the loan check to the Philadelphia Hockey Club.

Snider was at Fidelity Bank on the morning of June 3 to wire the full $2 million to Putnam, who was in Montreal to present the money to the league. And then the lights went out.

"There was a blackout in Philadelphia," Snider said. "Everything went dead. They couldn't wire [the money]." At approximately 10:23 AM, a power failure blacked out a 15,000-square-mile area from New Jersey south to Maryland and as far west as Harrisburg, Pennsylvania.

The NHL needed confirmation of the Flyers' money by 2:00 PM or all the hard work put in by Snider and others would go for naught.

At noon the power came back on, and Fidelity established a communication link with a bank in New York, which was able to wire the money to Royal Bank of Canada in Montreal. Putnam ran the $2 million check to the Queen Elizabeth Hotel, saving the day—and the Flyers—for Philadelphia.

"How could something like that happen?" Snider said with a laugh that only 40-plus years of success can allow. "It happened. That's how we started."

Suprimeau

When the 2004 playoffs started, the Flyers were an aging, injured group going into battle with an inexperienced goaltender in Robert Esche.

The Stanley Cup Playoffs are like a two-month tap dance through a minefield. One wrong step and *Boom!*—the season blows up in your face. The Flyers needed someone to guide them through the tough spots. Far down the list of candidates, however, would have been team captain Keith Primeau.

Primeau had just seven goals in 54 games and was returning for the postseason after missing almost seven weeks with a concussion. More than that, his playoff resume was unimpressive—outside of his fifth-overtime goal against the Penguins in 2000, he had just nine goals in 110 playoff games.

But instead of the mild-mannered playoff pushover of years past, Primeau added a little extra to his orange and black No. 25 sweater—a cape and a new name, "Suprimeau."

His heroics started in Game 1 of the first round against New Jersey, as Primeau set up the series' first goal and then scored the game-winner in a 3–2 victory. He scored again in Game 4, and he dominated all series in the faceoff circle. Devils coach Pat Burns

Primeau's End

Keith Primeau never had the opportunity to build on his remarkable 2004 playoff run. The 2004–05 season was canceled due to labor strife, and then his career was ended by a concussion eight games into the 2005–06 season. Primeau had suffered three concussions between February and June 2004, and while the lockout helped his recovery, he remained susceptible.

Primeau tried different doctors, different medications, and different treatments, but nothing worked. He retired on the eve of training camp in 2006.

Today, Primeau stays active coaching kids and raising money for brain-injury research. But physical exertion still brings on post-concussion issues—nausea, dizziness, and cranial pressure. In 2009, he promised to donate his brain posthumously for the study of brain-related injuries.

said the only way to stop Primeau was with "a couple of bricks and some cement."

The second-round series with Toronto was tied 2–2 after the Leafs pushed the Flyers around in winning Games 3 and 4 in Toronto. An unhappy Primeau called a team meeting prior to Game 5.

"He stepped up in the meeting and laid some things on the line," goalie Sean Burke said. "He told us he would be great today and told us to jump on for the ride."

And what a ride it was. Primeau entered the night of May 2, 2004, with just five goals in 49 playoff games as a Flyer. When the final horn sounded, he had nearly doubled that total.

With the Flyers leading 2–0 but down a man in final minutes of the first period, Primeau turned a Bryan McCabe giveaway into a shorthanded goal. Then 44 seconds into the second, he redirected a Simon Gagne pass past goalie Ed Belfour. And 3:50 into the third, he finished a give-and-go with Gagne to complete his first playoff hat trick. He also had an assist, won 10-of-15 faceoffs, and was dominant in all situations.

He didn't have a point in Game 6, but he had the series' most important assist. When Darcy Tucker's crushing hit on Sami Kapanen left the Flyers' forward wobbly and lost on the ice, Primeau reached over the bench wall and hooked him off the ice, which allowed Jeremy Roenick to jump on and score the series-clinching goal.

The magic continued in the Eastern Conference Finals against the Tampa Bay Lightning. Down 2–1 in the series heading into Game 4, Primeau again rode to the rescue. He set up John LeClair's first-period goal, and with the Flyers up 2–1, he turned a Dave Andreychuk giveaway into a shorthanded goal that went down as the game-winner in a 3–2 victory.

A loss in Game 5 put the Flyers' season on the line heading into Game 6 at the Wachovia Center, but once again Suprimeau saved the day.

He set up Gagne's first-period goal and then scored his eighth of the playoffs to put the Flyers up 2–1 after one. But as the game entered its final minutes, Tampa led 4–3. In the last two minutes, the Flyers were pressuring, and defenseman Mattias Timander jumped on a loose puck at the point. He fired a shot that pinballed off two Tampa players and dropped onto Primeau's right skate on the left post. In a play that was one part Pelé, one part Gretzky, he kicked the puck across the goal line, circled behind the net, and tapped it in for a remarkable game-tying goal with just 1:49 left.

"I kind of directed it with my skate, and then I thought, 'Oh, don't go in,'" Primeau said of his magical goal. "I wanted it to go in, but I didn't want it to go in, because I was thinking, 'They are going to review it, and it's going to be disallowed.' And all of a sudden, it kept coming across the crease and I was coming out the other side and I got an easy whack at it."

In overtime, Primeau started the play that ended with Gagne's game-winner.

"I know how many people remember the fifth-overtime game, but [the] most memorable game for me was Game 6 against Tampa Bay," Primeau said. "I was so much more involved offensively on the score sheet from start to finish, as opposed to just scoring an overtime goal. That game I remember very vividly, especially being at home. It was such a great atmosphere. That's a point in time I'll never forget."

That the dream died in a Game 7 loss that saw Primeau go scoreless in no way diminishes his effort. "Probably the best individual performance that I had seen by a Flyer," said the *Courier-Post*'s Chuck Gormley, who has covered the team since 1990. "He literally carried that team on his shoulders."

In 18 games, Primeau had 16 points, and his nine goals made him the first player in NHL history with at least 100 playoff games to match his career goal total in just one postseason.

22 Watch the Game That Would Never End

Watching a near seven-hour hockey game isn't the easiest thing to do. You need a good amount of food and drink, a comfy chair, a strong constitution, and lots of time.

"I've seen the replays of the overtime," Chris Therien said. "I never have [watched it all]. I just don't have that much time any more."

"I never watched the game from the beginning to end," Simon Gagne added. "I think they do a good job to show the best parts of the game [on television]. It was a long game."

Game 4 of the Flyers-Penguins conference semifinal, May 4, 2000, started at 7:38 PM and ended at 2:35 AM. Pop in the DVD and push play. There's Olympic hockey icon Herb Brooks leading the Penguins, and Craig Ramsey, the substitute, coaching the Flyers. The Flyers won the opening faceoff.

The first big moment of the game came just 2:22 in. Alexei Kovalev pounced on a John LeClair turnover, carried the puck just over the blue line, and fired a rocket low and to the left of goalie Brian Boucher and into the back of the net. It was the Penguins' first shot of the game.

The Flyers got the game's first power play moments later when Darius Kasparaitis went off for high-sticking, but they failed to cash in. It was the same fate for the Penguins when first Daymond Langkow and later LeClair were penalized.

The Flyers carried the play in the second period, outshooting the Pens 12–8, but they failed to take advantage of penalties by the Pens' Peter Popovic early and Kasparaitis late.

Penguins goalie Ron Tugnutt was a brick wall, but the Flyers finally found a hole early in the third. Martin Straka sat in the penalty box for slashing. On the ensuing faceoff, Langkow beat Jan Hrdina on an offensive-zone draw and pushed the puck back to Eric Desjardins. He fired a slap shot through traffic that suddenly changed course right into the net. The goal light went on, but the referees weren't sure. Did the puck hit LeClair? Was his stick over the crossbar? Was it played with a high stick? The referees conferred with the video replay official. The puck might have hit LeClair's helmet, or his stick up high, but the evidence was inconclusive. It was a good goal, and the game was tied 1–1.

It was 4:47 of the third period. It was going to be a long time before that score changed.

By the start of overtime, you could feel the energy ramping up. The Flyers certainly felt it as the game nearly ended moments into overtime when LeClair stole the puck from Tugnutt, went behind the Pens' net, wheeled in front, and passed to Langkow, whose one-timer rang off the crossbar.

The teams traded chances and went up and down the ice, but things started to meld together. One overtime became two, which faded to three, then four and into five.

There were a few penalties and scoring chances—14 shots total in the first overtime—but eventually it became slow-speed skating with the occasional whistle—but no commercials! This led to easily the funniest line of the night, when ESPN broadcaster Steve Levy read a promo for *SportsCenter* coming up next—"Whenever next is."

When the fifth overtime started, it was obvious the players were out of gas. "After the second overtime, third overtime period, we're out of power gels, power bars, Gatorade," Keith Primeau recalled. "We were literally looking for food to come into the locker room because you needed to get something into your system."

Midway through the period, everything changed. Dan McGillis chipped a puck along the right wall to Primeau, who

Gagne's Extra Gas

While players were dead tired during the five-overtime marathon Flyers-Penguins 2000 playoff game, there was one player fairly fresh at the end—Simon Gagne.

"I don't think everybody knew I broke my finger [in Game 3]," Gagne said. "I couldn't squeeze my stick. We asked the team doctor to freeze my finger before the game, but he put too much, it was too numb. I couldn't feel my hand, so I couldn't feel my stick. I did maybe one or two shifts in the first, went back into the locker room, didn't play the second, didn't play the third. We went to overtime, and the numbness started to go away. I said it's good, I can go back and play. I put back my skates, played the overtime."

Despite barely playing in regulation, Gagne still played 27:28—a lot, but a far cry from teammate Dan McGillis, who played a game-high 61:05.

grabbed it at center ice and entered the Penguins' zone. Kasparaitis stepped into his path.

Said Primeau on the Flyers' 40th anniversary DVD, "Two other times earlier in the game I had gone wide on Darius Kasparaitis only to get cut off at the net, so I faked like I was going to go outside on him again, and once he crossed his feet over I was able to pull the puck back on my forehand and get a shot off."

The puck was sitting nearly on the faceoff dot when Primeau cocked and fired. It was the 130th and final shot of the night, and it found beloved dead space between Tugnutt's left shoulder and the crossbar.

The total time of the game was 152:01, making it the longest of the modern era.

It was a long watch—time to stretch the legs and crack the back. Maybe that butt-print will come out of the couch in time. But it was worth it—although maybe Gagne's got it right when he says he just watches the end of that game.

"You just want to make sure we still win the game at the end," he said.

23 The Spectrum

The Flyers aren't an Original 6 team, but with their history, passionate fans, and success, they certainly have the feel of one. And their first home, the Spectrum, was a big part of that.

Credit Bill Becker, who worked for the company that designed the Flyers' uniforms, for naming the building. "I'm thinking about how this building will host a number of different events," Becker said in *Full Spectrum*. "I thought of color and this being a stadium or auditorium, and 'Spectrum' popped into my head and out my mouth."

For their presentation to ownership, Spectrum was turned into an acronym—SP for sports, E for entertainment, C for concerts, T for theatrics, R for recreation, and UM for stadium.

The original plan also called for the seats to play off the "display of colors" motif, with four shades of fabric ordered—blue, apple green, magenta, and orange. Thankfully, that plan was scrapped in favor of a uniform dark red when the fabric company couldn't get the colors right.

That wasn't the last problem the Spectrum had. On February 17, 1968, a 100-foot long by 50-foot wide piece of tar paper blew off the roof, leaving sheet metal exposed and letting the sun shine through.

The building remained open as repairs were done, but two weeks later more wind blew off more tar paper and roof decking, leaving three different holes, the largest measuring 20 feet by 40

The intimacy of the Spectrum and the rowdy fans who packed it made Philadelphia an especially tough place for visiting hockey teams. (AP Photo/ Julia Robertson)

feet. The city shuttered the building, and the Flyers were forced to play the last month of the regular season on the road.

That was the last physical problem with the building. The only other problems over the years were for the opposition. Some even came down with a Flyers-specific illness—the Philadelphia Flu.

During the 1970s, no team had a greater home-ice advantage than the Flyers.

"The Spectrum—it's dark, the music is intimidating, they're intimidating, and of course over the boards come all their tough guys," said Dave Maloney, a Rangers defenseman during the 1970s.

Bill Barber thought playing in Boston was just as tough for his team, but it gave him a clue as to what opposing players felt coming into the Spectrum.

"I don't think they rested too well in the afternoons," Barber said of visiting players. "Just like us when we were going into Boston. When we played in Boston we knew we were going to have a battle on our hands; it was going to be a physical game. You don't rest that well. I know coming into Philly we might have compounded that problem by a couple marks. I talked to the players on other teams in that era, and they had some sleepless afternoons."

The Flyers clinched their first Stanley Cup at the Spectrum on May 19, 1974, and on January 11, 1976, they beat the Russian Central Red Army team there. On December 20, 1979, they tied the NHL record for consecutive games without a loss in a 1–1 tie with Pittsburgh.

The next generation of Flyers tried to keep the Spectrum as intimidating and special a place as possible.

"Early in my career, that was the Dave Poulin–Brian Propp–Mark Howe–Brad McCrimmon era," said Detroit legend Steve Yzerman. "It was quite intimidating for me as a teenager. They were a very good team, as well. It was a fantastic building; the fans were on top of you."

The Flyers went to a pair of Stanley Cup Finals in the mid-1980s, with the most memorable moment coming in Game 6 of the 1987 Finals against the Oilers. Down 3–2 in the series, J.J. Daigneault's goal with 5:32 left snapped a 2–2 tie and forced Game 7 back in Edmonton.

The Flyers played their final game at the Spectrum on May 12, 1996, a 2–1 double-overtime loss to the Florida Panthers in the second round of the playoffs.

In 1,138 regular-season games at the Spectrum, the Flyers were 699–296, with 143 ties. In 29 seasons they won 12 division titles and played for the Stanley Cup six times. They also hosted a pair of All-Star Games (1976, 1992).

When it was announced the Spectrum would close for good, the cry rang out for one more game at the old barn. So a preseason game against the Carolina Hurricanes was played there on September 27, 2008. Most of the former captains came back for the event, and it was a grand celebration of the old building.

Many a tear will be shed the day the place one critic panned as "The Fish Can on the Delaware Flats" meets the wrecking ball.

24 A Choking Situation

The Stanley Cup Final is the ultimate crucible. The pressure of playing for the greatest trophy in sports reveals things in people that maybe even they didn't know was in them. That includes players playing far above—or below—their talent level and expectations.

The same can be said for coaches.

Terry Murray, who coached the Flyers to the 1997 Stanley Cup Final, felt the pressure in a major way—and buckled.

The Legion of Doom-led Flyers were heavy favorites to win the Cup. It was believed their size and skill would carry them past the smaller Red Wings.

It didn't go so well, however. The Wings exploited the Flyers' goaltending tandem of Ron Hextall and Garth Snow, and coach Scotty Bowman devised a master plan of using his Grind Line of Kris Draper, Kirk Maltby, and Joe Kocur—which on average was 4 inches shorter and 34 pounds lighter than Eric Lindros, John LeClair, and Mikael Renberg—and finesse defensemen Nicklas Lidstrom and Larry Murphy against the Lindros line to boost the Wings to a 3–0 series lead.

Murray, however, could see things breaking down before that.

"I saw this team really struggling to break though the pressure of the event," he said. "It wasn't just the spotlight of the Stanley Cup Final—it was a heat lamp. We started off here in Philadelphia, and for two or three days before the first game, this is where all the media was because Detroit was coming here. They [Detroit] came the day before the game, had their press conference, and played Game 1. We had three days of intense pressure."

That pressure built with each loss. Following a 6–1 defeat in Game 3, Murray tried to explain what was happening. For guidance, he looked to the other bench.

"I remember very clearly when Detroit played the New Jersey Devils [in the 1995 Cup Final]," Murray said. "And [the Devils] killed them; they shut them down. As great a team as Detroit was, they [New Jersey] gave them no sniff whatsoever. And Scotty Bowman, in the media press conference following that series, went after his team and his players big-time. But it was a learning process and they broke through. A lot of the players [who] were key players on that hockey team over the next several years [scored] a lot less points, [had] a lot less individual statistics, became more of a team, and look where they ended up. They became a great franchise."

Murray tried the same tact. After practice on the day between Games 3 and 4, he tore into his team. Then he went into the daily press briefing. His answer to a simple question about forechecking changed the entire atmosphere of the series.

"When we weren't playing in those games in the Final the way we had in the games in the three previous series, my history and looking back over the difficulties of breaking through, and reading about it and talking with sports psychologists over the years, it was a situation where you failed," Murray said. "It's really hard to break through right away. So in the press conference when I was asked the question by one of our beat writers about our forechecking, I kind of expanded on it. I said we're not getting it done, it's a situation that's so intense right now, it's a choking situation. It's unfortunate but we have to, as a young group, you have to go through this sometimes in order to come out the other side."

All that was heard by the gathered media was "a choking situation." The silence that followed Murray's answer was broken by the collective sound of jaws smacking on the floor.

"All of us couldn't believe those words would come out of a coach's mouth," said Chuck Gormley, the *Courier-Post* beat writer who was at the press conference.

The writers ran back to the Flyers' locker room to ask the players how they felt about being called chokers by their coach.

"Nobody likes to be called that," Eric Desjardins said that day. "I don't want to start a big war in the paper, but of course it hurts. It hurts to hear that."

"I don't think anybody liked it," Hextall said years later. "The media made a bigger deal and twisted it more than it was meant to be.... Not a big issue to me."

It was a big issue to others. The Flyers lost Game 4, and days after the series ended, Murray was fired. Outside of a 2-1/2-season stint with the Florida Panthers—where he was hired by his brother, Bryan—Murray was passed over for dozens of head coaching jobs before the Los Angeles Kings hired him in 2008. He believes that 1997 press conference followed him like a scarlet letter.

"It was the wrong thing to say," Murray said. "Maybe it was a deer-in-the-headlights kind of effect. Maybe that statement would have been more appropriate. But it was the reality of the situation."

25 Vengeance!

After the Flyers' historically awful 2006–07 season, GM Paul Holmgren set about remaking the team. He traded for Kimmo Timonen and Scott Hartnell and spent big money to give them new contracts, as well as free agent Danny Briere. He traded for Joffrey Lupul and Jason Smith, and during training camp Smith was named captain.

They also started the season with noted tough guys Jesse Boulerice, Steve Downie, and Riley Cote on the roster.

And to market this bunch, it was Holmgren who coined quite an apropos line.

"Early [that] summer I had a meeting with Paul Holmgren and [club president] Peter Luukko, and we were discussing the marketing for the upcoming season," said Shawn Tilger, the Flyers' senior vice president of business operations. "Paul mentioned that the theme the hockey operations department was using with the players was 'Back with a Vengeance.' Immediately, we thought it was the perfect marketing theme for the season."

Tilger had no idea how right he was. The Flyers, who had been stomped by the other 29 clubs in 2006–07, planned on gaining vengeance through any means necessary.

Their quest started before the regular season. In a preseason game September 25, Downie launched himself like a cruise missile, exploding on the head of Ottawa's Dean McAmmond. McAmmond was left with a concussion, and Downie was suspended for the first 20 games of the season.

In the third game of the regular season, Boulerice attempted to feed Vancouver's Ryan Kesler his stick by cross-checking him in the neck. The blow earned Boulerice a 25-game suspension.

Days later there was another vicious hit, this time by defenseman Randy Jones, who unintentionally drove the Bruins' Patrice Bergeron face-first into the boards chasing a puck. Bergeron suffered a broken nose and a season-ending concussion; Jones received a two-game suspension.

When the teams met again a month later, there was another incident. When Bruins defenseman Andrew Alberts went to his knees to play a puck, Hartnell barreled into him and his hip crunched Alberts' head into the boards. Hartnell earned a two-game suspension.

A game against Dallas on December 1 was marred when Cote left his feet to elbow Stars defenseman Matt Niskanen in the head. Cote earned a three-game suspension, and Holmgren received a call from the league offices.

Colin Campbell, the NHL's head disciplinarian, had seen enough.

"One or two things can happen, even three—but five? Gary [Bettman, commissioner] and I felt it was time to address it with Paul and say, 'You have to address this with your players, with your team,'" Campbell told ESPN.com following the Cote suspension.

Campbell's message to Holmgren was to keep your players in line or else the fines and suspensions won't be limited to the players.

"I think five incidents in the first quarter of the season is probably high. It's unprecedented," Campbell said. "Are we saying the coach or the general manager have instructed the players to play this way and be more physical? Not at all. But there has to be some responsibility or accountability at some point in time on the coach, GM, or organization."

The message was received loud and clear, and while the Flyers still played a physical style, there were no more suspensions the rest of the season.

And even without terrorizing the rest of the teams in the league, the Flyers got their vengeance with a surprise run to the Eastern Conference Finals.

26 Flyers Fall to the Fog

Fred Shero was known as the Fog because some of those around him always thought he seemed like he was in his own world.

But on May 20, 1975, the fog really rolled in.

It was Game 3 of the 1975 Stanley Cup Final. The Flyers were going for their second straight championship, but the conditions couldn't have been more different than the previous year. Rather than being the plucky expansion underdog to the Boston Bruins, this time the Flyers were the heavy favorite against a Buffalo Sabres team in just its fifth year of existence.

While the Flyers had the LCB Line of Reggie Leach, Bobby Clarke, and Bill Barber, who had combined for 106 goals and 265 points in the regular season, the Sabres had the famed French Connection—Rene Robert, Gilbert Perreault, and Rick Martin, who totaled 131 goals and 291 points.

The biggest advantage the Flyers had on the Sabres was in net, and they showed it by limiting the Sabres to one goal each in winning the first two games.

Game 3, however, was different. The average temperature in Buffalo in May is about 60 degrees, but a rare heat wave enveloped the city. The Sabres' home, Memorial Auditorium, didn't have air conditioning. The heat from the outside, plus the screaming throng of 15,863 inside raised the conditions at ice level to 90 degrees. The ice literally started melting under the players' skates, creating an eerie fog more suited for a horror movie.

"It was weird," Bob Clarke said. "It was 90 degrees outside and no air conditioning in the building. It was tough, not only because of the fog, but you'd get dehydrated. Those were the days where you weren't told to drink to water, you were told not to drink water. They always thought you'd get bloated from drinking water. Wash your mouth out but don't swallow it. You had dehydration problems."

The game was stopped 12 different times during regulation so the players could skate around to help the mist dissipate. Arena workers with bed sheets also joined in.

Both coaches told their skaters to shoot anytime they had the puck because the goalies likely couldn't pick up the puck through the fog.

It worked for the Flyers as Gary Dornhoefer and Don Saleski scored in the first 3:09 of the game, but the Sabres answered with two of their own. After two periods, the Flyers led 4–3.

Beyond the paying crowd, there was another spectator watching the game—a bat. The winged rodent flew back and forth over the ice until Sabres forward Jim Lorentz, waiting for a faceoff, slashed the bat into the afterlife.

"It was dive-bombing the crowd, and a couple of times it came near the ice and I remember [Bernie] Parent taking a couple of swings at it with his goal stick and missing," Lorentz told the website Sabreslegends.blogspot.com.

Lorentz did the work, but now someone was needed for clean-up duty. As players and referees stood and watched, Flyers forward Rick MacLeish scooped up the bat and dropped it in the penalty box. In a span of 366 days, MacLeish went from scoring the Stanley Cup–winning goal to scooping up roadkill.

Back to the game—Bill Hajt scored in the third period to force overtime. Late in the first extra session, Perreault sent the puck into the right corner. It bounced off the wall, where Robert one-timed it from along the goal line between Parent's skates for the winner.

"It's almost impossible to score from that angle," Robert said in a 1999 interview. "But I shot at the net, hoping somebody could get the rebound. It seemed to me he [Parent] wasn't ready for the shot. It went between his legs."

"I didn't see Perreault's pass," Parent said. "I saw Robert's shot too late for me to come out and stop it."

While the Flyers lost that night in the fog, they ultimately were able to fight through the mist to claim their second straight Stanley Cup.

27 The Winner from the Kennel

Fred Shero was known for practicing specific game-related situations. His theory was his players then would be prepared for anything that might happen in a game.

One of those drills involved winning puck battles behind the net, coming in front, and jamming the puck into the goal. It was a drill they did during the final 15 minutes of every practice during the 1974–75 season, with the players receiving $5 rewards for scoring.

One of the players least expected to earn any goal-related rewards was Bob Kelly. The rambunctious forward known as the Hound was part of the Broad Street Bullies' core of tough guys. If Dave Schultz was the leader of the gang, Kelly was his first lieutenant.

"If I was going to war, I would want him leading the charge," Joe Watson said of Kelly in *Walking Together Forever*.

"He's got something that's hard to come by," Shero said in a 1973 interview. "No coach in the world can make a guy do what Kelly does. It's not in his contract. It comes from within him."

Kelly did have some skill. He had a pair of 21-goal seasons as a junior and had at least 10 goals in eight of his 10 seasons with the Flyers. Still, he wasn't going to play on a scoring line. Not usually, at least.

Clement Scores, Then Gets Traded

When Bill Clement scored the final goal of the 1975 Stanley Cup Final, he was a Flyer in name only.

Earlier in the day, GM Keith Allen had agreed to trade Clement, defenseman Don MacLean, and a first-round pick to the Washington Capitals for the first pick in the 1975 NHL Draft. The Flyers used the pick on center Mel Bridgman.

As Game 6 of the 1975 Stanley Cup Final reached the third period scoreless, Shero was growing worried. The Flyers had been shorthanded five times in the first two periods, and since Shero used his top-line players to kill penalties, he could see them wearing down. When the teams came out to start the third period, he broke up the LCB line, sending Kelly over the boards with Clarke and Leach.

"Freddie wasn't sure," said Kelly. "It was [assistant coach] Mike Nykoluk who came to him and said put the Hound in there. He said I don't know, but he stuck me out there and it paid off."

Clarke won the opening faceoff. Leach dumped the puck into the right corner, and Kelly, streaking diagonally across the ice, beat Buffalo's Jerry Korab to the puck. Korab pinned Kelly to the glass and momentarily had possession of the puck, but Clarke bumped Korab and Kelly grabbed the loose rubber. He bulled from behind the net and jammed a backhand under goalie Roger Crozier for the game's opening goal 11 seconds into the period.

"He just went barreling in there," Clarke said. "The puck was behind the net and he just went barreling in. Korab went to check him, and I stepped in front of Korab so Hound could come out. I don't know if Buffalo was even expecting him to try to score."

When Kelly returned to the bench, he had a short message for Shero:

"I told Freddy he owed me $5," he said.

Bill Clement scored an insurance goal with 2:47 left, and the Flyers flew home with their second straight Stanley Cup.

The second Cup was far sweeter for Kelly, who had missed the 1974 Final after tearing knee ligaments in the semifinals against the Rangers.

"You have to be there in the end to feel like you made a contribution," Kelly told reporters.

28 Hextall Shoots...He Scores!

When Ron Hextall came into the NHL, he revolutionized the way goalies handled the puck. There had been goaltenders who could move the puck around, but not until Hextall arrived had a goaltender been regarded as a third defenseman.

"When we went into Philly or played Philly, it was always about being careful about where you put the puck on the dump-in," said Red Wings great Steve Yzerman. "You've got to keep it away from the goaltender, that's what we always talked about.… He had such an impact on the game. You couldn't just throw it in and assume you were going to get it. You had to throw it in with a purpose."

If a team wasn't careful, it could be caught in an odd-man rush. Or worse.

Late in a game against the Boston Bruins on December 8, 1987, the Flyers were ahead 4–2 after Brian Propp scored with 2:27 left in the game. The desperate Bruins pulled goaltender Reggie Lemelin for an extra attacker and dumped the puck into the Philadelphia end.

"The situation couldn't have been better," said Cam Neely, who was on the ice for the Bruins. "We were down one or two, pulled the goalie, it was late in the third period.... He had *carte blanche* to fire the puck down there."

Hextall played the puck just in front of the goal line to the right of the net. With a flick of his wrists, the puck took off. It bounced just inside the Boston blue line and skidded into the goal, just inside the right post.

The players jumped off the bench to congratulate Hextall. They drew a bench minor for too many men on the ice, but it was the happiest penalty they ever had to kill.

"The media kept asking me are you going to score, and I said 'Yeah, I'll score at some point,'" Hextall said. "It wasn't something I thought about. I felt like I was going to [but] it's not like it was high on my priority list. It wasn't like it was something I was going out to do."

When it did happen, however, it was wonderful.

"I remember when I scored the whole team came off the bench, it was like we were kids in a candy store," Hextall said. "The fact the whole team was excited was a thrill to me."

He did it again in the 1989 playoffs against the Washington Capitals. When Washington's Scott Stevens shot the puck into the Philadelphia end, Hextall stopped it behind the goal, came out the other side and saw a gaping net 200 feet away. And seconds later, history was made a second time.

"Somebody told me the other day that it had been over 100 games since I had scored," Hextall joked after the game. "I guess it was time."

29 Firing Bob Clarke

No person in the history of the Philadelphia Flyers has had a bigger impact on the franchise's success than Bob Clarke. Whether it was captaining the team to a pair of Stanley Cups or building a team that went to the Cup Final twice in his first three years as a GM, Clarke's impact was felt at all levels of the organization.

The Flyers without Bob Clarke is like City Hall without the William Penn statue.

After that 1987 Cup Final run, however, things started to backslide. In 1987–88 they slipped from 100 points to 85, lost in the first round of the playoffs, and Clarke fired Coach Mike Keenan. Paul Holmgren replaced him, but the slide continued. They finished fourth in the Patrick Division in 1988–89 but made a stirring run to the Wales Conference Finals.

In 1989–90, things completely fell apart. The team finished sixth in the Patrick Division and with just 71 points missed the playoffs for the first time since the 1971–72 season.

It was the culmination of bad trades and worse drafts. Clarke deals that sent away stalwarts like Peter Zezel, Doug Crossman, Dave Brown, and Brad McCrimmon brought little in return. His drafts were even worse, as only nine of the 35 players selected between 1985 and '87 ever played in the NHL. He picked center Glen Seabrooke in the first round in 1985, passing on Joe Nieuwendyk and Mike Richter. In 1986, he took defenseman Kerry Huffman at No. 20, bypassing Adam Graves. Drafts in 1988 and '89 were no better, as the only player to see significant time in Philadelphia was goalie Dominic Roussel, a third-round pick in 1988.

"I didn't do a good job that last year," Clarke admits. "There were things that I did that weren't good."

Worse, the fans had started to turn on Clarke, chanting "Bob must go." Team president Jay Snider heard it; he also believed there was a difference in philosophy between himself and Clarke.

"Bob's philosophy is that if you get to the playoffs, anything can happen," Snider said in *Full Spectrum*. "My dad's philosophy from Day 1 was to measure everything against winning the Cup. I'd much rather go into the playoffs with a 100-point team than an 80-point one because by and large, I'll have a better chance of winning the Cup. Bob agreed the goal is to win the Cup, but to do that you have to make sure you get into the playoffs every year. In my mind that leads to short-term deals. That was our fundamental difference. I felt the organization was deteriorating. I have to be convinced that there is a game plan that works, and that's where things broke down between Bob and me."

Snider told Clarke to outline his plans for the future, but when they met in Snider's office April 16, 1990, Clarke never had a chance to go over his notes. Snider told the face of the franchise it was time for a facelift. He asked Clarke to stay on in some yet-to-be-named position, but Clarke refused.

"I remember getting out of his office and standing out on the street there and going to the hot dog stand there and buying a Diet Pepsi and thinking, 'What the [heck] am I going to do now?' You're 40 years old, you got four kids, none of them in college yet, and you don't have a job. [Ed] Snider was real good to me financially. I wasn't broke, but I still had to work. And you've had basically your legs cut off. This is my team. This is my life—the Flyers are my life."

Ed Snider, 3,000 miles away in California, watched the squabbles between his son and the man he treated like a son, but there was little he could do. "It was like having two sons that were squabbling," he said. "I tried to patch things up and I couldn't."

30 Who Named the Legion?

Jim Montgomery isn't a name most Flyers fans—or most hockey fans in general—would recognize. But if not for the fourth-line center, who played a grand total of 13 games with Philadelphia, one of the enduring legacies of the club might have gone entirely different.

Montgomery arrived in Philadelphia on February 10, 1995, after Montreal waived him. That transaction was overshadowed by the arrival of another couple of players from the Canadiens the day before—John LeClair and Eric Desjardins.

Montgomery's first game as a Flyer was the second for LeClair and Desjardins, and obviously he was the difference as the Flyers skated to a 3–1 victory in New Jersey just two days after LeClair and Desjardins' debut was a 3–0 loss to the Florida Panthers.

In his next game, Montgomery picked up his first assist, on a Chris Therien goal, in a 5–3 win against Washington.

Meanwhile, the Flyers' new top line of Eric Lindros, LeClair, and Mikael Renberg was starting to build chemistry.

"It was really impressive how they could take over a whole game and put a team on its heels," Montgomery said. "It was so rare to see a line with that speed and size and that much skill."

Putting three big, skilled, physical players together made things difficult on opposing teams. Things had started during the New Jersey game, when Lindros went to center a pass and saw LeClair blocking Devils goalie Chris Terreri like a lunar eclipse. It was the harbinger of things to come.

"That was the game where things started to go with Renny and Eric," LeClair said. "We had a game with lots of chances. I scored my first goal as a Flyer and you could tell there was some good chemistry there."

Watching Lindros (6'4", 240 pounds), LeClair (6'3", 233 pounds) and Renberg (6'2", 215 pounds) run over, around, and through their Devils counterparts, Montgomery told a reporter, "They look like the Legion of Doom out there."

While Montgomery takes the credit, he knows the real origin of the name.

"It's my best friend growing up, Tommy Cacioppo," Montgomery said. "We played hockey growing up, and he was a Flyers fan and I was a Canadiens fan, and we'd go at each other. When I got traded there, we were both big-time Flyers fans. He stared talking to me on the phone about that line, it's incredible to watch them on the ice. I said you should see it up close. To watch them do their stuff on the ice, it's almost like the other team is doomed when these guys start to roll. Then Tommy said, 'They're like the Legion of Doom,' from wrestling at the time."

Montgomery wasn't a fan of pro wrestling but thought the name fit.

"I thought the Legion of Doom made sense," Montgomery said. "There were only three of them, but with the size of them it's like they were a legion."

They certainly rained down doom on opposing teams. And Montgomery had one of the best seats in the house to see it.

"They were fun to watch," Montgomery said. "They were a big part of Flyers history."

After five years out of the playoffs, the Legion led the Flyers to the 1995 Eastern Conference Finals and the 1997 Stanley Cup Final. Montgomery, however, only was part of the '95 run—he played eight regular-season games and seven more in the playoffs.

"The run to the semifinals where we lost to the Devils in six [games], just watching the maturation of that young, talented team start to come together," Montgomery said. "For me, regretfully, it was my last time with them. I knew they were building something special, and you could tell it was going to be something special for a long time."

31 Jonesy the Lifesaver

Keith Jones was a role player during most of his nine NHL seasons. That role was agitator, energy player, and locker room cut-up.

One additional role Jones played—lifesaver.

On April 1, 1999, the Flyers played the Predators in Nashville. During the contest, team captain Eric Lindros complained of soreness in his chest and side. It didn't seem anything out of the ordinary in those days. Most teams couldn't match Lindros' dominance without clobbering him with sticks and elbows—and when the opposition was a second-year club like the Predators, the number of cheap shots generally was higher.

After the game, Lindros received ice and electrical stimulation to relieve any pain, and then he and a few teammates went for a late snack and some drinks. Still sore, however, Lindros made it an early night and returned to his room at the Renaissance Hotel.

Jones, Lindros' road roommate, had been out with the same group. When he got back to the hotel, Lindros was awake, watching television, and still complaining of soreness in his chest. Jones wrote in his autobiography, *Jonesy: Put Your Head Down and Skate*, that Lindros took some Advil and tried going to sleep.

Jones recalled in his book hearing the bathtub running a few times during the night, but that didn't surprise him. "I don't think much of it, because when you play hockey sometimes guys will hop in the tub and try to give the body some relief, so I just assumed that's what Eric was doing."

When he woke early the next morning, Jones discovered Lindros still in pain. He called trainer John Worley but got no answer. That's because Worley hadn't returned from spending the night at a local hospital with Mark Recchi, who was suffering from concussion-related issues.

Jones finally spoke to Worley about 7:30 AM. He described Lindros' issues to him, and the trainer said he would come up to their room after he cleaned himself up. Jones then went down for breakfast, but when he returned to the room, Lindros looked terrible.

"I come back up and Eric is back in the tub, pale, and in even worse shape than he had been," Jones wrote. "I say to him, 'Something is wrong here. Maybe it's something internal. I'll go get John right now. I think we got to get you to the hospital.'"

As Jones walked to the elevator, Worley stepped out. They walked back to the room, and with Lindros in Worley's capable hands, Jones gathered their things and went to the team bus.

Worley called GM Bob Clarke, and they discussed having Lindros fly home so the club's doctors could examine him, but Worley reconsidered and instead called an ambulance, which took Lindros to Nashville Baptist Hospital. In the emergency room, Lindros complained of shortness of breath and pain in his chest. X-rays revealed a collapsed lung due to internal bleeding. Three liters of blood—half his blood volume—had filled Lindros' chest cavity, causing the lung to collapse. A chest tube was inserted between two ribs to drain out the blood. As the blood ran out, Lindros' breathing returned to normal.

Lindros returned to Philadelphia a few days later, but it brought to a boil the ever-simmering feud between the club and the Lindros family. Bonnie Lindros, Eric's mother, accused the club of trying to kill Eric by putting him on a plane before fully understanding his injury, and Carl Lindros said there was almost no chance of Eric playing again that season, doctors be damned.

"We did everything right," team chairman Ed Snider said nearly 10 years later. "And the mother said that Bob Clarke tried to kill her son."

For his part, Jones doesn't really like the lifesaver label.

"Did I save his life? I don't know," Jones wrote. "I just noticed he wasn't looking good and left it up to the medical staff to take care of it. I get a lot of credit for something that I'm not sure I deserve. I guarantee you everyone's intentions were to make sure the right thing was done to help Eric."

32 Foppa Goes Floppa

The Flyers had to watch from afar as Peter Forsberg—a player they drafted and then traded as part of the Eric Lindros deal—became for a time the best player in the NHL. He won a pair of Stanley Cups, a scoring title, and a league MVP award in 10 seasons with the Colorado Avalanche.

When the opportunity came to sign Forsberg in the days after the end of the 2004–05 lockout, GM Bob Clarke moved mountains—sending Jeremy Roenick to Los Angeles—to fit Forsberg's two-year, $11.5 million contract under the new league-mandated salary cap.

Coming the day after the club signed big-ticket defensemen Derian Hatcher and Mike Rathje, the move shocked the hockey world and made the Flyers immediate Stanley Cup favorites.

"I think starting this year we're a pretty good team," Clarke said in the days following Forsberg's signing. "I'd say we're one of the teams that can compete for it. But so much can happen along the

When Peter Forsberg was healthy, he was a dynamic presence for the Flyers. The problem was that he wasn't healthy very often in his two seasons in black and orange. (AP Photo/ Chris O'Meara)

road that I can't say we're closer to a Stanley Cup than anybody else right now."

Clarke's hesitation wasn't just hubris—it became reality.

Things started ominously when Forsberg missed his first training camp because surgery was needed to remove an infected bursa sac in his ankle.

When Forsberg did play, he was outstanding. He had 56 assists, 75 points, and a plus–21 rating—but it came in just 60 games. He helped linemates Simon Gagne and Mike Knuble have career-best scoring outputs. But lots of time was missed to groin injuries and a controversy over him being too hurt to play for the Flyers but

Forsberg's Bounty

Peter Forsberg may have been elsewhere, but he had a lot to do with the Flyers' run to the 2008 Eastern Conference Finals.

When the Flyers traded Forsberg to Nashville on February 15, 2007, they received forward Scottie Upshall, defenseman Ryan Parent, and a 2007 first-round pick.

In the summer of 2007, the Flyers took advantage of the Predators' financial woes by giving back Nashville its pick for the rights to defenseman Kimmo Timonen and forward Scott Hartnell. Upshall, Parent, Timonen, and Hartnell combined for 46 goals and 117 points in the regular season, and six goals and 21 points in the playoffs.

healthy enough to win a gold medal with Sweden at the 2006 Olympics.

The 2005–06 season ended in playoff disappointment as the Flyers were dispatched in six games by the Buffalo Sabres. The next season Forsberg was named captain, the first time in his NHL career he had the 'C' stitched on his sweater.

"It can be a burden," said Keith Primeau, who captained the Flyers for five years. "It's a big responsibility, and not everyone is cut out to carry that responsibility."

Forsberg seemed to wilt under the pressure, starting with his reluctance to take part in a shootout in the home opener—he claimed he wasn't comfortable with his sticks, despite scoring a goal earlier in the game. Things didn't go much better from there. Losses piled up, and Forsberg's chronically sore feet made his presence on the ice a continuous question.

"Everything was fine at the pregame skate and then you'd come in in the afternoon and all of a sudden there's an extra guy there that wasn't there in the morning," Knuble said. "I'm playing because Peter called and said he wasn't feeling it, or his ankle was bad or whatever. It's tough on the players, just for the continuity of the lineup and all that. He's one of your main guys. You really look to count on him to do well. Sometimes when he's in and out, it would be tough on guys; you have to juggle lines. It affects more guys, guys have to move around. Plus, you wanted to win a lot, and he offered a great chance to win."

Add in the issue of his impending free agency, and it made a mess of a season that much harder to stomach.

The Forsberg situation—Would he play? Would he sign a new contract?—came to a head on February 15, 2007. After taking warm-ups with the team prior to a game against the Toronto Maple Leafs, Forsberg was pulled out of the locker room and told to take off his uniform—he had been traded to the Nashville Predators.

"It was literally five, seven minutes before the game," Knuble told reporters. "I've never seen that, a guy getting yanked out of the locker room as you're tightening up your skates."

Forsberg's departure was as shocking as his arrival.

33 A Carnival Atmosphere

Ever want to score on a Flyers goalie? Drop the GM in a dunk tank? Beat the team goon in boxing?

Well, Flyers fans have the opportunity to do just that, and more, every year.

It's the Flyers' Wives Fight For Lives Carnival, and since the first event was held on a snowy day in 1977, it's become a can't-miss event.

The first Carnival raised more than $95,000 and saw about 8,000 tickets sold for about $6 apiece, despite a snowstorm that blanketed the area. Since then, the Carnival has raised more than

$23 million for charities across the Delaware Valley. It's also become the envy of other sports teams in Philadelphia and beyond.

"Our neighbors here, the Eagles and Phillies, both do festivals that they sort of copied a little bit from this," said Mary Ann Saleski, wife of former Flyer Don Saleski, who now serves as senior vice president of the Comcast-Spectacor Foundation, which oversees the charitable activities of the Flyers and Sixers. "The Boston Bruins Foundation now has a carnival, they do pretty well. We've actually been talking with a couple other [NHL] teams. Tampa Bay is interested in learning how to do it, the L.A. Kings are interested. We're the NHL expert on carnivals. It would be really fun to sort of brand that in hockey."

Players who join the team are no stranger to the Carnival. Keith Primeau said he and his wife, Lisa, knew of it when Keith was playing in Carolina. Lauren Pronger knew of the Carnival when she and her husband, Chris, were in Anaheim, and she quickly involved herself in the planning of the 2010 Carnival.

"It has received a lot of recognition and notoriety, and it's recognized around the league by the fans, by other organizations, by other players, as a tremendous event," Keith Primeau said.

Ian Laperriere got his first look at the Carnival in January and was overwhelmed.

"I heard of it when I signed here," he said. "I talked to Riley Cote, he was really involved. They all said wait until you see the Carnival, it's really something. Every team has something different, but this one is huge.... They say it's big, you'll see it. But until you see the way it is, it's hard to really measure. Now I know what it is, and I can even appreciate it more."

The genesis for the Carnival was Dr. Isadore Brodsky, who ran the cancer center at Philadelphia's Hahnemann University Hospital. Brodsky was looking to raise money and turned to his brother-in-law, Sylvan Tobin, for help. Tobin was a minority owner of the Flyers and set up a meeting with Brodsky and team owner Ed

Snider. Ed Golden, the team's public relations director, came up with the idea of a carnival.

The players' wives, many of whom were Canadian citizens and couldn't hold full-time jobs, were put in charge of the event.

"It gives the wives an identity," Mary Ann Saleski said. "When you're involved in sports, it really is about your husband. There's a family, but it's a way to get involved in the community. Not everybody has children, so [for] the younger wives that don't have kids yet, it's really a way for them to learn and get involved. I try to teach them that what you do off the ice and how you sort of create your identity in the community is really who you are as a person. They really love it."

"It's just amazing for us to be able to come to this great city that accepts us and our husbands and boyfriends," said Holly Cote, Riley's wife, who co-chaired the 2010 Carnival. "It's nice to be able to give back. I know it's just a little, but it's good to be able to be a part of the community and give back to everybody. It's wonderful. We love it."

All the money raised at the first Carnival went to the Hahnemann cancer center, which became prophetic when, months later, Barry Ashbee died from leukemia. Brodsky was his doctor.

The Carnival was re-dedicated in Ashbee's memory, and a majority of money raised is earmarked for the Barry Ashbee Research Laboratory at the Isadore Brodsky Institute for Cancer and Blood Diseases at Hahnemann. Brodsky died in October 2007.

"It used to be after Barry died for about 15 years, all the money just went to leukemia research at Hahnemann," Saleski said. "We gave millions there and you realize there are so many deserving, worthy charities around that it's almost sometimes bad to try to be good because you can't ignore everyone. So now we give to dozens of charities every year."

The Carnival has changed with the times. Besides the traditional opportunity for autographs and pictures with current and former Flyers, the 2010 event featured a 40-foot inflatable slide, Wii Boxing, live music, and raffles for prizes like a team-signed motorcycle, a new Toyota Corolla S, and lunch with the Prongers at the Capital Grille. Tens of thousands have enjoyed the Carnival over the years, and the folks who run the Carnival have enjoyed every second of it.

"We were all getting traded, moved away," Saleski said, "but every time someone would come onto the team, they knew that one of the things that was important was Flyers' Wives and the Carnival. And here we are, 33 years later."

34 Crosby the Flyer Killer

Not since Eric Lindros arrived in Philadelphia in 1992 had a player joined the NHL with as much fanfare as Sidney Crosby when he debuted with the Pittsburgh Penguins in 2005.

Prior to Crosby's arrival, the Penguins were pretty bad. Mario Lemieux had retired and Jaromir Jagr had forced a trade out of town, leaving the Pens a bottom feeder. From 2001–04, the Flyers were 9–3 with four ties against their Pennsylvania neighbors. The rivalry was almost like hammer vs. nail.

That all changed with Crosby's arrival.

In just his second visit to Philadelphia, Flyers defenseman Derian Hatcher gave Crosby a special greeting—a cross-check in the mouth that broke some teeth and split his lip. The bloody Crosby was incensed that no penalty was called—well, he was whistled for unsportsmanlike conduct for whining about the non-call. He took that anger out on the Flyers.

That night, Crosby returned to score the overtime winner. That moment started his run of using the Flyers as his personal punching bag.

It didn't help that fans—as well as coach Ken Hitchcock and center Peter Forsberg—accused Crosby of diving and whining to referees.

Crosby is booed so loudly and lustily every time he steps on the ice in Philadelphia, you'd think he performed some unspeakable criminal act. The louder the fans get, however, the more it seems to add to his personal fire.

As a rookie, Crosby finished the season with seven goals and 14 points in eight games, but the Flyers managed to win six of the eight games.

The following season, as the Flyers suffered through the worst season in franchise history, Crosby and the Penguins had no problem kicking a team when it was down—and they kicked hard. He had his first NHL hat trick early in the season, and later he had a goal and five assists in an 8–4 Penguins win. The Flyers went 10–6–2 against the Pens that season, as Crosby alone had seven goals and 16 points.

Against Flyers Mario was Extra Super

Sidney Crosby isn't the first Penguins superstar to have his way with the Flyers. Mario Lemieux gave his own special agita to Flyers fans over the years. In 71 games, he had 51 goals and 124 points.

The lowlight for Flyers fans had to be Lemieux's NHL-record day in Game 5 of the 1989 Patrick Division Finals when he had a remarkable five goals and eight points in a 10–7 Penguins victory.

Lemieux only faced the Flyers twice in the playoffs (1989, 1997), and while he had 12 goals and 20 points in 12 games, the Flyers won both series.

The better Crosby plays, the more belligerent the fans get, but the louder those fans scream, the more it seems to drive Crosby to shut them up. He'll never admit it, but Crosby relishes wearing the black hat in Philadelphia.

"I don't really know anything different," he said after scoring in regulation and in a shootout to beat the Flyers in Philadelphia on December 17, 2009. "That's the way it's been for five years."

One time, on the morning of a Penguins-Flyers game during the 2009–10 season, Crosby and a reporter were discussing how a week earlier, the Islanders' Brendan Witt had been hit by a car outside the team hotel, and Witt remarked how shocked he was that bystanders—that Philadelphia people—were so helpful and caring. The reporter asked Crosby if he thought he'd get the same treatment. Crosby laughed and replied you certainly wouldn't see skid marks behind the car that hit him.

For two straight playoff seasons, Crosby was the car that ran over the Flyers' Stanley Cup hopes. When the teams met in the 2008 Eastern Conference Finals, Crosby had two goals and seven points as the Flyers fell in six games.

The following season, the teams met in the first round, and in the six games Crosby scored four times, including—to the chagrin of 20,072 at the Wachovia Center—a pair in the clinching game.

In his first five seasons, Crosby has 24 goals and 32 assists in 32 games against the Flyers—he has more multi-goal games (eight) than games he's gone scoreless (six). His 56 points against the Flyers is the second-most against any team he's played, but it's a near-guarantee he hasn't had more fun scoring those points against any team other than the Flyers.

35 Chelios' Dirty Hit

One of the hot-button topics in the NHL today is hits to the head. The league seemingly is on a never-ending quest to find a middle ground between keeping players safe while keeping good physical play in the game.

The issue isn't a new one. Look at the Flyers' 1989 Wales Conference Finals series against the Montreal Canadiens for evidence.

Midway through the second period of Game 1, Brian Propp skated into the corner in his end to clear the puck. Montreal defenseman Chris Chelios followed him and left his feet to deliver a devastating elbow to Propp's jaw. The blow drove Propp's head into a metal glass support, knocking him unconscious. Propp dropped like a rock, with the back of his head bouncing off the ice like a basketball. When medical personnel removed Propp's helmet, blood poured out of the winger's head.

Propp was placed on a stretcher and taken to Montreal General Hospital, where he was diagnosed with a concussion and a cut lip. No penalty was called on the play.

Chelios' lame reasoning to reporters after the game was Propp "was coming around the net and had just got rid of the puck when I hit him—I don't know how."

Video replays showed just how—it was about as dirty a hit as you'll see.

At the time, Propp said the only vengeance needed was winning the series. "It's too important just to go out looking for revenge," he said. "We're looking for a win. That's the best way to get revenge."

Propp returned for Game 3, but it didn't help as the Flyers fell behind 3–1 in the series. Dave Poulin's overtime goal in Game 5 forced the series back to Philadelphia for Game 6.

Scott Mellanby opened the scoring, but the Canadiens scored the next four goals. Propp's score with 6:05 left made it 4–2, but it was too little, too late. With nothing left to do but look to next season, the Flyers' focus went from winning to revenge. Ron Sutter fired the first blow, taking a run at Chelios, but the attempted clobbering only earned Sutter two minutes in the penalty box for high-sticking.

Ron Hextall, who had sat out Game 1 due to injury, was next.

With 1:37 left in the game, Chelios brought the puck in offside. As the referee blew the play dead, Hextall rushed out of his crease and clobbered Chelios, knocking him down and punching him. Two referees tried to separate the pair; when they came apart, Hextall was missing his jersey, and Chelios couldn't skate away fast enough. Hextall kept screaming at Chelios and threw his blocker at him.

As Chelios was ushered off the ice through the Zamboni chute, fans pelted him with trash and chanted, "We want Chelios!" Chelios stayed in the locker room during the postgame handshake line for fear of further antagonizing the situation.

"You never know what to expect with Hextall," Chelios said after the game. "But I saw him and was ready. I was fortunate I didn't get a skate in the head or anything."

Hextall was unrepentant for his action. "Did you see what he did to Brian Propp? Come on, I think we owed him something," Hextall said after the game. "God almighty, he just about took [Propp's] head off. I think that's good enough reason."

More than 20 years later, Hextall still doesn't have any problem with what he did.

"It was just a dirty hit," he said. "I respect the hell out of Chris Chelios, but that was a dirty hit. And obviously it could have been a lot worse for Proppie than it was, but it was bad. I have an attack mentality, and someone did something to one of my foot soldiers. I felt like there had to be retribution."

For that retribution, Hextall was suspended for the first 12 games of the 1989–90 season—at the time, it was the fourth-longest ban in NHL history.

It's also a decision that still bothers Propp. "Chelios never got anything for [the hit]. Hextall threw his blocker, and he gets suspended for 12 games at the beginning of the next year, which really hurt our club. That was the most ridiculous thing I've ever seen the league do."

Propp also remains steamed by the hit. "I know it was [a cheap shot]," he said. "If you want to take a look at it, it's on YouTube.

"At the time I was the leading playoff scorer. There was no remorse, nothing.… I have no respect for him."

36 From the Locker Room to the Board Room

When the Flyers were knocked out of the 1984 playoffs by the Washington Capitals, Bobby Clarke didn't have much intention of retiring. He was 34—old in those days—but thought he had another season or two left in him, especially in a reduced role that saw him more as a checker than scorer.

But when the season ended, club president Jay Snider fired coach/GM Bob McCammon and had the perfect candidate in mind to fill the GM slot—Clarke.

"I still intended to play," Clarke said. "I think I was still one of the better players when Washington beat us. In those days 34, 35 was getting a lot older for a player, but defensively I was still a really capable player, capable of helping this team."

Clarke was smart enough to know, however, that the offer wasn't going to last forever, and he was going to be a former player far longer than he was going to be an active one.

Bobby Clarke wasn't ready to retire when he was offered the job as Flyers GM in 1984, but he was smart enough to know it was a pretty good opportunity for him. (AP Photo/RBK)

"Had I kept playing, which I could have done, I don't know, maybe I would have stayed in hockey—scouting, coaching. I had no vision of what I was going to do. Jay Snider offered me this position. I knew I could play for a few more years, but I knew the end was coming. If that's what the Flyers thought was right for me, then okay."

The shaggy mane of hair was tamed and trimmed. The false teeth that always seemed to end up in teammates' beer mugs stayed in their owner's mouth. The uniform went from hockey sweater and skates to suit, tie, and dress shoes. And Bobby was shortened to the more professional sounding Bob.

Clarke's first job was to hire a coach—something he admits he had no idea how to do.

"Jay Snider did all the interviews," Clarke said. "I wouldn't know how to interview someone." Clarke signed off on Mike Keenan's hiring a few days after taking the job.

Clarke did know, however, how to build a team. In one of his first moves, he traded Darryl Sittler to the Detroit Red Wings for Murray Craven and then named Dave Poulin captain.

With Keenan in charge of the youngest group of players in the league, Clarke sat back and watched things unfold. Tim Kerr, Brian Propp, Poulin, and Ilkka Sinisalo all scored 30 goals, Mark Howe and Brad McCrimmon solidified the defense, and Pelle Lindbergh won the Vezina in goal. The team marched through the playoffs but lost to the dynastic Edmonton Oilers in five games in the Stanley Cup finals.

The following season was marred by the tragic death of Lindbergh in a drunk-driving accident, but the team still finished with 53 wins—the same as the season before—and again won the Patrick Division, but they lost to the Rangers in the division semifinals.

In 1986–87, with rookie goalie Ron Hextall, the Flyers went on a magical run that again ended in defeat to the Oilers in the Stanley Cup Final. Hextall won the Vezina Trophy and the Conn Smythe Trophy as playoff MVP.

"It was a fast ride there," Clarke said of his first three seasons. "Things were happening so fast, we were winning all the time. It was so good."

It wasn't all good, however. Disputes between the players and Keenan became too much for Clarke to take, and he fired Keenan after the 1988–89 season. Clarke himself was dismissed in April 1990.

Getting fired, he said, ended up being one of the best things that happened to him.

"Losing a game tore me apart and I couldn't do nothing about it and I didn't know how," Clarke said. "I didn't know how to handle the job as the GM.... You try but you don't really know."

Clarke landed in Minnesota, where his North Stars went to the Stanley Cup Final in his first season. He returned to the Flyers for a short time in 1992 but left in '93 to run the expansion Florida Panthers. Clarke returned one more time to Philadelphia on June 15, 1994. Again, success followed immediately as the Flyers went to the Eastern Conference Finals his first season after a five-year post-season absence and the Stanley Cup Final in 1997. He retired eight games into the 2006–07 season.

The immediate jump from the ice to the front office isn't an easy one, but Clarke was incredibly successful. In 17 full seasons, Clarke's Flyers teams went to the playoffs 16 times, reached the conference finals seven times, and made the Stanley Cup Final three times.

37 The Saddest Streak

When the Flyers and win streaks are discussed, the immediate thought is the 35-game unbeaten streak from the 1979–80 season. But the most games that team won consecutively was nine.

The longest win streak in team history is 13 in a row, set from October 19 to November 17, 1985. That month-long stretch was the longest in the lives of the players who went through it, and it had nothing to do with what happened on the ice.

Bisecting that streak was the tragic loss of goaltender Pelle Lindbergh in a senseless drunk-driving accident. While the incident claimed just one life, the hole it left in those left behind never has been filled.

"I still have a picture of Pelle in my office," Brian Propp said.

The win streak started five games into a season that began with great expectations. A season earlier, the youngest team in the league, playing under a first-time NHL coach and first-time-anywhere general manager, had gone to the Stanley Cup Final. Every important member of that team had returned older and wiser for the experience.

They opened the season 2–2 and finished a two-game homestand with a 7–3 rout of the North Stars. The next day they beat the Blackhawks in Chicago 5–2, and returned home with a 3–0 defeat of the Whalers.

They blasted Vancouver 7–4, and then swept through the province of Quebec, beating the Canadiens and the Nordiques and came home to smash the L.A. Kings 7–4, to push the streak to seven games.

Wins at the Rangers, and at home against the Blackhawks, and Bruins on Saturday, November 9, put the win streak at 10 games and allowed the Flyers to enter a five-day stretch between contests on a high.

That all ended, however, in one awful instant. After a night of drinking, Lindbergh lost control of his turbo-charged Porsche and collided head-on with a concrete wall. He died November 11, when he was removed from life-support machines.

"We were poised to go to the Final again that year, and he was the guy [who] was going to lead us there," Dave Brown said of Lindbergh. "There's no plan on how to get through things like that. Something like that happens, you lose your No. 1 goalie, and most of all a friend, it sends the whole team into turmoil. What do you do? He was dead. You just try to cope with it after that."

Following the Bruins win, Coach Mike Keenan had given the players two days off. Instead, they reported Monday morning, November 12, to the Coliseum for practice.

Gretzky's Donation

Following Pelle Lindberg's tragic death in 1985, the Flyers were inundated with flowers and other notes of support. The club asked people who wanted to honor Pelle to donate money to a fund created to support Lindbergh's sister, Ann-Christine, who was fighting cancer.

The only opposing NHL player to make a donation was Wayne Gretzky.

"There was nothing else to do," Tim Kerr said. "Getting back out there on the ice was somewhat of a distraction at the time. It was the only place we could go where it wasn't an issue for a while."

It also served the practical purpose of getting the team ready to play again. Just because a player died, the NHL wasn't going to shut down. And not only did the Flyers have another game, it was a highly anticipated rematch with the Oilers.

"Personally you grieve, but you know you have to move on," Brown said. "You have to get up the next day and do what you have to do. Pelle would have wanted us to move on. Not forget him, but move on. What else are you going to do? There's nothing else you can do."

It was a tentative start, but as play wore on, the game became the thing and all the other stuff moved to the back burner. But once in a while, emotions would bubble to the surface, like when Mark Howe scored the game's first goal late in the first.

"I came back to the bench and remember sitting down and almost crying," Howe said.

The game was tied 1–1 going into the third period, but Ilkka Sinisalo and Propp scored to put the Flyers ahead 3–1, and after the Oilers got within one goal late, Brad McCrimmon's goal clinched a 5–3 victory.

It was a win and two points, but it was so much more for the men who went through it.

"Winning or losing was not a factor," Keenan told reporters. "I'm just so proud of the way they played."

Two nights later the Flyers won in Hartford to set the club record with 12 straight wins. One night later, November 17, Murray Craven scored in overtime to beat the Islanders to push the record to 13.

The streak ended November 19 in a rematch with the Islanders. Rather than dwell on it, Kerr told reporters, "That's okay. We'll just start another [streak]." That group of Flyers had learned there were worse things to lose than a game.

38 Because Freddy's Philistines Doesn't Have the Same Ring

Ask most sports fans in the Delaware Valley what the names Jack Chevalier and Pete Cafone mean to them, and it's likely you'll get a blank stare or shrugged shoulders.

But without them, what would we call the Flyers of the mid–1970s?

Back then, there were a number of Philadelphia daily newspapers that covered the Flyers at home and on the road, including the *Philadelphia Bulletin*. Chevalier was the *Bulletin*'s Flyers beat reporter. And in 1972 the Flyers, like many teams, were not good away from home. In fact, when the Flyers arrived in Atlanta for a game against the Flames on January 3, 1973, they were 2–13–5 on the road.

For second-year coach Fred Shero, that wasn't near good enough. The days of the Flyers being the league's favorite guest were over. When he was hired by the Flyers, Shero had talked about how his teams would attack in five-man groups. What he didn't say then was that sticks and pucks were only part of that attack strategy.

Shero discussed that strategy with Chevalier over lunch in an Atlanta hotel restaurant. A few nights earlier in Vancouver, the Flyers and Canucks had engaged in a memorable brawl that saw the Flyers charge into the stands after a fan who had grabbed Don Saleski.

The Flyers had been piling up the penalty minutes—something that didn't bother Shero in the least. "We have no Rocket Richards on this team," Shero said. "Hitting is our game." That hitting, the coach believed, was going to neutralize the home-ice edge teams had when the Flyers came to town.

"So many clubs are tough only in their own rinks," Shero told Chevalier. "But [Dave] Schultz gave us courage on the road. You can't measure the value of a man like that.

"We'll win our share on the road this year. I guarantee it."

A few hours later the players backed up their coach as the Flyers stormed Atlanta like they were General Sherman's army. The Flyers had 43 penalty minutes to the Flames' 17 but cruised to an easy 3–1 win.

In his dispatch for the *Bulletin* after the game, Chevalier wrote, "The image of the fightin' Flyers is spreading gradually around the NHL, and people are dreaming up wild nicknames. They're the Mean Machine, the Blue Line Banditos, and Freddy's Philistines."

On the flight home, however, Chevalier called in a change to his story. Take out Blue Line Banditos. Insert Bullies of Broad Street.

Cafone was the editor who took Chevalier's call. He wrote the now-famous headline: "Broad Street Bullies Muscle Atlanta." So it was in the early morning hours of January 4, 1973, that the Broad Street Bullies were born.

The players weren't all that fond of the nickname, but they eventually realized it had some value.

"Having the nickname the Broad Street Bullies and some of the criticism directed toward us, it brought us together," Schultz said. "Wouldn't tear us apart. 'Hide the women and children, here come the animals.'…We'd go on the road and someone would do something, we'd take care of it. If they think we're a tough, dirty team, let's live up to our reputation."

The Flyers finished that season 7–9–2 on the road, and then went 22–10–7 away from the Spectrum in 1973–74 and 19–12–9 the following season, both of which ended with the Flyers hoisting the Stanley Cup.

39 Catch the Flyers Live Anytime

One of the hallmarks of the Flyers is the way the team interacts with its fan base. And one of the biggest ways they do this is by opening their practices to the general public.

The Flyers were one of eight teams in the 2009–10 season that advertised their practice schedule on their website, and almost every home practice is held at the highly accessible Virtua Health Flyers Skate Zone in suburban Voorhees, New Jersey.

All the information for practice times and dates is easily accessible on the team's website—it's right there under the regular-season schedule—and they practice at about the same time most days, so fans can set their schedules in advance. And the fans do flock to the Skate Zone.

Some take an early lunch, some visit on their day off from work. Many bring their kids, or school groups will stop by. It's not uncommon to see 75-100 fans—minimum—at every practice, regardless of the day of the week or time of the season. And on certain days—training camp, weekends, during the playoffs—the sounds of pucks, sticks, and skates can be drowned out by the clanging of many pairs of feet running for a seat on the metal bleachers that line one full side of the rink.

It's fun, it's free, and it gives fans who might never get the chance to have the opportunity to see their hockey heroes at ice level.

Ian Laperriere played in St. Louis, New York, Los Angeles, and Colorado before coming to Philadelphia, and he said the daily crowds in Voorhees are far different than anything he's seen elsewhere.

"At the beginning of the year, most of the cities you play in, they're there because they want to see what the new team looks like," he said. "But here it's like that every day. There's a bunch of people there every day. Sometimes I wonder if they work. I know what I do and I know why I'm there, but sometimes it's like, 'Holy cow, what are you doing here every day?'

"Believe me, it's not like that everywhere. In L.A. we had a couple, in Denver we had a couple. But packed like that every day? It's unheard of. I've never seen it before."

The players might not show it every day, but they certainly appreciate the fans' presence. "That type of fan support is always welcome," Chris Pronger said. "It's what makes this team so special."

"There's not a day we have practice that there's not a fair amount of people watching," GM Paul Holmgren said. "It's pretty neat, and it speaks volumes to the passion of the fans and their loyalty to the team."

Holmgren said there are even regulars like at a local tavern. "A lot of times it's the same people [who] are there to watch that I've seen over the years," he said. "I wave to them, and they ask questions about what's going on. I think it's important to acknowledge them."

Obviously the fan base feels engaged, because day after day, season after season, they're always there.

40 Big Fish, Small Island

There was a time in the early 1990s that Eric Lindros was the third-most well-known hockey player on the planet behind Wayne Gretzky and Mario Lemieux—and this was before Lindros ever played a game in the NHL.

At 6'4" and 250 pounds, scouts looked at Lindros and saw Gretzky's skills packed into Lemieux's body with Mark Messier's mean streak. There's a reason Lindros was called the Next One.

When the Flyers acquired Lindros, WIP sports radio broke into its top-rated afternoon show, hosted by Howard Eskin, to broadcast live the decision rendered by arbitrator Larry Bertuzzi.

And sporting goods stores couldn't stock enough No. 88 sweaters and T-shirts.

"They had already put him up on that pedestal," Eskin said of Lindros. "The fans thought the Flyers had the next Wayne Gretzky. It wasn't just they were going to win one [Stanley] Cup, it was they were going to win multiple Cups. They had put the Flyers in the same realm as the Edmonton Oilers when Gretzky was there and they won all those Cups."

Looking to avoid a maelstrom of publicity surrounding Lindros, the Flyers opted to stay with a deal previously signed to hold training camp in 1992 in O'Leary, Prince Edward Island, an area best known for hosting the Prince Edward Island Potato Museum.

With the museum as the second-biggest draw in town, it's no surprise every practice at the 1,200-seat O'Leary Recreation Center was sold out.

"There wasn't much going on," Rod Brind'Amour recalled. "Looking back on it, it was a good experience...you like to do things once and see that part of the country, it was nice to go there as a team, [but] I wouldn't recommend doing that again."

Chuck Gormley, the longtime Flyers writer for the *Courier-Post*, covered Lindros' first camp. He said the hope for privacy backfired, as the Canadian media was more prevalent in O'Leary than it likely would have been had the team stayed in Voorhees.

"I remember that training camp, there were people lined up to see him," Gormley said. "It was clear that if that training camp had taken place in Voorhees, he would not have gotten the attention he got up in PEI, yet that was what they wanted to escape. They wanted to take him to PEI to say it's a quiet little town and you'll be able to start your NHL career here. And it was bedlam. They couldn't fit enough people in that tiny arena. And there were fans lined up outside. I signed someone's yearbook."

41 The Passion of the Fans

Over the years, Flyers fans have earned a reputation for an attitude and behavior that matches their hometown hockey team's play—rough, nasty, and belligerent. But they also are passionate and loyal—also hallmarks of the franchise.

The fans weren't always so in love with their hockey team. A mid-day parade down Broad Street to welcome the players to town in 1967 was sparsely attended, at best.

"About halfway down to the Spectrum, I swear to gosh, there was this guy there giving us the finger," Joe Watson recalled in *Full Spectrum*. "He yelled, 'You'll be in Baltimore by December.' I'll bet there were 20 people, tops, all the way down Broad Street, who

That's the Ticket

To celebrate the 40th year of the franchise, in 2007–08 the Flyers decided to honor their fans by allowing them to be part of the game—so to speak. Season-ticket holders were encouraged to e-mail the team their best Flyers-related picture, and 44 would be printed on tickets—one for each preseason and regular-season home game.

"One thing we realized is, the fans are what make the organization," said Shawn Tilger, the club's senior vice president of business operations, "so why not do a tribute to the fans, especially the season-ticket holders?"

actually stood there to watch. All the rest were people on lunch hour wondering who the hell we were."

They learned fast. The Flyers won the Western Division in their first season, and that certainly caught the fans' attention. Then came the era of the Broad Street Bullies.

In a town whose most famous athlete is fictional palooka turned champion boxer Rocky Balboa, it's no surprise the fightin' Flyers caught on fast.

At the same time, the players appreciated just what their fans gave them.

"They played a huge part," said Bob Clarke of the fans who packed the Spectrum. "The noise would start in the warm-ups. They'd be abusing the opposing team, and they'd go the whole game—they were either cheering for us or abusing the other team. The noise would never end. I think it was scary for a lot of teams."

It was those fans who created the hockey epidemic called the Philly Flu.

One of those germs that infect visiting hockey players is a gentleman by the name of Dave Leonardi. While that name might not ring a bell, if you've watched a Flyers game any time in the past 35 years, you've seen him and his signs. Dave Leonardi is the famed "Sign Man."

Leonardi became a hockey fan before the NHL came to town, watching games on TV in the 1950s and going to minor-league games at the old Cherry Hill Arena. Not long after the Flyers arrived, he became a season-ticket holder. Despite sitting ice-level near the visiting goal, Leonardi noticed his onslaught of verbal abuse was being missed by the players. A friend suggested he make a sign.

"I made one for [Dave] Schultz, one for [Bob] Kelly," Leonardi said. "Gene Hart noticed one of the signs I had and mentioned it on radio. I was encouraged to make more signs, and people knew who I was, bringing signs to games. They said Gene Hart mentioned a guy with a sign, and he was the guy who named me 'Sign Man.'"

From "Ilkka Score-a-Gola" to "Start Your Bus," from "Have a Nice Summer" to "Asham Smash-em," Leonardi has signs for almost every player and nearly every in-game occurrence. He's got one that says "B48 Bingo" for when Danny Briere scores, and after a Claude Giroux game-winning shootout goal, out came "Claude Reins."

Leonardi said he brings about 90 signs with him for regular-season games, and more than 100 for the playoffs.

The Flyers appreciate Leonardi's efforts. The day of his wedding in 1989, he and his bride left the ceremony to catch a game at the Spectrum. On the Jumbotron scoreboard, the club flashed a congratulatory message. That message came back during the 2007–08 season when the Flyers honored season-ticket holders by putting them on the tickets, and a picture of the message to the happy Leonardi couple made it onto a ticket.

Over the years, the players who have come through Philadelphia understand just what their loud, loyal fans can do for them, and absolutely appreciate it.

"A bunch of games driving over the Walt Whitman Bridge, you're feeling very average," Rick Tocchet said. "Some games you don't feel good, your legs are tired. Driving to the game, you get out of your car, you're walking in, you're getting dressed, you're trying to pump yourself up, but you just don't have that life. As soon as you hit that warm-up and you see the people on their feet screaming and yelling, and the first shift they push you through, they push you to get your legs; they push you through those games where you don't feel good. So yeah, they are the seventh man."

42 Flyers 4, Communism 1

During the 1970s, the Flyers were the NHL's most hated team. They were the rampaging animals, the big bad Broad Street Bullies, punching a bloody swath through the league. They wore the black hat and relished the role.

Following their second straight Stanley Cup, the Flyers were booked as the final opponent for the touring Russian Central Red Army team—the Red Menace's troops that were invading North America. It was more than just a series of exhibition games. It was a battle to see whose version of hockey was better, whose political system was better—whose quality of life was the "right way."

"It was awful important for us to beat them," Bob Clarke said. "If you're a competitive person, you wanted to beat them bad because of what was going on.

"Everybody hated the Russians. Society hated the Russians in those days."

On the hatred scale, however, the Flyers rated just above the Russians. So when it came time to pick sides, hockey fans across

Flyers look to Russia

What's well known is the Flyers' refusal to draft Eastern bloc players during the days of the Cold War. What might be less known is which NHL team drafted the first Russian-born and -trained player—that would be the same Flyers.

In the ninth round of the 1975 draft, the Flyers picked Viktor Khatulev, a 6'3", 200-pound forward with a bad temper and a history of on-ice incidents. Khatulev had scored the gold medal-winning goal for the Soviets at the 1975 World Junior Championships, and despite knowing the chance of getting him out of Russia was slim, the Flyers picked him.

Khatulev spent most of his career playing in his native Latvia, and didn't know he had been drafted until 1978.

North America, who loathed all things black and orange, held their noses and rooted together.

"We were hated," Ed Snider recalled, "and suddenly all of Canada wanted us to win."

It wouldn't be easy, however.

"It was their All-Star team against our regular franchises, and they were winning," Snider said. "They came in here and we were the defending Stanley Cup champions. We were the team that everybody was hoping would finally beat these sons of bitches."

The Russians had beaten the Bruins and Rangers, and even the mighty Canadiens had only managed a tie. Suddenly, Philadelphia, the cradle of liberty, was the last bastion of hope. And on January 11, 1976, orange and black flew proudly next to the red, white, and blue.

The mood at the game was incredibly tense. Soviet officials demanded Spectrum ushers remove any signs that disparaged the Russians, and fans picketed outside the arena and handed out leaflets that explained Soviet human rights atrocities.

Inside the Flyers' locker room, the players admitted the game had a different vibe than a usual January game. "That was a little bit of pressure on the players," Dave Schultz said. "Wasn't a league game or a playoff game, but they were the Red Army. They were a great team."

Flyers coach Fred Shero respected the Soviet style of play and put in a game plan he thought would neutralize their immense speed and skill. "Once you had the patience and discipline to just wait, they had to bring the puck to you eventually," Clarke said. "They could keep going backward all they wanted, but they have to come forward at some point if they want to score. And once they started coming forward, we took them physically, and then they weren't so eager to come forward."

The Flyers hit the Russians every chance they got, with the resounding blow being Ed Van Impe's head-high hit on Valeri Kharlamov, who was considered one of the best players in the world.

"He basically ran into my elbow with his head," Van Impe joked in *Walking Together Forever*. "I've always said I just couldn't understand how a world-class player would have wanted to do such a thing."

The Russians screamed for a penalty, and their players gathered by the bench.

"They pulled all the players over in front of the bench, and they didn't want to come off for the faceoff," said Lou Nolan, the longtime PA announcer who was stationed next to the Soviet bench. "I remember talking to Lloyd Gilmour, he was the referee. We said it [the delay] is an intimidation factor, and he said yeah, I know—give them two minutes for delay of the game. When I announced that two minutes for delay of the game, they went berserk and that's when they left."

Led by coach Konstantin Loktev, the Russian team left the ice.

Snider huddled with NHL President Clarence Campbell and NHLPA boss Alan Eagleson, who had planned the tour, to figure out what to do.

"We went down, and they said we're not playing," Snider remembered. "They won't play, they're going to leave. I said, 'What's the status of the payment for this tournament?' They said we haven't given them anything yet. They get the check tonight for all the games. I said to tell them you're not going to pay them. I think we were the eighth game, and it was only like $25,000 a game in those days. They were supposed to get a couple hundred grand, but they hadn't been paid anything yet. It was supposed to be settled that night, so I said just tell them they're not going to get paid for the tour. They told them, they started huddling, then they came back and said, 'We play.'"

The Russians returned after a 17-minute absence, but it was obvious their hearts weren't in it.

"I played against them in '72, they were really tough," Clarke said of the famed Summit Series. "I knew a lot of those players, they were on that team." When the same team came to the Spectrum, however, Clarke said, "They were scared to death."

The Flyers walked off with a 4–1 victory, but they had accomplished so much more. They had beaten the stinkin' Russians, they had beaten Communism, and they had proven the dominance of all things North American.

"Probably the only time the league was cheering for us," Clarke said with a smile. "To this day."

43 J.J. Daigneault's One Shining Moment

The most wonderful thing about playoff hockey is that greatness is just a puck-bounce away.

J.J. Daigneault played just 114 games for the Flyers, but his place in team history is cast forever. It was May 28, 1987—Game 6 of the Stanley Cup Final. The Flyers had to win or their season was over. No pressure, right?

Daigneault had missed most of the playoffs with an ankle injury. He returned after a five-week absence for Game 3 against the Oilers but made little impact.

His teammates, however, were doing lots of good things. They rallied from a 3–0 second-period deficit to win Game 3 and came back from a 3–1 second-period hole in Game 5 to remain alive in the series and force Game 6 back at the Spectrum.

Brad McCrimmon was the hero in Game 3. It was Rick Tocchet and Brian Propp in Game 5. Who would step up in Game 6?

The Flyers, like they did the first five games of the series, fell behind as Kevin Lowe and Kevin McClelland scored 10 minutes apart in the first period, and the Flyers trailed by two after one period.

Slowly the Flyers chipped away. Lindsay Carson scored the lone goal of the second period, and then Propp's power-play goal at 13:04 of the third tied it.

Moments later, after Daigneault did a nice job checking Jari Kurri and helping send the play the other way, he skated off for a change. Coach Mike Keenan, though, told him to stay on. Meanwhile, Kurri had intercepted a Peter Zezel pass and tried to clear the Edmonton zone, but his weak attempt didn't make it to the blue line.

"Mark Howe was coming off and I wasn't sure," Daigneault told reporters. "I looked to the bench, and everybody said, 'Keep going.' I was pretty far away—about 20 feet—when I saw the puck."

As the puck dribbled to the left point, Daigneault controlled it just inside the blue line.

"I looked at the net, and my thought was to just put the puck on the net," Daigneault said. "Scott Mellanby was going by the front of the goal, and it's tough for the goalie to see the puck when he's screened like that. It was a pretty long shot."

All Oilers goalie Grant Fuhr saw was Mellanby's back and then the red light.

The roof remained on the Spectrum—but just barely.

"It was something that's hard to explain," Tocchet said. "It's a sudden rush of euphoria for everybody.... I remember the magnitude of it all. I had 14 buddies drive down in a Winnebago for that game. They said it was deafening. It was incredible. Whether you're an 80-year-old grandmother or a 5-year-old kid, they had the same reaction."

The goal came with 5:32 left, and after rookie goalie Ron Hextall made the lead stand up, the Flyers went back to Edmonton for Game 7. Daigneault made no impact, and the Flyers lost. He split the next season between the Flyers and AHL Hershey, and in November 1988 he was dealt to Montreal.

While Daigneault never became a star with the Flyers, his singular moment won't ever be forgotten.

44 When Animals Attack

The Flyers were just hitting their Broad Street Bullies stride when they played the Vancouver Canucks on December 29, 1972. There was the usual brutal action, but on this night things went far over the line.

During a fight between Bob Kelly and Jim Hargreaves, Don Saleski began pounding Canucks rookie Barry Wilcox, and at one point Saleski had him around the neck. When their brutal dance took them near the glass, a Vancouver fan took being the seventh man a little too literally.

This fan—a local dentist—reached over the glass and grabbed Saleski by his long, shaggy hair and tried to lift him off the ice.

"What I've heard is the fan thought I was really going to hurt this guy, the guy was in danger, so he reached over and pulled my hair to try to stop me from hurting him," Saleski says today.

While Saleski said he had no idea what was happening, his teammates certainly did.

Backup goalie Bob Taylor, sitting on the bench next to where the action was, jumped off his seat and into the stands. Other teammates saw what was going on and followed Taylor into the crowd.

"I couldn't let him do that to Donny," Taylor said after the game. "Everything would be all right if the fans would keep out of the action on the ice."

Barry Ashbee was next into the stands after Taylor, followed closely by Ed Van Impe and Cowboy Bill Flett. After Flett pulled Taylor out of the crowd, he remarked, "That's the first time a Cowboy ever saved an Indian."

Seven players were charged with various crimes, including Saleski, whose only crime, apparently, was having long hair.

"I was one of the only players on the team that didn't go in the stands, and I was guilty by association," Saleski said, "because all I had was somebody pull my hair and I ended up being arrested for assault and everything else. I was a victim."

They got over the incident fairly easily. When they returned to Vancouver in February, the Flyers again pounded the Canucks, which led to this memorable line from Moose Dupont, who uttered it in his Quebecois accent:

"We don't go to jail, we beat up der chicken forwards, we score 10 goals, and we win. And now de Moose drinks beer."

In June the Vancouver 7, as they were called—Van Impe, Ashbee, Taylor, Flett, Saleski, Joe Watson, and Ross Lonsberry—were all fined $500 each, except for Lonsberry, who successfully appealed and wasn't fined. Taylor received a 30-day jail sentence, but it was changed to a suspended sentence on appeal.

"Bobby Taylor, a fan or what he thought was a fan, grabbed him from behind and he turned around and slugged a guy and knocked him down about three rows," Saleski said. "It was a cop, so that was pretty serious."

45 Rock 'Em, Sock 'Em Tocchet

The best players in Flyers history generally had two common traits—toughness and skill. Few epitomized those qualities more than Rick Tocchet.

Tocchet was a sixth-round pick in the 1983 NHL Draft. The forward's skating was a major issue during his junior days in the Ontario Hockey League with the Sault Ste. Marie Greyhounds, and his other skills did little to distinguish him. He was drafted mostly as a favor to Greyhounds GM Sam McMaster, who had been a Flyers scout.

"Tock's skating was off…he had a high kick to his stride so it looked like he wasn't a good skater," Bob Clarke said. "But he became an effective skater by hard work. He had a fierce, fierce determination to make it. There was nothing that was going to stop him, nothing was going to get in his road to making the Flyers, making the NHL."

That started in 1984, when Tocchet was part of a young nucleus that included Peter Zezel, Murray Craven, Dave Poulin, and Pelle Lindbergh. The youngest team in the league, under a first-time NHL coach in Mike Keenan and a first-time-ever GM in

Clarke, advanced to the 1985 Stanley Cup Final. Tocchet had 14 goals, 39 points, and 181 penalty minutes. The next two seasons, he had more than 280 minutes in the sin bin.

After the 1986–87 season, however, Clarke called him in for a career-changing chat.

"I had him in and told him he couldn't fight anymore," Clarke said. "For me, he was a really, really good team player, [but] he was fighting too much. It got to the point where someone pissed him off and he'd beat the shit out of him or want to fight him. I said if we only want guys to fight, Rick, I'll get someone who can only fight. You've got to play hockey and only fight when someone bothers a weaker member of your team. You can't fight for yourself because you're too good a player. You don't have to prove to us you're tough. Prove to us that you're a good player, that you can score."

Tocchet took the advice to heart and set out to change himself from a fighter who could score a little to a scorer who would fight a little. "In my third year, I went home for the summer and Mike

Zezel the Ladies' Man

During the mid-1980s, the favorite player of every Flyers fans' wife or girlfriend was Peter Zezel.

"If we'd go out to get something to eat, usually the girls would go to Peter and the guys would come to me and say nice fight," Rick Tocchet said.

Zezel, who passed away from a rare blood disease in 2009, was always one of the more popular players on his teams—and not only with the ladies.

"The marketing people loved him," Tocchet said. "The one thing with Peter, and I always respected this about him, he would never turn down going to a hospital or talking to a kid…. He was a special guy."

Keenan said, 'I need more from you on the offensive end.' I went home and my dad made downstairs in the basement a shooting gallery. He used a parachute and I would shoot 200, 300 pucks a day. I had a chance to go to the Team Canada [Canada Cup] training camp, which was huge for me. I just started to realize how I was going to score—I had to be in front of the net. I didn't have a quick shot, I wasn't a talented guy where I could go down the wing and deke everybody out. I just kind of knew what I had to do, and I tried to become good at that, whatever qualities I had."

In 1987–88 he scored 31 goals and started his career ascent. He had 45 goals in 1988–89 and 37 the season after; he still fought, but now he was scoring goals at a high rate. And when Ron Sutter was traded, Tocchet was given the captaincy for the 1991–92 season.

"It's a big thrill because of the history of it," Tocchet said. "It means a lot. They don't just throw a 'C' on your chest. It was something…I hate to use the cliché of passing the torch, but it's something you make sure you have some dignity with. It was special."

The special feelings didn't last long, however, as the fading Flyers traded Tocchet on February 19, 1992, to the Pittsburgh Penguins, who he helped win a Stanley Cup as a second-line complement to Mario Lemieux and Jaromir Jagr.

After stops in Los Angeles, Boston, Washington, and Phoenix, Tocchet returned to Philadelphia during the 1999–2000 season. While his skills had subsided, Tocchet still played a major role on and off the ice in helping the team reach the 2000 Eastern Conference Finals, scoring five goals and 11 points in 18 playoff games.

He retired following 2001–02 season after a preseason knee injury limited him to just 14 games. He retired with 440 goals and 2,972 penalty minutes, making him one of just five players in NHL history with 400-plus goals and 2,000-plus penalty minutes.

46 The Seven-Year Five-Day Deal

By late 1989, the Spectrum was starting to show some age, and Ed Snider began investigating constructing a new home for his hockey team. Sixers owner Harold Katz, whose basketball team was a tenant in Snider's hockey home, had begun discussions with officials in New Jersey about building his own place on the Camden waterfront.

Philadelphia Mayor Wilson Goode knew what Katz was doing and envisioned Snider doing something similar. Not wanting to lose the capital both sports teams brought in, Goode told Snider at a Police Athletic League dinner in November 1989 that a deal for a new arena in Philadelphia could be approved in five days.

Snider reached out to Katz, and the pair agreed to work with Philadelphia officials on a new building. The site agreed upon was JFK Stadium, which had fallen into disrepair. With the city near bankrupt, Goode agreed to give the land to Snider and not assess property taxes in exchange for the club paying construction costs and financing the arena privately.

New Jersey officials caught wind of the deal prior to its announcement and raised their offer from a flat $100 million to 80 percent of construction costs. Katz and others pushed for the New Jersey deal, but Snider used a map to show why staying in South Philadelphia was the best plan.

"We were in the best location in the Delaware Valley," Snider said in *Full Spectrum*. "The subway and I–95 are right there. I was reluctant to go to another location that I thought was less desirable."

City politics came into play, however, and the deal constantly was being changed. Plans for a 21,000-seat building with a

The Name Game

The Flyers' second home has changed names like the team changes coaches.

In September 1994, CoreStates Financial Corp. spent $40 million to buy the naming rights to the new building, as well as the Spectrum. The contract was for 29 years. The names lasted four.

First Union merged with CoreStates, and on September 1, 1998, the buildings were renamed for First Union. Then on July 28, 2003, Wachovia Security's purchase of First Union meant another new name for the buildings.

And on July 1, 1010, the building became known as the Wells Fargo Center, reflecting Wells Fargo's 2008 purchase of Wachovia Security.

parking garage were scrapped; the city was going to charge Snider for the land; the property tax abatement would last only five years.

A contract was approved by Philadelphia City Council on July 7, 1991, but a year later, no construction had started. Late in 1993, Snider tore up his deal with the city and with Katz, who he had grown tired of dealing with. Katz almost immediately made a deal with New Jersey governor Jim Florio for an arena on the Camden waterfront, but when Florio lost his re-election bid to Christie Whitman, that deal died.

Meanwhile, Snider finally found funding for a new hockey home from Prudential Power Funding Associates, who gave him $140 million. With money in hand, Snider and Katz again agreed on a deal for the teams to share a new building, and on February 1, 1994, the new arena—named Spectrum II—was announced. On June 23, the Philadelphia City Council approved the agreement, and ground was broken September 13.

On August 31, 1996, the CoreStates Center was finished— only seven years after Wilson Goode's five-day promise.

"From the time I had the idea to build the Spectrum to the time it was completed was 16 months," Snider recalled. "Construction was 11 months. On the same parking lot, that building cost $6.5 million to build. This one cost $200-and-something [actually $210] million. The agreements with the city and everybody else for [the Spectrum] was about [3-4 inches] thick; the agreements for this building filled a whole conference room. Same city, same parking lot, same circumstances. Just the workmen's compensation for this building cost more than that building [the Spectrum] to build."

47 Gene Hart—The Cheap Alternative

Reaching out to the fans is one of the most important jobs a sports broadcaster has. It's the broadcaster's job to not just tell the fans what's happening on the ice but to explain why and to say it in an impactful yet entertaining way.

And when it comes to an expansion team, that broadcaster not only has to know the game but has to be able to teach a fan base about the new sport. All of which made Gene Hart the perfect choice—not that anyone realized it at the time.

"I'd like to think the Flyers selected me because I had the best audition tape around," Hart once told the *Philadelphia Inquirer*. "But I was expedient. They had to buy radio time. They had no contract. They wanted someone who could do hockey, and I kept sticking my face around. Obviously, the Flyers' budget wouldn't allow them to bring in some high-priced import from Canada, so they penciled in the local native sports guy from South Jersey, despite his being fat, unknown, and one of the world's worst dressers."

Over the next 35 years, Hart became a hockey minstrel, spreading the gospel of the great game over the airwaves, at charity luncheons, and at golf tournaments throughout the Delaware Valley.

"Gene was a fabulous ambassador for our sport," Islanders Hall of Fame broadcaster Jiggs McDonald told the *Philadelphia Inquirer*.

Early on, Hart also was a full-time school teacher. Oftentimes Hart would return home from a road trip with enough time to drop his suitcase, freshen up, and then get to school.

"A lot of people don't realize that for about 10 years, he would do games on the road and then take a red-eye back to New Jersey to teach school the next day," Ed Snider said.

Hart wasn't the only person showing up at school exhausted. Young hockey fans would stay up well past their bedtimes, sneaking their radios into bed to listen to Hart's call on Flyers games.

"I would fall asleep with Flyers games," said the one-named Eklund, the anonymous proprietor of the popular hockey website Hockeybuzz.com. "I would put the [radio] underneath my pillow."

It didn't take long for Hart's voice to become synonymous with hockey in Philadelphia. He called every game from 1967 until his retirement in 1995.

"Gene Hart taught us the game," legendary Philadelphia broadcaster Bill Campbell said in Hart's obituary.

But Hart wasn't solely a broadcaster. His interests were wide and varied. He loved the opera and learned a number of different languages—including Russian, which came in handy when the Central Red Army team visited in 1976.

"We had a luncheon that the league put on in what was the Blue Line Club that's now called Ovations," Snider said. "The Russian players were on one side, and our players were on the other.... So Gene taught me how to say in Russian, '*We welcome you to our fair city*' and '*We hope you're enjoying yourselves,*' something like that. So I practiced and practiced, got up, and I said, '*We're looking forward to the game tonight, may the best team win,*' and I sat down. Gene said, 'Did you forget?' I said, 'I looked at those son of a bitches and I couldn't welcome them.'"

Hart was as beloved a member of the team as any player. When the Flyers decided to go with separate television and radio broadcasts in 1988—for years the club had simulcast the radio feed on TV—Hart was pushed to radio. Fans complained, and in a 1993 survey sent to season-ticket holders about how to improve the team, the suggestion most often heard was for Hart to be back on TV.

Hart retired following the 1994–95 season, and in 1997, the cheap alternative was inducted into the Hockey Hall of Fame.

Hart passed away July 14, 1999, but his legacy remains.

"When you think of Gene Hart," Snider told the audience at Hart's funeral, "you think Flyers."

48 The Rifle Shoots 5

The legend of what happened on May 5-6, 1976, has grown to big-fish-story proportions. Was Reggie Leach drunk the night he scored five goals in a playoff game against the Boston Bruins? Was he hung over? Did he hate Fred Shero? Was Shero going to bench him?

Leach entered the playoffs with a team-record 61 goals, and he combined with linemates Bob Clarke and Bill Barber for a remarkable 141 goals and 322 points.

Leach's outstanding play carried right into the postseason. He scored the Flyers' first goal of the playoffs and had six goals in seven games in the first round against the Maple Leafs.

He scored a goal in the last four games of the Leafs series, and that carried into the next round against the Bruins. His goal streak was at eight going into Game 5.

The Drive for Five

Only five players in the history of the NHL have scored five goals in a playoff game, and the Flyers have been involved in the three most recent occurrences. On April 22, 1976—two weeks before Reggie Leach's five-goal game—the Maple Leafs' Darryl Sitler scored five times against the Flyers in Game 6 of the teams' quarterfinal series. The Leafs won 8–6 but lost in Game 7.

And on April 25, 1989, Mario Lemieux had a hat trick 6:55 into the game, four goals in the first period, and an empty-netter for his fifth goal in a wild 10–7 Penguins win in Game 4 of the Patrick Division Finals. The Flyers, however, won the next two games to win the series.

The Flyers led the series 3–1, but all was not well in Flyer-land.

Leach and Shero had always had a tenuous relationship, with Shero constantly pushing Leach to work harder so he could get full value for his tremendous skill. The night before Game 5, however, something happened.

"We stayed at a hotel down in Valley Forge the night before that game," Leach said in *Walking Together Forever*. "I got into a big argument that night with one of the coaches, so I got drunk and went home."

The next day, when Leach no-showed for the morning skate, teammates found Leach passed out in the basement of his Cherry Hill home. They tried coffee and a shower to revive him, but that didn't work. A few more drinks, however, seemed to do the trick.

"I had a couple of beers to revive me and told him [Clarke] to take me to the rink so I could play," Leach said.

The hair of the dog seemed to work well enough, but when they arrived at the Spectrum, Shero wasn't going to let Leach play. "When we got to the Spectrum, Freddy saw what shape I was in, and he wasn't going to play me," Leach said. "Clarkie told him, 'Let him play. He will probably score a bunch of goals.'"

Even half in the bag, Clark knew what Leach could do. The pair had been playing together since they were teenagers, and played the same way in 1976 they did in 1966—Clarke the distributor, Leach the high-scoring gunner.

"He was, for me, the best pure goal scorer that I had ever played with," Clarke said. "Giving him the puck was easy. I always used to tell him, if I want to shoot the puck I won't pass it to you, but if I pass it to you, you shoot it. He could score from anywhere at anytime. Two or three [a game] was nothing for him. He had six or seven one night in junior."

That particular night against the Bruins, it was like Leach was skating against junior players again.

He scored three times on backhanders—to the short side, the wide side, and under the crossbar. Three times he scored after he crossed from right wing to left. He scored the game's first goal, and after the Bruins tied it, he put the game away with a second-period natural hat trick.

He became the first Flyer to score five in a game, and he's one of five players ever to score five in a playoff game.

Leach finished the series with nine goals in five games. He had a 10-game goal-scoring streak and a record 19 goals in 16 playoff games. Even though the Flyers lost the Cup to the Canadiens, Leach was rewarded with the Conn Smythe Trophy as playoff MVP.

49 From the Checking Line to the Front Line

Ben Stafford never played an NHL game, but his contribution to the Flyers' organization is impossible to overlook.

Stafford signed with the club in 2001 after graduating from Yale. He never rose above the AHL level, but he had a number of memorable moments with the Phantoms, and in his last game, he helped the club clinch the 2005 Calder Cup.

"He could play on your fourth line or your first line," John Stevens, who coached Stafford on the Phantoms, told NHL.com. "He could play five minutes or 15 minutes, and he was your best five-minute player or your best 15-minute player. He was willing to do whatever he could do to help the team."

Stafford, however, is now playing with a new team—the U.S. Marine Corps.

Stafford, a native of Edina, Minnesota, retired from hockey following the Calder Cup to enroll at Jefferson Medical College at Thomas Jefferson University in Philadelphia.

"I wanted to play hockey for as long as I could, and I would have kept playing if I thought I had a good shot at being a consistent NHLer. That didn't seem to be happening," Stafford told the *Philadelphia Inquirer* in an April 2009 interview. "I was doing well in the AHL and enjoyed playing for the Phantoms, but I had other things on my mind, i.e. medicine and the military. I knew 2005 would be my last season before the playoffs started. Winning the Calder Cup was an added bonus on my way out."

While Stafford played and studied, the atrocities of September 11, 2001, stuck with him. That's why early in his second year of medical school, he dropped out and enlisted in the Marines.

"It was something he'd been thinking about for a long time, even when he was playing hockey," Ben's wife, Ali, told NHL.com. "Then he got into medical school, but even when he was in medical school he felt he still really wanted to do this."

For Stafford, his decision was an easy one. Informing family and friends, though, wasn't so simple. Ali described telling Ben's parents as "a weird time."

"A lot of people ask me why I became a Marine, and I can comfortably say that it was the right decision," Stafford told the *Inquirer*. "Leading infantry Marines in a combat zone has been, and will most likely always be, the greatest honor and privilege of my life."

Others tried talking him out of doing this, but they quickly realized that Stafford was set in his path.

"He feels strongly about it," said Flyers equipment manager Derek Settlemyre, who held that post with the Phantoms during Stafford's time there. "Anything you say he comes back with an answer. That's what he believes.... Any point I had, he countered."

"He's got real strong beliefs as a citizen of this country, and he feels it's part of his duty to serve this country," Stevens said. "He was a history major, he's a well-educated guy. He feels this obligation to serve his country. I certainly think you have to respect him for that. I think that's what made him such a team guy. I think it's somewhat ironic that he scored the winning goal in our championship game, but he's just that guy [who] always has a good reason for what he does. He was a firm member of our team. He's a firm citizen. After talking to him, you had a real appreciation for what he wanted to do."

Stafford never is far from his former teammates who have graduated to the Flyers. Trainer Jim McCrossin had dog tags made up for some of the players on that championship Phantoms team, and he leads the effort to send care packages to Stafford and other Delaware Valley residents serving in the military.

McCrossin talks to Stafford as often as he can, but it isn't often enough.

"He said he was in Iraq for a while, then he said he couldn't tell me where he was so I didn't ask," McCrossin told NHL.com. "I just know one time he said, 'Jimmy I'm hunting the bad guys.'"

50 Scrapping in Sandals

Hockey players are a superstitious lot. They'll wear a certain T-shirt under their jersey, yank on a certain hat after a game, or tape their stick the same way every day. It's easier to break a bone than to break their ritual.

During the 1987 playoffs, Montreal forward Claude Lemieux had developed his own ritual—before he left the ice for warm-ups, he would shoot a puck into the opposing team's net. The Flyers caught wind of this before the teams met in the Wales Conference Finals and made it their goal to keep Lemieux from reaching his.

Leading the battle for the Flyers was defenseman Ed Hospodar. When Lemieux tried to score before Game 3, Hospodar blocked the shot and returned fire into the Montreal goal. Prior to Game 4, Hospodar and backup goalie Chico Resch turned the net backward before leaving the ice. When they did the same thing before Game 5 at the Spectrum, Montreal defenseman Chris Chelios skated down and turned the net the right way to indulge Lemieux.

In Game 6, Hospodar and Resch waited until Lemieux left the ice before returning to the locker room. Suddenly Lemieux and Shayne Corson reappeared, skated out with a puck and went toward the Flyers' net.

Hospodar didn't appreciate the ruse. He jumped back on the ice, chased Lemieux down and began pounding him. At that point, a Flyers equipment manager ran into the locker room to tell the other players what was going on. Players from both teams spilled back onto the ice ready to fight, but many weren't dressed for the occasion. Some had no shirt on, some weren't wearing skates. Doug Crossman ran out in a pair of sandals.

"I was in the dressing room, I think I had my skates off," Rick Tocchet recalled. "Our trainer came running in, 'There's a brawl, there's a brawl.'"

"We'd all gone off the ice and after that we piled out there and everyone went at it," Dave Brown added. "I've never seen anything like that before."

One of the players who missed the festivities was Ron Hextall. When coach Mike Keenan saw Hextall ready to rumble, the coach restrained him and shoved him back into the locker room. Not knowing what would happen to the players involved, Keenan knew Hextall was the player he could least afford to lose.

It took referees—who were also still getting dressed—more than 15 minutes to break up all the action and get the players back to their locker rooms.

The players were fined a combined $24,500, and Hospodor was suspended for the remainder of the postseason.

51 Not a Bad Start, Kid

Through the 2009–10 season, 5,895 skaters have suited up for at least one game. That means there were 5,873 debut games. Of all those thousands and thousands of players, none have had a better first game than Al Hill.

Hill played 221 NHL games over parts of eight seasons—all with the Flyers. He had 95 points in that time, so he was far from a Gretzky-esque scorer. But on February 14, 1977, he accomplished something not even the Great One did.

In a game at the Spectrum against the St. Louis Blues, Hill scored a pair of goals and handed out three assists in a 6–4 Flyers

Bladon's Great Fight

Darryl Sitler. Rocket Richard. Wayne Gretzky. Mario Lemieux. Paul Coffey. Bernie Nichols. Peter Stastny. Bert Olmstead. Anton Stastny. Bryan Trottier. Tom Bladon.

Which name doesn't quite fit? Yup, that would be Bladon, who on December 11, 1977, became one of 10 players in NHL history—but the lone defenseman—to score at least eight points in a game.

Bladon had four goals and four assists against the short-lived Cleveland Barons in an 11–1 Flyers win.

"Tom had a really good shot, he could really shoot it," Bob Clarke said. "Just a good, honest hockey player, with good skills—could pass it good, shoot it good. That was just one of those nights."

win, and in the process he set an NHL record for most points by a player in his first game.

It wasn't an easy trip for Hill to reach the NHL—literally.

"I was playing in Rochester [New York] the night before and playing for Springfield [Massachusetts], and we bussed all the way back. It was a long drive, was snowing like crazy," recalled Hill, now a pro scout for the Flyers. "I just got back to my apartment and Walter Atanas, who was one of the scouts for the Flyers, was living in Springfield and he gave me the call and said you're going up [to the NHL] tomorrow, be ready. I got a plane ticket for you, and I'm going to pick you up at 7:00 in the morning, and I'll take you to the airport.

"Got to the airport and it was snowing like crazy, and I didn't think I was going to make it. And it was snowing in Philly, too. I ended up flying, made it to the airport, took a cab over [to the Spectrum]. Barely made it over in the cab because there was a lot of snow that day."

He got to the building about two hours before the 7:35 PM start. Hill had little time to get dressed and ready to go.

"Freddie Shero had a thing with new guys coming up that he'd always play them the first shift," Hill said, "so I ended up starting the game with Bob Clarke and Bob Kelly."

Hill scored that first shift, which got the ball rolling on his remarkable night.

"I had a good start and the momentum got going and everything I touched seemed to go in the net, either by me or someone else," said Hill. "One of those nights that everything worked out great."

Was the bar set for a promising NHL career? Not quite.

"That's where you're hoping the expectation wasn't going to be doing it every night because I knew it wasn't going to happen," Hill said. "The next game I played, against the Rangers, I should have had three goals. I had three point-blank shots, and I got stopped on every one. That's the way it goes.

"I never really was that kind of player. I had points in junior, but nothing like getting five in my first game in the NHL. That wasn't me. I had 41 points that year in the American League, so I wasn't exactly ripping it up down there, either."

After two more NHL games, Hill was returned to Springfield.

More than 30 years later, Hill is surprised to find his name in a unique spot in the NHL record book.

"I never would have thought it would have lasted this long," he said. "It gets brought up everywhere I go. That's what I'm known for more than anything, that first game. But it's still a nice thing to have."

JR Style

Jeremy Roenick's introductory press conference showed Philadelphia Flyers fans just what they were getting. Roenick gave owner Ed Snider a big hug and said, "Mr. Schneider, thank you very much." After saying a few more words, he lifted an imaginary Stanley Cup over his head.

Loud, over-the-top public displays were just another day at the office for Roenick, who admitted, "I'm not afraid of a camera or microphone. I really enjoy it."

"The thing I remember about him the most is the disco ball," Keith Primeau said. "We listened to music before games, but he literally had a disco ball placed in the room and he would turn on disco music and start dancing to it. It was very different from the norm and so very JR."

He dressed as Bobby Clarke one year for Halloween—skating out for pregame warm-ups with a curly blond wig, fake missing teeth, Cooperalls, and a No. 16 jersey. Another time, he hit the glass during warm-ups to knock a fan's beer off the ledge. Roenick then got a $5 bill from a trainer, slid it to the fan between the panes of glass and told him to have another drink on JR."

Those are just some of the examples of Roenick doing what he could to make the fans feel special. It's something that happened to him when he was a 7-year-old going to Hartford Whalers games, and he always felt a duty to pay it forward.

"I was standing up against the glass and Gordie [Howe] scooped up a stick full of ice and dumped it on my head," Roenick said. "He acknowledged me. I thought that was the coolest thing of all time. It happened 32 years ago, and I still remember as if it was yesterday. Gordie didn't think anything of it, but I did. That's why I make sure that every time I'm on the ice I try to give two seconds to as many people as I can. Whether it's throwing pucks over the glass, making eye contact or giving a wink, I acknowledge as many people as I can. I want them to know we're there playing for them."

Roenick wouldn't just make nice to the fans. His constant quotes and quick quips kept reporters' notebooks filled. And even when he couldn't talk, Roenick still made for good copy.

Yes, JR, It's Still News

Jeremy Roenick only played three seasons in Philadelphia, but he so loved the attention the Flyers' beat writers lavished on him that when he decided to retire, it was in the form of a text message to the *Philadelphia Inquirer's* Tim Panaccio on July 4, 2007.

"I'm retiring. Is that still news?" was the message, and yes, it certainly was, as media across North America picked up the story.

It was short-lived news, however; two months later Roenick unretired to play two final seasons with the San Jose Sharks.

In a game at Madison Square Garden on February 12, 2004, Roenick was drilled in the face by a Boris Mironov slap shot. The blast left him bloodied and down on the ice for several minutes. Finally, a woozy Roenick got to his feet, and in classic JR style, waved to the cheering MSG crowd as he left the ice. And the man who never walked away from an interview was conducting them on his cell phone in the ambulance on the way to the hospital until a Flyers PR official finally ripped the phone from his hand.

Roenick suffered a broken jaw and a concussion, and he contemplated retirement. He eventually returned and danced his famous jig after scoring the series-clinching overtime goal against the Maple Leafs in the second round of the 2004 playoffs.

That would be Roenick's final shining moment with the Flyers, as he was traded to Los Angeles following the lockout to make cap space for the signing of Peter Forsberg. He bounced from the Kings to Phoenix to San Jose before retiring following the 2009 playoffs.

Roenick left an impression on those who were privileged to be around him.

"JR was a special kind of player and a special kind of person," Primeau said. "He treated everybody the same. I think that's what makes people respond to him. He was a real down-to-earth guy and very warm and kind."

Fans felt that, as well.

Dave Leonardi, aka Sign Man, had become friendly with Roenick, who had appreciated some of Leonardi's signs.

"I was in San Jose for a ski show and he had 499 goals and I got a ticket to the game by myself, and as soon as I got the tickets I went to my hotel room and bought some magic markers and a piece of paper and made a sign that I was here to see 500," Leonardi said. "I went to the glass at warm-ups and he was stretching and I yelled around the glass and he said, 'What are you doing here?' I said, 'Read the sign.' And in the second period he got the [500th] goal." Leonardi can be seen in the background of the highlight video wearing a Flyers Orange Crush T-shirt.

53 Friday Night at the Fights

When the Ottawa Senators visited the Wachovia Center on March 5, 2004, there was a different kind of atmosphere in the building. Not only were the teams fighting for Eastern Conference supremacy, it was the first time they were meeting since Sens winger Martin Havlat had cross-checked Mark Recchi in the face. Havlat was suspended for his stick-work, but the Flyers were more interested in meting out their own justice.

Early on, however, the Senators were the ones throwing around the body. A hit by Ottawa's Shaun Van Allen knocked Joni Pitkanen out with a concussion, and Marian Hossa left Chris Therien with a shoulder injury following a collision along the wall.

The Flyers were losing players but were winning the game and were leading 5–2 when, with 1:45 left in the game, it turned into 1973.

Donald Brashear and Senators tough guy Rob Ray started the festivities. The pair were tangling in front of the Flyers' net when Brashear shoved Ray, who responded by elbowing Brashear in the head. Brashear than began raining left hands down on Ray's face, and then a nasty right cross opened a vicious gash over Ray's right eye.

While Brashear watched Ray skate off, two Senators—Todd Simpson and Brian Pothier—jumped Brashear from behind, with Pothier throwing punches over a linesman. When Patrick Sharp tried to intervene, Simpson knocked him down and began pounding him. Danny Markov jumped in and began scrapping with Simpson.

At the same time, Senators goalie Patrick Lalime began shedding his gear and skated into the fray, heading right for Flyers netminder Robert Esche, who provided a more than willing combatant. At the same time, Branko Radivojevic was tossing Van Allen around, and the brave Simpson, all 6'3" and 215 pounds of him, showed his courage level by poking at 5'10", 180-pound Sami Kapanen.

When officials restored order, Brashear, Markov, Esche, and Radivojevic stood in the tunnel leading to the locker room watching the replays on the center-ice scoreboard, and Brashear continued to jaw at the Senators as they skated off.

Round 2 began at the drop of the next puck, when Senators tough guy Chris Neil first speared soft second-year winger Radovan Somik, then began throwing punches at him. Neil easily buried Somik, who at least got in one good punch, but Neil got at least one cheap shot in after he knocked down Somik.

Meanwhile, Sens gargantuan defenseman Zdeno Chara, all 6'9" of him, made a beeline for another non-fighting Flyer, 6'1" defenseman Mattias Timander. Chara rag-dolled Timander for a bit before officials broke it up.

Meanwhile, In Hocky Action...

The monster brawl game against the Senators in 2004 featured some non-fight-related milestones. Danny Markov's first-period goal was the 10,000th in Flyers history, making them the fifth team—and first expansion club—to reach that milestone.

It also was the 1,000th game of Tony Amonte's career.

Only three seconds had dripped off the game clock.

Round 3 came on the next faceoff between centers Michal Handzus and Mike Fisher. The bigger Handzus, though, got a little overzealous and allowed Fisher to use his leverage to flip Handzus down onto his back in what could have been a scary scene. Instead, the Flyers' Czech ironman skated off as part of the seventh major fighting incident of the night.

After all that, another three seconds had dribbled away.

Finally, a hockey game interrupted the fights, which caused the fans to boo lustily. Only in Philadelphia. But they wouldn't have to wait long for Round 4.

After a Flyers dump-in, Recchi laid a solid hit on Senators defenseman Wade Redden, who responded by grabbing the nearest Flyer, which happened to be John LeClair.

While those two big bulls wrestled around in the Ottawa end, back at center ice Recchi and Bryan Smolinski threw down their gloves and went at it, with the tenacious Recchi pounding Smolinski with right hands before Smolinski landed a right cross and both players ran out of gas.

This time, 24 seconds had elapsed, leaving 1:15 of game action remaining, which was just enough time for one final throwdown.

At the next drop of the puck, Ottawa center Jason Spezza went after Sharp, which turned out badly for Spezza. As Spezza came forward, Sharp caught him and threw a few right hands, and when

Spezza went down, Sharp landed on top of him and got in another good shot before the officials could separate them.

After Sharp and Spezza were sent off and the teams lined up for the faceoff, there were as many players left on the Flyers' bench—Alexei Zhamnov, John Slaney, and Tony Amonte—as there were coaches. There were just two players left on the Ottawa bench, Hossa and Antoine Vermette.

All the while, the player around whom all the venom centered, Havlat, sat safely in the penalty box, sent there by coach Jacques Martin to serve a penalty.

The final tally showed a number of NHL records—most combined penalty minutes, 413; most penalty minutes in a period, 409 in the third; most penalty minutes for a team in a game, 213 for the Flyers; and most penalty minutes for one team in a period, 209 for the Flyers in the third.

54 Do the Guffaw

Brian Propp scored more than 400 goals with the Flyers, and after many of them came the oddest of celebrations—the Guffaw.

While Propp popularized the motion—a short right-to-left wave and then extending the arm straight up—the move was originated by comedian Howie Mandel.

Propp first saw Mandel do the Guffaw at an Atlantic City comedy show in the summer of 1986. Looking for a way to stand out from the crowd, Propp decided he would do the Guffaw after he scored his first goal that season.

"I had the usual crowd of players congratulating me after the goal," Propp wrote on his website to describe the origin of his celebration. "Then as I broke away from the pack and headed to center ice, I put my right glove under my left arm and did the Guffaw as I skated toward center ice. I have always said the word 'guffaw' as I was doing it…. Well, I scored another goal in that game and went right back to center ice and did the Guffaw again."

Mandel—a Canadian and a hockey fan—learned Propp was Guffaw-ing after his goals and called Propp before a playoff game in 1987 to give his stamp of approval.

"I thought Turk [Evers], the equipment manager, was playing a joke, but sure enough, it was Howie Mandel on the line," Propp wrote. "He thought it was great that I was using the Guffaw and he didn't mind if I used it. That was a thrill for me to get his approval."

Propp took the Guffaw with him to Boston, Minnesota, and Europe for a few seasons, and even in retirement he still uses it today, whether it's to celebrate a goal in a Flyers Alumni game or a birdie on the golf course. Propp ran for political office in New Jersey in 2008, and it's a certainty he would have Guffaw-ed as part of his acceptance speech had he won.

"I have been very proud of my signature mark, and it is a lot of fun to watch young children at the hockey rinks and other places copying the Guffaw," Propp wrote. "I love it when people show their personality and emotion in a happy way."

 **55 Bookmark Flyershistory.net**

The Internet is a fabulous place, and anyone who uses it has found their pet places for whatever it is they're looking for.

For Flyers fans, there's really no better place to go than Flyershistory.net.

Can knowing who the Flyers traded to acquire Trent Klatt settle a bar bet? Wondering who the Flyers beat in the 11th game of their record 35-game unbeaten streak? Need to know who was on the Flyers' 1978 training camp roster? Flyershistory.net has all those answers and much more.

(If you're wondering, the answers are Brent Fedyk to the Dallas Stars on December 13, 1995; the New York Islanders 5–2 on November 10, 1979; and such luminaries as Dana Decker, Mike Ewanouski, and Gord Salt.)

The site was developed and is maintained by Peter Anson, a resident of St. Catharine's, Ontario. In addition to every box score—regular season and playoff—the site has a bio page for every player who has ever worn a black and orange sweater, plus a list of every trade, every free agent signing, every in-season transaction, and more on an easy-to-navigate site.

Anson pledged allegiance to the Flyers during the 1975 Stanley Cup Final when he was 9 years old.

"The Sabres were a more skillful team, but the Flyers looked like they tried harder and it was cool that they could overcome a more skillful team with their work ethic," Anson said. "Been a fan ever since."

That fandom led him to create the site in September 1998 as a hobby when he wasn't at his real job as a computer programmer for a steel company.

"I started it off as a hobby, something I could do at home," Anson said. "I was always a stats hound as a kid. Originally the intention was to have an overview of each season and that was going to be it. As I was building it, I learned how to do more things, add scripts. Then I did a page on each player."

And that has built up to what it is today, with links to news stories, message boards, and places to buy Flyers merchandise.

Anson admits he'll never get rich off the site—he has ads, but in the two years he's had them, he estimates he's made about $30—it remains, in his words, "Just a labor of love."

Flyers fans who take the time to surf over to Flyershistory.net will feel the same way.

56 More Than a Nice Head of Hair

Folks in the Delaware Valley don't need to be hockey fans to know who Scott Hartnell is. The reddish-brown shrubbery sprouting from his head makes him hard to miss.

"You can't have hair like that and not have people notice eventually," former linemate Joffrey Lupul told NHL.com.

Hartnell trimmed about an inch off his curly locks in early January 2010, but he hasn't had a real haircut since his first week with the Flyers in the summer of 2007.

Family and friends don't complain, and neither does the Flyers' marketing department—there was even a Scott Hartnell Wig Night during the 2008–09 season.

"I don't want to say it's my trademark, but it's what I got going," Hartnell said. "It doesn't bother me too much. I just throw it in a ponytail to get it out of my face."

That's the kind of easygoing attitude that has made Hartnell a locker-room favorite during his three seasons in Philadelphia.

"The attitude of his life, he's always happy, positive," said Kimmo Timonen, who came to Philadelphia with Hartnell after being teammates with him in Nashville for six seasons. "I think his approach to his life and his respect for his teammates are huge. It's always positive. He's a funny person."

Scott Hartnell's long, bushy hair is just one reason he stands out. (Canadian Press via AP Images/Larry MacDougal)

Hartnell has no problem bringing the funny. Whether it's winning poker hands on the team plane, trying to knock down guys in practice, or being in the middle of a snowball fight during practice at the Winter Classic, Hartnell almost always is having a good time.

"It keeps things loose for sure," Hartnell said. "Keeps guys giggling around the room."

"There's a lot of those [funny moments]," Timonen said, "but you probably can't put those in the book."

One of the funnier moments came in a game against the Lightning on December 2, 2008. With 16.3 seconds left in the third period of a 3–3 game, Tampa forward Ryan Malone broke in alone on goalie Martin Biron. Hartnell, who had lost his stick earlier in the shift, gave chase but had no chance of catching Malone. With little else to do, Hartnell—to the disbelief of the 19,227 in attendance, as well as the players, coaches, referees, and anyone else watching—threw his right glove at Malone.

"That was goofy but it was pretty dumb," teammate Braydon Coburn said.

"Probably not my best moment as a Flyer, that's for sure," Hartnell said. "He [Malone] knocked my stick away 10 seconds before he went on that breakaway, so I had no stick. I was at the end of a shift, so my brain wasn't really functioning as it should. I was thinking of anything I could do to stop him from scoring and ended up throwing my glove. Looks kind of brain dead at the time, and it was a brain-dead move."

Malone was awarded a penalty shot, which Hartnell didn't watch as he had his head buried in his hands on the bench. Biron made a nice pad save to preserve the tie, and the Flyers managed to win in overtime.

Since the Flyers won, players were able to have a bit of fun at Hartnell's expense. The next day during practice, Lupul tossed his glove at Hartnell as he skated in on a breakaway. And the Phantoms had a Scott Hartnell Glove and Mitten Toss night later that month, as fans were invited to throw gloves and mittens, as well as hats and scarves, onto the ice for donation to Operation Warm, which collects cold-weather clothing for the needy.

"That's the kind of fun that we have here," Hartnell said. "You have to make light of certain situations.... Some things are serious, but you have to be able to joke around and have fun out of it."

57 Bibs, Bonnets, and Soothers

Flyers coach Bill Dineen knew Eric Lindros' first game in Quebec in 1992 would be a zoo of epic proportions, so he held him out of a preseason game there. But four games into the 1992–93 season, he had no choice—Lindros made his debut in Le Colisee in a scene not far removed from Russell Crowe's first appearance in the Coliseum in *Gladiator*.

Only instead of toga-wearing Romans, there were French-Canadian fans of all ages, shapes, and sizes wearing baby bonnets, bibs and diapers, and wielding pacifiers—called soothers in Canada. A Quebec radio station had given them out to fans, and those fans littered the ice with them during the game.

"It was the craziest thing I've ever seen at a hockey game," Dineen told Chuck Gormley in his book, *Orange, Black and Blue*.

Lindros was able to make a bit of a joke out of the situation, saying after the game, "I guess I'll have plenty of soothers if I ever have a baby."

Fans screamed all sorts of invectives at Lindros and his family—in French and English. They never got over the way Lindros refused to play for the Nordiques after they selected him with the first pick of the 1991 draft. Fans took it as a personal insult to every citizen of the province when he sat out a season and declared he was ready to stay out for another in order to force a trade.

Goalie Ron Hextall, one of the players the Flyers sent to Quebec in the Lindros deal, understood the fans' anger.

"I probably had as much hatred [for Lindros] as anybody in that building," he said in *Orange, Black and Blue*. "He was the one that got us all traded, and it's probably a good thing I was in goal.

"Really, what did people expect? Here's a guy who said I don't want to play for the Nordiques. If Eric got drafted by Philly and said he didn't want to play for the Flyers, I'd be furious at him. The reaction, to me, was appropriate."

Lindros ignored the jeers and scored a pair of goals, but Mike Ricci—also part of the Lindros deal—started a three-goal rally and Hextall played solid in net as the Nordiques won 6–3.

"Those people in Quebec were really passionate, and the hatred they had for Eric was incredible," said Kerry Huffman, also part of the Lindros trade, in *Orange, Black and Blue*. "Even the days leading up to the game were a circus. Hexy, Ricci, and I were talking before the game and we wondered if they might actually try to kill Eric. That's how nuts it got."

58 The Icemen Cometh

To say the Flyers had a bumpy entrance to Philadelphia would be a bit of an understatement. If a hockey team arrives in a town and no one bothers to greet them, did they really show up? That had to be the thought running through the minds of the original Flyers on October 15, 1967.

The "celebration" actually started the day before, when the team returned home from its opening road trip in California. Their arrival at Philadelphia Airport was met by a rousing 35 fans.

The next day a parade was planned to carry the new hockey heroes down Broad Street at lunchtime, ending at City Hall.

"We come to Philadelphia, they're having a parade down Broad Street to welcome us to the city," Joe Watson recalled, "and there's more people in the parade than watching it."

Among the no-shows was Philadelphia Mayor James Tate, who at least sent his regards.

The low turnout didn't bother Bernie Parent, however.

"It's understandable because nobody knew about the Flyers," he said. "What they wanted to do was introduce the players to the city, but it was the first step [of] a long journey. It wasn't an established team. It was something new in the city. I've always been the type of person, take one step at a time. That didn't bother me at all.... In my mind, I was [more] preoccupied with performing well than with how many people we had at the parade."

Later that day the team held an open practice at the Spectrum. A whopping 10 people took the club up on the offer, but those who stayed away missed little. A manufacturer's strike had delayed delivery of the boards, so shooting was kept to a minimum. Snider allegedly had to bribe a union worker to open the gates at the factory so his trucks could get the boards out.

On October 19, 1967, the Flyers played their first home game against the Pittsburgh Penguins. A crowd of 7,812 paid between $2 and $5.50 for tickets. The high prices were blamed for the poor turnout, but NHL president Clarence Campbell, on hand to drop the ceremonial first puck, said the league had to "charge luxury prices for a luxury product."

The Flyers won that night 1–0 on a Bill Sutherland goal. Doug Favell stopped all 21 shots he faced.

After beating the California Golden Seals in their second home game, Gordie Howe was brought into town a day in advance of the Flyers' first game against an Original 6 opponent, the Detroit Red Wings. It worked, as the first five-figure crowd—10,859—watched the Flyers fall 3–1.

Slowly, the guys with the toothless smiles and ice skates started to grow on folks. After a 4–1 win in Montreal on November 4, some 9,188 filled the Spectrum to see the re-match on November 5. After beating the Bruins at Boston Garden on November 12, 11,276 greeted the Flyers' return for a 3–2 win against the Rangers four days later.

The team went 7–4–3 in November and 7–5–1 in December as they moved into first place in the West Division, the home of the six new clubs.

In early February, the Flyers drew their first set of consecutive sellouts, as scalpers were getting $10 for $3.25 tickets. The Flyers didn't let the fans down, beating Chicago and Toronto.

A loss in Los Angeles on February 16 dropped the Flyers to 25–22–8, but there were worse problems at home, as a hole was found in the roof of the Spectrum. The roof was patched and the Flyers played three more home games, but on March 1 there were more problems with the roof, and the Flyers became the NHL's guest, playing "home" games in New York, Toronto, and Quebec City.

Despite all that, the Flyers still won the West Division, laying the foundation for future success.

King Kong Keenan

To NHL players, there was no middle ground with Mike Keenan—you either liked him a little or hated him a lot.

In four seasons with the Flyers, Keenan guided the club to a pair of Stanley Cup Finals and through the tragic death of Pelle Lindbergh. Off the ice, though, players openly seethed at their coach and seemingly hoped the axe would fall on his proverbial head at any moment.

Keenan had a strong resume when the Flyers hired him, having won championships in the AHL and Canadian college ranks. But even then his rough style was well-known. "Everybody I talked to said that his style would cause some problems with players," Bob Clarke said in *Full Spectrum*, "but that he had always won. I thought we needed discipline."

Keenan drove the players nuts. They would complain to Clarke, but as a young GM, all he could do was look at the results.

"Keenan was coaching and doing a real good job of coaching, but the locker room stuff, the off-ice stuff that was going on, there was a never-ending type of turmoil with Mike that I had never seen," Clarke said. "I had never gone through that as a player. I had no idea how to handle it, didn't know what to do. Everybody hates him, he's abusive to the players, and you talk to him about it, but the team kept winning. I was too new to know right from wrong. We're still winning—he must be right, I must be wrong."

Paul Holmgren worked under Keenan from 1985–88 and saw the coach at his best and worst. "It was an eye-opening experience for me to see the amount of time spent coaching that a man like Mike put into it," Holmgren said. "His energy and enthusiasm for the game was tremendous. And I think he gets a bum rap for the way he treated players. I think Mike cared for all of his players; he just wanted to push them. He did certain things to push certain players, and a lot of players maybe took it personal. Just knowing Mike the way I did over those three years I was able to work with him, he cared for each and every player that we had and cared about them a lot.

"I think there's a lot of guys [who] responded to Mike's style, and I think there were a lot of guys [who] didn't. You're going to have some that you get a good response from and some you don't get the response you want or need. Rick [Tocchet] is a guy that flourished under Mike. I think Scotty Mellanby, if you asked him his first year what he thought of Keenan, he'd say he hated his guts, but he pushed Scotty and made him a better player."

"He was pretty tough on me in certain respects, but he was very good to me in certain respects," Tocchet said. "I don't know if I would have made the NHL right away if it wasn't for Mike Keenan. I can honestly say that now. He got another level out of me. I wasn't the most talented player, but he was the biggest reason I played in the NHL."

While some players may have hated Keenan, they universally laud the way he handled the team in the aftermath of Lindbergh's death in 1985.

"He was magnificent," Dave Poulin said. "He was stellar. His feel of the pulse of the team and his decision-making process through that was just remarkable. He was at his best."

"Mike did an excellent job," Mark Howe added. "He got the guys together at his house a couple times.... He kept everybody together."

That was the yin and yang of Keenan.

"Mike was so cruel to some of the players that I had a couple players come in on their own crying—sit in front of me and cry—and said, 'Let me go home,'" Clarke recalled. "'I hate Keenan so bad, he's just so cruel to me'—men sitting in front of me crying. And then [Keenan would] come to my house for Christmas and he'd be sitting at the piano, playing the piano with my kids and his kid and singing, and you wouldn't know it's the same guy. My wife always loved him...but he could be so cruel to the players."

Clarke fired Keenan after the 1988 playoffs, and both realized it was the right move at the time. Keenan never showed the players how he really felt about them, and some never changed how they felt about him.

"Mike cared for the players," Clarke said. "It's not that he didn't care for them. I talked to him after he was gone, I was gone. We had a few talks, and he always felt the players would figure it out and respect him and like him later. But I don't think it happened."

60 | Know Your Philadelphia Hockey History

If ignorance is bliss, Philadelphia fans can be happy Ed Snider was a pretty clueless guy back in 1965. Otherwise there's no way the savvy businessman would have tried bringing professional hockey to Philadelphia.

"I was young and full of enthusiasm," Snider said in the video, *Twenty-Five Years of Pride and Tradition*. "I had seen hockey and loved it. I had seen its success in the six cities that had it. But I didn't realize the history of hockey in Philadelphia or in other places. Maybe if I had, I wouldn't have gone through with it."

Here's what Snider didn't know:

- The Flyers were not Philadelphia's first NHL team; it was the Philadelphia Quakers. Owned by former middleweight boxing champion Benny Leonard, he needed a temporary home for his Pittsburgh Pirates hockey team while a new arena was built, and he chose Philadelphia. The Quakers hold the distinction of having the worst record in league history—in the 1930–31 season, the team went 4–36–4; the four wins are tied for a full-season league-record low, and the .136 points percentage is the league's worst ever. Things were so bad Leonard folded the team after its one season in Philadelphia and had to return to boxing to make back the money he lost.

- Minor league teams didn't fare much better than the first NHL experiment. The Philadelphia Arrows probably were the best of a bad lot. Members of the Canadian-American League, they played at the Philadelphia Arena on Market Street from 1927–35. The team later became a minor-league affiliate of the New York Rangers and was renamed the Ramblers. The Ramblers lasted until 1941, were renamed the Rockets and folded in 1942.

- The Philadelphia Comets of the Tri-State Hockey League raced around for all of four months in the 1932–33 season, visible long enough to lose all 16 games they played.

- The Philadelphia Falcons of the Eastern Amateur Hockey League gave it two tries, playing from 1942–46 and again in the 1951–52 season. The second edition of the Falcons, however, didn't make it to the 1952 portion of the schedule— poor attendance led to the team being disbanded in December 1951. "The attendance this season to date has proven that there are not enough Philadelphians interested in hockey to warrant its continuance," said Philadelphia Arena president and general manager Peter A. Tyrell when he announced the Falcons' folding.

- The Philadelphia Rockets of the American Hockey League played from 1946–49. They barely survived that first season, however, going 5–52–7 for a points percentage of .133, an all-level record of futility that remains today.

- The Philadelphia Ramblers of the Eastern Hockey League played to little renown from 1955–64 before moving across the Delaware to Cherry Hill, New Jersey, and becoming the Jersey Devils.

Why Those Colors?

Ever wonder why the Flyers look like they're celebrating Halloween year-round? Take a look at the University of Texas—the alma mater of first team president Bill Putnam.

"The hot colors are always more attractive from a marketing standpoint," he said in *Full Spectrum.* "Since Detroit and Montreal already used red in their color schemes, the closest the Flyers could get was orange…. The fact that I graduated from the University of Texas, where the colors are orange and white, might have had something to do with the choice." Black was added as an accent.

There was a problem however—the NHL logo featured the same colors. Putnam offered to drop the black, but league president Clarence Campbell gave his okay and the black stayed.

A year later, Snider went about building his own hockey team. Against all odds, against a half-century of history, it worked. It shouldn't have, but somehow it did.

61 Four 50s for Kerr

Nothing really stood out about Tim Kerr's first three seasons with the Flyers. He had a pair of 20-goal seasons, but injuries limited him to just 153 of a possible 240 games.

"My first two years I had good years, scoring over 20 goals," he said. "The third year is when I had a knee injury. I rehabbed it and missed six weeks. Then my first game back it went out on me, and I had to have surgery on it. I worked with [trainer] Pat Croce all year long and really built up my leg strength, which had never been done before. I think that propelled me to the next year and the next level."

That next level started a run of historic proportions for Kerr.

Staying healthy for the first time, he scored 54 goals while playing 79-of-80 games. He came back in 1984–85 with another 54 goals, including five hat tricks and three four-goal games.

"He was a prototypical power forward," Rick Tocchet said. "When he gets position in the slot or in front of the net, you're done. That era, a lot of the defensemen were done when he got into that position."

Back-to-back 50-goal seasons had made up for the slow start to his NHL career, but Kerr felt he had to atone for his poor playoff performances. Prior to the 1985 postseason, he had just three goals in 19 games.

On April 13, 1985, in Game 3 of the Patrick Division semifinals, that all changed.

A Kerr tripping penalty led to a Willie Huber power-play goal that put the Rangers up 3–2 at 9:18 of the second period.

Over the next 8:16, Kerr more than made up for the penalty.

At 9:41 of the period, the Rangers' Mike Rogers was whistled for tripping Peter Zezel. On the ensuing power play, Kerr camped in front of the net and swept a Zezel pass past goalie Glen Hanlon to tie the game at 10:06.

Less than five minutes later, Murray Craven forced Hanlon into a giveaway that Kerr converted into the go-ahead goal at 14:58.

At 16:25, Bob Brooke was sent off for dragging Tocchet to the ice. On the next faceoff, Kerr won the draw back to Mark Howe. Hanlon stopped Howe's point shot, but Zezel threw the rebound in front, where Kerr shrugged off Barry Beck to score for the natural hat trick.

Another penalty on Brooke, who was called for roughing when he threw a punch at Craven, gave the Flyers another power play. Zezel carried the puck into the Rangers' zone, spun around Tom Laidlaw, and dropped a pass to Kerr in the high slot. His one-timer zipped under Hanlon's glove at 18:22 to give the Flyers a 6–3 lead, and they held on for a series-clinching 6–5 win.

Kerr set or tied four NHL records in that game. He still owns the marks for fastest four goals in a playoff game (8:16) and most power-play goals in a period (three). His four goals and four points in one period tied NHL records.

"It was one of those games where the puck was finding me," Kerr said in a drastic understatement. "When you're in the heat of the game you don't really follow up on what's going on. It was pretty quick how it happened.... It was kind of magical what happened there."

Kerr scored 58 goals each of the next two seasons, including a league-record 34 power-play goals in 1985–86. His 58 goals in 1986–87 made him one of 10 players in league history to score at least 50 in four straight seasons.

"It's an easy game to be a 20-goal scorer," Kerr said. "You have to score just once every four games. When you're counted on to score, there's extra pressure."

A shoulder injury in the 1987 playoffs and five subsequent surgeries pretty much ended Kerr's time as an effective player. Once nicknamed the Sultan of the Slot, he was more like a slot machine—a one-armed bandit.

He had 48 goals in 1988–89, but more shoulder soreness led to more surgeries, and he played just 40 games in 1989–90. He was selected by San Jose in the 1991 expansion draft and then was traded to the Rangers. After one final season with Hartford, Kerr retired after the 1992–93 season.

Kerr ranks third on the club's all-time list with 363 goals and sixth with 650 points in just 601 games. He's first with 145 power-play goals and 17 hat tricks. Almost all of his goals were scored a stick's width from the goal crease.

"There was no secret to where I was going to go," Kerr said. "For me it was a game within a game. That [the front of the net] was my territory."

62 Good-Time Roger Comes to Philly

Roger Neilson's NHL legacy was cemented long before he came to Philadelphia, but that didn't make his three-season stay with the Flyers any less eventful.

"Roger was friends with everybody, but nobody ever got close to Roger that I saw," said Bob Clarke, who hired him twice in Florida and Philadelphia. "You entered his world; he didn't enter yours."

Known as Captain Video and Rule Book Roger, Neilson was an innovator who knew every inch of the rule book and how to take advantage of it. Neilson existed so far outside the box he'd need the Hubble Telescope to see it.

Clarke knew all about Neilson's personality quirks when he hired him March 9, 1998, to replace Wayne Cashman.

"He'd go to WaWa and get his coffee or donuts, or Dunkin' Donuts, talk to the same guys almost every morning because they were all there at 4:00 in the morning," Clarke said. "He'd come to the rink and get all his work done for preparation for practice, then he'd work on his hockey school, then he'd work on something else. After practice was over he'd talk with the players and then he'd go home and sleep, then come back to the rink at night, then go home and sleep. Must have slept in two or three different bursts per day."

Neilson biked from his home in Medford to his office in Voorhees when he could. When he talked about the team's young French-Canadian forward, he pronounced the player's name Sy-mon Gag-knee.

The night of his first game, he needed Ron Hextall to help him find the coaches' office at the CoreStates Center

"He was standing right in front of it," Hextall said in the book, *Orange, Black and Blue.* "I thought, 'Oh boy, this really is Mr. Magoo.'"

Neilson even made a joke about cancer. Diagnosed with multiple myeloma in December 1999—the same disease that killed his sister just before he landed in Philadelphia—he first told his assistant coaches, Cashman and Craig Ramsey, and the next day he told Clarke. He even told Clarke of his plan to tell the players.

"'We put together this great video to show the team,'" Clarke recalled Neilson telling him in a *Philadelphia Daily News* story. "'We've got Chris Therien losing his gloves and his stick [in a previous game], and we got [video coach] Rob Cookson to edit in that bit from the Monty Python movie where the knight loses his legs and arms and just wants to keep fighting. The players are going to love this.'"

Only Roger

The list of funny Roger Neilson stories is endless, but Bob Clarke recalled a pair of classics:

"When he was coaching in New York, he had this dog, and he talked about this dog like it was his son or his friend. Said when he used to go on the road, 'I'd park my car and leave the window down, and Jack would just jump out the window and away he'd go and he'd come back and sleep in the car at night, and I'd come back home three days, four days later.' He said the dog could look out for itself."

And this one about Neilson and his longtime girlfriend from his days with the Panthers:

"His girlfriend lived in Texas, and she came down to see him. He's 60 years old. I come into practice one morning and the trainers are working on his neck, and I said, 'Roger, what the hell is the matter with you?' He said, 'Clarkie, she's in town and we were necking in the car last night and my neck is so stiff.' I said, 'Roger, you're 60 years old—can't you get a room?' He just laughed."

The players laughed right along with the joke—until Neilson told them of his illness.

Neilson left the team in February 2000 to have bone marrow surgery. He planned on returning for the 2000 playoffs, but that didn't happen. Neilson first joked that, "Clarke thinks [I should miss] the first round of the playoffs since we've gone out in the last two years," but the absence became permanent when the team reached the 2000 conference finals, and Clarke pronounced Ramsey the full-time coach.

Neilson had an acrimonious exit from the club that summer, and he died in 2003. But he left a lasting impression on those he coached in Philadelphia.

"Roger was the best coach I ever had," Therien said. "In terms of being a person and the way he would talk to the players, he just got it. He knew that some days just weren't going to be your day. He was like that. He didn't take you the next day and drag you through videotape for the next six hours. If you had a bad game, he'd be like, 'We'll get 'em tomorrow.'

"He was a great, great man. He was a terrific, terrific person. A man with high values, somebody the hockey world was really lucky to have as a coach and a person."

The Snipe Hunt

As long as there have been sports teams, there have been practical jokes pulled on new team members. In the hockey world, there's tape on the skate blades, shaving cream in the helmet, or the half-sawed stick.

In the early days of the Flyers, there was the Snipe Hunt.

A young Bob Kelly overheard Ed Van Impe and a few other veterans discussing hunting snipes—small birds that could only be caught at night. Kelly listened for a while, then he said he'd like to go hunting with the boys.

Van Impe said okay, and after teaching Kelly some snipe calls, a group of players met in a dark field in Delaware County. Van Impe gave Kelly a snipe-hunting tool—a hockey stick with a pair of Mrs. Van Impe's pantyhose on the end.

With a flashlight and his special snipe net, Kelly began beating the bushes and making ear-piercing snipe calls. Suddenly, a police siren sounded and officers arrived. They surrounded Kelly and were questioning him when one of the other players attacked one of the officers. A gunshot was heard, with the cop who was attacked yelling, "The guy ran away, but I hit him."

A terrified Kelly—thinking a teammate had been shot—was handcuffed, thrown in the back of a squad car, and taken to the stationhouse. He was fingerprinted, photographed, and thrown into a jail cell, just like any other law-breaker, until it was time to appear before a judge.

The judge told Kelly he could go home if he paid a $2,500 bail. He couldn't do it, and when the judge asked if anyone in the courtroom could serve as a character witness, a near-tears Kelly again said no. Thoughts of deportation to Canada, serious jail time, and the end of his hockey career flooded his mind.

At that point, the doors to the courtroom flew open and Kelly's teammates ran in. When he saw no one had been shot, he finally realized it was just a joke.

Kelly wasn't mad, however; he looks back at the elaborate prank with a measure of pride.

"That came from the Blackhawks, they did that to initiate the rookies," Kelly said. "If they're going to initiate you, they want you. For them to put that together, it was awesome."

64 Iron Man

Like the sun rising in the east, for nine years Rod Brind'Amour was that reliable presence in the lineup on a nightly basis.

Brind'Amour could do whatever was needed in any situation. Need a goal? He could score in the clutch. Need to preserve a lead? Brind'Amour was ready, willing, and able to throw himself in front of any shot. He could kill penalties and center your first power-play unit.

And he did it all night after night after night.

"He was very insistent on being in good shape and taking care of himself," Dave Brown recalled. "He was a really good player. He was a top-line player who could play in any situation. He was durable, he played a lot of minutes. He had a big heart for the game.... I know he was a guy [who] would be there every night for you."

When Brind'Amour arrived in Philadelphia prior to the 1991–92 season, he was seen as a skilled player whose hyper-intensity eventually would be his undoing. In the early 1990s, hockey players weren't gym rats; Brind'Amour, however, was far ahead of his time.

"The way he took care of his body was second to none," Chris Therien recalled. "He was the best, most prepared athlete you could find. His summer training, the way he prepared himself for games, that's what sticks out to me."

Brind'Amour worked out longer and harder than any of his teammates, and when he got to Philadelphia, it started to show in his performances. He played all 80 games in 1991–92 and had his first 30-goal season. His career just took off from there. In Brind'Amour's first eight seasons with the Flyers, he missed just one game, playing a remarkable 621-of-622 games, including a club-record 484 in a row.

"It never really fazed me that it was that big a deal until I couldn't play, and then everyone started talking about it," Brind'Amour said. "I remember getting a special note from Pat Croce, that I still have, when I got the mark. Then I said I guess this is pretty impressive. That never really occurred to me that it was that big a deal. It's your job—if you can play you get out there and do it."

Brind'Amour might not have thought so, but his teammates saw it as a very big deal.

"He was a very reliable guy," Brown said. "Probably because he was in such great condition he never got hurt. He wanted to be in the lineup. I'm sure he played many nights where he was hurting, but he still played through it. He was that kind of guy. Hard to get him out of the lineup. He really would have to have been hurt to get out of the lineup."

Brind'Amour's legendary work habits made an impression on his teammates.

"He was a great example for younger players because he was always in great condition, always working out," Brown said. "It was a good leadership thing for him. The other guys saw it and they had to do it, no doubt about that. It was a good example."

Playing mostly in a second-line role behind Eric Lindros, Brind'Amour had 230 goals and 593 points in his first eight seasons, and he was a big part of the Flyers' return to prominence after a five-year playoff drought that ended in 1995.

Brind'Amour's remarkable consecutive games played streak finally ended when the 1999–2000 season started. He broke his foot blocking a shot in the preseason, and the injury sidelined him for nearly three months. He returned, played 12 games, and then was traded to the Carolina Hurricanes for Keith Primeau.

More than 10 years later, No. 17 Brind'Amour sweaters remain a frequent site at Flyers games, a tribute to his enduring popularity.

"To be honest, that's the one thing that surprises me about this game," Brind'Amour said. "I'm kind of shocked by it, too.... I've always said the Philadelphia fans have treated me so well. They liked the way I played. I still get fan mail from people in Philadelphia upset I got traded. It makes you feel good that you were liked. I didn't realize it as much when I was playing there. Makes you feel good. Just goes to show what kind of fans you have in that city."

"When you think of Roddy, you think of the Flyers," John LeClair told the *Philadelphia Daily News* the day of the trade. "No matter what day it was, he came to work hard. Roddy did a lot of things for us."

Black Sunday

There are certain times that a ringing phone means only bad things. So when the call came around 8:00 AM on a Sunday morning from the Flyers' public-relations staff, you knew something big was happening.

That's about the time the folks who cover the Flyers learned of a major overhaul of the hockey operations department—Sunday morning, October 22, 2006.

Out was GM Bob Clarke, who was retiring from a second stint that was starting year 13 and most assumed would last for much longer. Also out was Coach Ken Hitchcock, who was being fired with his team at 1–6–1.

People around the team could sense the end was near—at least for the coach—following a 9–1 evisceration in Buffalo on October 17 after which second-year center Mike Richards said,

"The character on this team is not showing right now." No one disagreed with him, least of all chairman Ed Snider.

"A performance like that will not be tolerated," Snider ranted. "The whole damn team stinks."

Watching from home, Snider wanted to act the minute the final horn sounded. He talked to Clarke, assistant GM Paul Holmgren, and Hitchcock. Two days later, on the Flyers' version of Black Sunday, Snider accepted Clarke's resignation and replaced him with Holmgren. In Holmgren's first move as interim GM, he fired Hitchcock.

"Homer called me into his office and said he was making a change," Hitchcock recalled. "When you're not winning, the pressure starts and then the evaluation has to start—how good is the team, and can it play better for another coach. The Flyers thought they could play better for another coach."

That other coach was John Stevens, who was just a few weeks into his first season as an NHL assistant. His quiet demeanor allowed him to play good cop to Hitchcock's abrasive, task-master style that seemed to turn the younger players on the team against him. Plus, Stevens had coached some of those young players—Richards, Jeff Carter, R.J. Umberger, and Joni Pitkanen among them—to a Calder Cup in 2005. And as a former NHL player, Stevens could relate to the veterans.

The big shock, though, was Clarke quitting—not a firing, as Snider insisted.

"This is why I respect Bob Clarke so much," Snider said. "I have always known I would not have to fire Bob Clarke, that he would fire himself."

If Clarke had his way, it would have happened over the summer. He said he felt like a bystander at the 2006 draft and seemed to have less and less interest in doing his job.

"I don't know what happened to me," he said. "I knew I wasn't very efficient at the draft. Over the course of the summer I was leaving the office early, I didn't want to get involved in the decisions I was supposed to be involved in. I probably should have made the decision then, but I thought once the season starts I'll kick back into gear, but I didn't."

Instead, Clarke started looking for a way out. He first offered his resignation to club president Peter Luukko on October 10. Luukko told him to sleep on it, but Clarke was firm in his belief that Holmgren could do a better job.

"In a way, it was typical Bob," Luukko said. "Right or wrong, Bob always knows what he wants to do, and he convinced me it was time. He's the ultimate Flyer, the ultimate warrior. And when Bob Clarke said it's time, it's time."

66 Meet the Voice of the Flyers

Of all the changes the Flyers have made over the years, from coaches to players to homes, there have been very few constants.

One of them has a very unmistakable voice. Whether he's announcing the starting lineups, calling a goal or a penalty or telling fans, "The Flyers are going on the PEEEEEECOOOOOOOO power play," almost every Flyers fan knows the voice of Lou Nolan.

A warm, genial man who sells securities to banks in his day job, Nolan was a hockey fan long before the Flyers came to town. Growing up in Southwest Philadelphia, he would attend Philadelphia Ramblers games with a friend and play street hockey with broken sticks glued together.

When the Flyers arrived, Nolan parlayed a friendship with PR director Joe Kadlec into a job in the press box handing out statistics. When the Flyers' public-address announcer left in 1972, Nolan moved down to ice level. And after more than 1,800 games, he's still going strong.

If there's been a memorable moment in Flyers history over the last 35-plus years, there's a good chance Nolan witnessed it. From Rick MacLeish's goal in Game 6 of the 1974 Stanley Cup Final to J.J. Daigneault's remarkable score in Game 6 of the 1987 Final, from the Russians walking out to Keith Primeau walking around the net to score against Tampa Bay in Game 6 of the 2004 Eastern Conference Finals, Nolan has seen it all from his "office" at center ice.

"You can't really be in a better place than where I sit," Nolan said.

When he first started, Nolan didn't have the benefit of instant replays to help with his goal announcements.

"TVs weren't around like there are [now], there were no replays," he said. "I'd hear a roar and I'd be writing, I'd hear another goal, write it down, announce it. Must have missed 90 percent of them back in those days."

He also didn't have the benefit of protective glass around him like there is today, so over the years he was dinged by his share of errant pucks and sticks.

"We all got hit at some point," he said. "A puck hit me in the head once—it was deflected, those are the ones you don't see. I was awake but I was sort of incoherent. As soon as I got hit, the producer said, 'Lou, let's go down to him.' I had a live mic then. Bobby Taylor and Gene Hart were the guys, they said, 'Lou, are you okay there?' I said something but my tongue wouldn't work. When it finally came out, I said, 'I'm okay, honey,' because my wife watches all the games. I got home and I expect this big thing at the door—she didn't see it at all, she was asleep."

Nolan also got to hear some of the fine conversations that went on in the penalty boxes. One time, Daymond Langkow was sent off for high-sticking when the stick was knocked out of his hands, flew

Close Call

When Lou Nolan walks across the ice to his center-ice box, generally he's the only one out there. But one night in 1999, it wasn't the easiest trip. After handing out the end-of-season awards, Nolan began the trek to his box.

"The guys aren't on the bench, and I start walking across the ice diagonally to my box," Nolan said. "In my ear, I hear, 'Oh hell, here come the players.' I say to myself no problem—the players will skate around me. But all of a sudden I see a number, No. 3."

It was Dan McGillis—he was skating backward and didn't see Nolan.

"Dan turns around and I swear to God he turned around about a foot from me and looked me in the eye," Nolan said. "He grabbed me and we went around in a circle once or twice and then he let go and I drifted to the boards, seeing my life pass before me. The guys on the headsets laughed for about 10 minutes."

through the air, and clipped another player. When Nolan asked him how he did it, Langkow replied, "Jedi mind trick."

He also listened to Bobby Clarke list his objections to penalty calls. "He never thought he had a penalty or deserved one," Nolan said with a laugh.

One of his favorite moments came late in Game 6 in the 1974 Final against the Bruins, when the Flyers were moments away from their first Stanley Cup.

"When [Bobby] Orr got the penalty in Game 6 [holding with 2:21 left] and he was adamant saying, 'I didn't deserve the penalty,'" Nolan said, "and the fans knew at that point that we might win, it carried through. That's when we all stated looking around and saying this is going to happen."

Nolan said that moment was one of the loudest times he can remember at the Spectrum, which always had its own special buzz.

"You could actually feel the noise, you could feel the vibrations," he said. "The headsets had all kinds of static in them. It would just overwhelm you. It built. When you thought it couldn't get any louder, it would get louder. It was incredible. The guys on the ice had a rough time talking to each other. It was amazing."

Today, Nolan can be seen making the same long walk out of the Zamboni chute across the ice to his spot between the penalty boxes. And his voice will continue to play a major role for the Flyers.

67 Sami Kapanen—Eight Feet of Heart in Five Feet of Body

Since the days of the Broad Street Bullies, the Philadelphia Flyers have epitomized tough-guy hockey. Usually it was Dave Schultz or Dave Brown or Donald Brashear brawling their way to fan-favorite status. But pound for pound, the toughest man ever to pull on a Flyers jersey might have been Sami Kapanen.

Listed generously at 5'10" and 180 pounds—those measurements had to be taken when the Vantae, Finland, native was in full game uniform—he had no reverse gear. Kapanen never let his size slow him down.

"He's the toughest little guy in the league," Jeremy Roenick once said of Kapanen. "He's as tough as anybody I've ever met."

"As far as heart and determination, there was nobody I could compare him to," Keith Primeau said. "I would look at him and would wonder why he wouldn't go around the traffic, but it wasn't in his nature. He played much bigger than his size. He's a guy I truly respect as a player and a person."

Kapanen transformed from a scoring forward to a checking winger when he arrived in Philadelphia in 2003. He also became an ace penalty killer and a respected voice in the locker room.

Despite his small stature, Sami Kapanen is one of the toughest players ever to suit up for the Flyers. (AP Photo/Chris O'Meara)

That versatility and toughness was put to the test during the 2004 playoffs. A number of injuries on the blue line left Coach Ken Hitchcock short on capable replacements, so he turned to Kapanen, the team's best defensive forward.

"He was the first guy to put his hand up," Hitchcock joked at the time. "I have no idea what he's going to do. I hope the other team doesn't have a clue, either."

Hitchcock said the move showed a devotion to the team that spoke volumes about Kapanen's character. "He went back there as a favor," Hitchcock said. "We had run out of bodies, and he went back there and gave us a dynamic that we didn't have.... His competitiveness allowed him to go back and play defense.

"Toronto was trying to do everything they could to take him out of that series."

The Flyers' second-round series against the Leafs was a highly physical affair, highlighted by an epic overtime collision in Game 6. Trying to hold the puck in the offensive zone near the point, Kapanen stretched to make a play, leaving himself vulnerable. Toronto's Darcy Tucker, never one to pass on a head shot, arrived with a hit more felt then seen.

The force of the blow lifted Kapanen off his feet and turned him parallel to the boards, dasher-height off the ice. For a split second he remained airborne, caught between Tucker and the wall. When Tucker skated away, Kapanen, like Wile E. Coyote, fell with an audible splat.

Kapanen tried getting up, but while his body was in Toronto, his head was somewhere else. In his daze, Kapanen needed a GPS to find his bench. He began to stumble toward center ice, but Primeau opened the bench door, and with one skate on the rink, used his stick to hook Kapanen back toward the bench like he was reeling in a marlin.

"I could see he had no clue as to where he was," Primeau told reporters. "He wasn't sure which way he was facing."

That Kapanen at least tried to get off the ice won the Flyers the series—when he got off, Roenick jumped on, the Leafs couldn't get out players to defend him, and he scored the series-clinching goal. A still-dazed Kapanen remained on the bench during the celebration.

"To me, Sami Kapanen, that whole sequence of events, was just amazing," John LeClair said. "I think that really turned things around. As a player, as a teammate of Sami's, everyone knew the heart he had. That was a big lift."

It wasn't until after the first game of the conference finals against Tampa Bay that Kapanen said he watched the clobbering.

"I've had better days than that," he said with a laugh.

Kapanen played 13 games on defense in that 2004 playoff run. He had two goals, four assists, and was a plus–1 in more than 18 minutes of ice time per game.

"He just didn't go back and play defense," Hitchcock said, "he played the second-most minutes on our team on the back end, which is pretty incredible."

 **Nearly Neely**

Any Flyers fan who watched Cam Neely's crash-bang style with the Boston Bruins in the 1980s had to think, "Man, he would look good in orange and black."

Oh, how close you were to having just that.

"Both teams had very similar styles in play, and still to this day similar styles of play," Neely said. "When you went into Philly or Philly came into Boston, it would be a tough game. My style of play would have suited Philly as much as Boston."

The Flyers certainly thought so. Neely, the ninth pick of the 1983 NHL Draft, had fallen into disfavor in Vancouver by 1986—he dipped from 21 goals in his second season to 14 and was a minus–30 in 1985–86—but Flyers GM Bob Clarke saw a giant amount of talent packed into a 6'1", 218-pound body with hands that had multiple positive uses.

"You're looking at having two Rick Tocchets in your lineup—that wouldn't have been too bad," Clarke told NHL.com. "Neely's a Hall of Famer, and I think Tocchet will be. Dominating, physical players."

Clarke worked with his counterpart on the Canucks, Arthur Griffiths, and a deal was lined up—the Flyers would send forwards Brian Propp and Rich Sutter, defenseman Dave Richter, and a 1986 first-round draft pick to the Canucks for Neely, defenseman J.J. Daigneault, and a 1986 first-round pick.

"Arthur Griffiths, who was doing the deal, had kind of agreed with us on what the deal would be," Clarke said.

Griffiths told Clarke the Vancouver hockey department was going to discuss the deal one last time but that it likely was going to happen.

While Clarke waited, the Canucks made other plans. They signed Boston free-agent center Barry Pederson, who had averaged 32 goals in his first five full seasons. In those days teams had to offer compensation for signing another club's free agent, and the Canucks offered Neely and their 1987 first-round draft pick. The Bruins were only too happy to accept.

Pederson played four seasons with the Canucks, topping out at 24 goals in his first season. Neely went on to score 344 goals in 525 games in Boston, including three 50-goal seasons, en route to enshrinement in the Hockey Hall of Fame and a place as a Boston icon.

"It was obviously an extremely lopsided deal," Clarke said. "You get Cam Neely and a first-round pick that turned into Glen Wesley. Barry Pederson, who was pretty much done at the time…we had a lot better deal on the table and Arthur Griffiths took it off.

"It was a major deal for us, some pretty good players from our team going out there. It would have helped them a lot more than Barry Pederson would have."

Neely never realized just how close he was to landing in Philadelphia. He remembered going to dinner the day of the trade to Boston and hearing a story from his agent about another team that was interested, but Neely didn't really believe him. He never learned the full story until a reporter informed him of it in 2009.

"I was out to dinner with my then-agent at the time, Alan Eagleson, and with my parents, and I think he was trying to make me feel good about being traded and told me there was another team interested," Neely told NHL.com. "He was telling me this story, 'I knew that Bobby Clarke was interested in trading for you. When I heard you were traded, I called Bobby Clarke and congratulated him, and then he [Clarke] said no, it's Boston.'"

Clarke looks back today with a bit of what-might-have-been whimsy.

"[It was] that close—in our mind anyway," Clarke said. "Not Arthur Griffiths. I thought it was coming, but it didn't work out for us. Worked out for the Bruins."

Making the Best of It

When the Cam Neely deal fell apart with the Canucks, Flyers GM Bob Clarke still was able to make something out of his hard work. He sent defenseman Dave Richter, forward Rich Sutter and a 1986 third-round pick to Vancouver for defenseman J.J. Daigneault and a 1986 second-round pick.

Daigneault spent just one full season in Philadelphia, but his goal against the Oilers in Game 6 of the 1987 Stanley Cup Final remains one of the biggest in club history.

69 The Forgotten GM

Here's one Flyers general manager's resume: Drafted Peter Forsberg and Mike Ricci. Traded for Mark Recchi and Rod Brind'Amour. Delivered Eric Lindros to Philadelphia.

Not a bad tenure, eh?

Those were just some of the moves Russ Farwell was able to pull off during his four seasons with the Flyers, 1990–94. However, Farwell's short stay in Philadelphia is more remembered for being part of a five-year stretch out of the playoffs.

"We started over twice," Farwell said. "There were a lot of things building-wise that I'm not ashamed of, but we had four years out of the playoffs."

Farwell arrived after Bob Clarke had been fired. He had scouted part-time for the team for a few years while working as owner and GM of the Seattle Thunderbirds of the WHL.

"I got a call from Keith Allen, would I be interested," Farwell said. "I worked with Keith and scouted for them and had a relationship and that was the interest. The Flyers had fallen a bit but they had a great history and a tradition, and it was one of the most desirable jobs in the league."

After evaluating the team in his first season, he got busy at the 1991 draft. With the sixth pick, Farwell listened when his scouts recommended a Swedish center named Peter Forsberg.

"When we picked Forsberg, we knew we were picking the best guy," Farwell said. "I heard some snickers, but they [scouts] stood up and said this guy is the best player.... We just felt he may have been born in Sweden, but he's more Saskatchewan than Saskatchewan guys. They can hardly handle him in his hockey because he plays so hard and so tough. We felt he was the ideal guy."

European Scare

On the Flyers' 1990 draft board, they had a Czechoslovakian winger rated as their top player, but when their pick came at No. 4, the Flyers passed on Jaromir Jagr in favor of Canadian center Mike Ricci. GM Russ Farwell believed he'd never be able to justify to his fan base taking a European player that high.

The Penguins took Jagr with the next pick, paired him with Mario Lemieux, and won a pair of Stanley Cups. Ricci, a serviceable player, was dealt in the epic Eric Lindros deal, and he won a Stanley Cup with the 1996 Colorado Avalanche.

After the draft, Farwell went to work making the roster his. In a three-team deal with the Oilers and Kings, he got offensive-minded defenseman Steve Duchene. During training camp he sent Ron Sutter and Murray Baron to the Blues for the 21-year-old Brind'Amour, who St. Louis thought was too tightly wound to have long-term success. Then a month into the season, he sent Murray Craven to Hartford for Kevin Dineen. Late in the season, he sent Rick Tocchet, Kjell Samuelsson, and Ken Wregget to the Penguins for Recchi.

Then came the 1992 draft, and the Lindros soap opera went into high gear. Farwell had made every player in the organization available with the exception of Recchi and Brind'Amour. He had no interest in moving Forsberg, either, but when Forsberg told the Flyers he would need another year of development in Sweden, Farwell believed his hands were tied.

"If we could have gotten him to come that year, we would have gone a different direction," Farwell said. "He turned us down, didn't feel he was ready, and we were a little desperate."

So when Farwell added Forsberg's rights to a package that included Ricci, Duchene, Ron Hextall, Kerry Huffman, Chris Simon, a pair of draft picks, and $15 million, Lindros became a Flyer.

While Lindros' arrival sparked the club to a new level of popularity, it set back Farwell's rebuilding effort. Farwell also had issues almost from the beginning with the young star.

"Every dealing had to go through the family," Farwell said. "We couldn't get momentum and fit him in as part of the team. Then the little things that happened with him and some of the stands we took that alienated me with the family, and I was seen as a villain. The last year I was there the mom wouldn't speak to me. The problem was she had a direct line to Ed Snider, and she would call and complain about this or that. And he would call and say, 'Is this right?' I thought I had left that behind when I left junior."

While Lindros and Farwell feuded, Lindros built a solid relationship with Clarke, who had returned just before the Lindros deal. Lindros made it no secret he was disappointed when Clarke jumped to the expansion Panthers, and was thrilled upon his return in 1994. That spelled the end of Farwell's tenure with the team.

"When I left, Bob Clarke was seen as the answer and they [Lindros family] worshiped Bob.... When I left, Bob was flat-out the answer, he was golden. Everything was good.

"And as soon as Bob did what I tried to do and make him accountable, he became the villain to the family."

70 Oh No, Chemo!

It safely can be said that no other goalie in Flyers history ever stopped to pick up his glove mid-game while a puck flew over his head and into the net.

That odd moment pretty much captures Roman Cechmanek's time in Philadelphia.

One Flyers teammate described Roman Cechmanek as having a personality similar to his playing style: "Erratic and unorthodox."
(AP Photo/Bill Kostroun)

"I think his personality was very similar to his goaltending style," Keith Primeau said. "Erratic and unorthodox."

During his three seasons with the Flyers, most fans don't realize Cechmanek holds team records for lowest single-season goals-against average (1.83, 2002–03) and career GAA (1.96), and his 20 shutouts are second only to Bernie Parent's 50.

No, what most remember with Cechmanek are the *Ripley's Believe it Or Not* moments. Like that game in the 2003 playoffs against the Maple Leafs where he was more worried about his glove than the puck. Or the previous postseason, when he completely melted down against Ottawa, skated to his bench during a stoppage, and began screaming at his teammates.

"I vaguely remember it, too, because I was caught up in the moment, I really wasn't paying attention to Roman," Primeau said. "Whether he was lambasting the players, the coaches, wanting more from us, wanting out of the net, I'm not sure."

Those teammates responded the next day by using Cechmanek's head for target practice during practice. "We did that more than once," Primeau said. "Pucks ended up high."

Primeau believes Cechmanek was one of the last players who could be lumped into the old stereotype of European players that didn't place the same amount of value on the Stanley Cup as North Americans did.

"He came over late in his career," Bob Clarke said. "I think it was just to see if he could play in the NHL. I don't think he ever had a goal of winning the Stanley Cup. He just wanted to see what the NHL was like. He'd play great during the season, but when the season ended, that's when he ended. Playoffs didn't seem to mean anything to him."

The numbers bear Clarke out. Cechmanek posted three of the seven lowest single-season regular-season GAA's in team history, with his worst being a 2.05. But in the playoffs, well, odd things would happen, and while his 2.33 postseason GAA is good, he won just one playoff series.

"He played well during the [regular] season, was one of the best goalies in the game during the season," Clarke said, "but come playoff time, he goes for shit. How are you going to tell that? Just can't figure it out, can't plan it."

After the 2003 playoffs, Clarke decided enough was enough and shipped Cechmanek to the L.A. Kings. Cechmanek spent one season there before returning to Europe.

"We allowed with a lot of goaltenders to have a separation from their team," Clarke said. "They're their own position. Even when I was playing, Bernie [Parent] had his own room…we allowed it for the goaltenders. We've allowed goaltenders to be separate from the team but still be part of the team. We made that excuse [goalies are odd] for them. We did that with [Cechmanek]. As long as he stops the puck, I don't care, I don't care if anyone talks to him. You wouldn't want that with the rest of the players. His only job is to stop the puck. He doesn't have to cover for anyone else or do anything else, just stop the goddamned puck. You can separate a goaltender from his teammates if you want to, and we had to [with Cechmanek]. We didn't have anybody better. And he was good, he was a really good goalie—until playoffs."

71 Into the Abyss

The Flyers have done lots of things as an organization, but over all their years, they never had finished last in the NHL—until the 2006–07 season.

Even before the season started, there were signs of disaster. After getting smashed in the 2006 playoffs by the Buffalo Sabres, the problems were obvious—an overall lack of team speed, especially on defense, as well as scoring depth.

After spending big on free agents coming out of the lockout, GM Bob Clarke picked through the bargain bin starting July 1, 2006. That bin must have been in a pet store, because he came out with a bunch of mutts. Among the additions were forwards Brad Tapper, Randy Robitaille, and Mark Cullen, and defensemen Lars Jonsson, Jussi Timonen, and Nolan Baumgartner. And to make matters worse, Clarke traded valuable, versatile center Michal Handzus to the Blackhawks for walking disaster Kyle Calder.

One Final Loss

The 2006–07 season was so bad the Flyers even lost after the season ended. Despite having better than a 50 percent chance to win the 2007 Draft Lottery, the Flyers lost that, too.

The Chicago Blackhawks had the league's fifth-worst record and the least chance of winning the top spot, but the ping-pong balls bounced their way, as they jumped ahead of the Flyers to claim the first overall pick. Since teams only can move back one spot, the Flyers automatically received the No. 2 pick.

With that first pick the Blackhawks selected Patrick Kane, who went on to win the 2008 Calder Trophy, made the 2010 U.S. Olympic team, and scored the Stanley Cup–clinching overtime goal in Game 6 of the 2010 Final against the Flyers. With the second pick, the Flyers chose James van Riemsdyk.

And with the retirements of Eric Desjardins and Keith Primeau, there was a distinct lack of leadership in the locker room. That left the captaincy for injury-prone Peter Forsberg, who wore the "C" about as comfortably as a man riding a bike without a seat.

The Flyers lost four of their first five games leading into their first visit to Buffalo since the playoff disaster, and this meeting went worse than the previous spring—Sabres 9, Flyers 1.

A steaming Ed Snider demanded changes, ranting, "The whole damn team stinks." Clarke responded by waiving three players, forwards Petr Nedved and Niko Dimitrakos and Baumgartner, his prize defense addition, but that did nothing to change their fortunes.

That led to Black Sunday, October 22, when Clarke resigned and Coach Ken Hitchcock was fired. Paul Holmgren moved up to the GM chair, and John Stevens slid from assistant to head coach. They won their first game under the new regime, but that was the high point as the Flyers lost 21 of their next 27 to embed themselves in the bottom of the league standings.

Holmgren tried to shuffle the deck, but he still came out with losing cards. In separate deals with the Islanders, Randy Robitaille and Freddy Meyer were dealt for Alexei Zhitnik and Mike York. Zhitnik was serviceable, but the out-of-shape York was a waste.

There also was the never-ending Forsberg soap opera, as injuries and his impending free agency made him a constant media magnet. It overwhelmed and annoyed his teammates, with one going so far as to tape off his dressing stall as a "media no-fly" zone.

After multiple attempts to re-sign him, Forsberg was traded in one of a number of moves Holmgren made during the season as the locker room needed to be refit with a revolving door. The Flyers set a club record by dressing 49 players, including five goalies.

The losses continued to pile up, making the season resemble a slow-speed 82-car pileup. It mercifully ended April 8 with a 4–3 defeat of the Sabres, but the club's 40th anniversary season was a record-setting one—their 48 losses and 56 points set club marks for futility, as did a 13-game home losing streak.

72 Stastny Hat Trick

For years during the Cold War, the Flyers were adamant that they would never sign a Soviet-bloc player.

Years before the Berlin Wall came down, however, the Snider Wall crumbled. On November 18, 1977, the Flyers announced the signing of defenseman Rudy Tajcnar, a defenseman on the Czechoslovakian national team who had defected to Switzerland after an issue with police in Switzerland.

The 5'11", 200-pounder spoke no English and was sent to the club's American Hockey League team in Maine for seasoning.

The Flyers signed Tajcnar with the help of Louis Katona, a Czech expatriate living in Canada. Katona told Flyers GM Keith Allen there was more talent at home. The Flyers gave Katona $20,000 to arrange the defection of three hockey-playing brothers from Czechoslovakia—Peter, Marian, and Anton Stastny.

Allen gave Katona five-year contracts worth $1.25 million each for Peter and Marian and a five-year deal worth $850,000 for Anton.

Katona and Peter met first, and Peter admits now he was intrigued by the offer, but he said at the time defecting wasn't in his best interests. "At the time I had no interest whatsoever to leave," Stastny said. "I had a large family—brothers, parents, sister. It would cause them a lot of hardship. That was the basic reason."

Even meeting with Katona, Stastny says, was a huge undertaking. "Louis was one of the famous 007s running around, trying to sign the whole national team," Stastny recalled. "People were afraid because the KGBs were with the national team. The national team was the pride of the regime. But all of a sudden some players had left.... Then they were watching, they were more careful, very vigilant. They used all kinds of tactics. They let you know you're being watched. Be careful who you're talking to, who you're meeting. They assigned some stranger, he was friendly but he was there as a KGB agent, the guy who was supposed to spy and watch and create an element of fear and being vigilant of what you're doing because you're being watched."

Stastny wasn't ready then, but by 1980, the atmosphere had changed greatly, as a dispute led to officials threatening to remove him from the national team.

"They threatened my future, my career, my chance to play for the national team which was the summit, the peak, the most important honor," he said. "That changed the game completely. They basically made the decision for me by threatening me."

Stastny ranked his options, with the Quebec Nordiques squeaking ahead of the Flyers.

"Philadelphia at the time had a pretty strong team, and I wasn't sure I would get a shot," Stastny said. "Quebec was out of the playoffs, was on the East Coast, it was in Canada. I had played there in '76 [Canada Cup].... Huge interest for the game. Was a hockey country. They loved the club, the sport itself.... But mostly they finished 20th out of 21 teams, so I knew we would get a fair shot, and that's all I really wanted."

Stastny cold-called the Nordiques, who recovered from the shock fast enough to land all three brothers.

"I had a very good feeling about Quebec City, about Canada altogether, that somehow came to put them as No. 1," Stastny said. "Probably second was Philadelphia.... If Quebec had said no, I would have gone to Philadelphia."

73 Work Out Like Chris Pronger

Year in and year out, there's always one list you'll see Chris Pronger's name near the top of—average ice time per game.

It doesn't matter if he's a 25-year-old winning Hart and Norris trophies, or at the hockey-old age of 35—he's still out there for upwards of 24 or 25 minutes per game, 75–80 games a year, plus playoffs. Last season, at 35, he was fifth in the League at 25:55 per game and tops in the playoffs at 29:03 per game.

So how does he do it? In short, an intense commitment to hard work, both in season and out.

"Once the season is done I don't take a lot of time off," Pronger said. "I don't feel very good [being inactive]. Sometimes

A fierce commitment to off-ice work is what has allowed Chris Pronger to remain a top defenseman into his mid-30s.
(AP Photo/Lynne Sladky)

your body needs some time off, but even though I'm taking some time off, I'm still riding the bike. I might not be riding as hard, but I'm still doing something to stay active, keep moving. Allowing some of the bumps and bruises and injuries to heal but still trying to stay a little active, not allow things to seize up and tighten up on you. Once the training regimen starts, it's 4–5 times a week 'til the season starts."

When he gets in the gym, his generally jovial mood turns serious.

"First off, I'm not in the gym to talk. I'm not there to socialize," he said. "People can be in the gym for six hours and do nothing.

I'm in there to work. I'll get in there early and maybe I'll do a 30-, 35-minute bike ride, fairly hard, or I'll do the arc trainer, that's a really good cross-training workout, and then get 15 minutes of stretching in before I meet with my trainer, then I'll do an hour of strength. Some days it'll be all strength, some days it'll be strength and stamina. It varies; we set it up as we go. Maybe do some sprint work after that, some quick-feet drills, followed by some more stretching, then a [protein] shake and I'm done."

Pronger admits his commitment level wasn't always as high as it needed to be. But early in his career, he figured it out.

"It was probably after my first year in St. Louis," he said. "Al MacInnis had a trainer he was using, and he suggested I meet with him. He was in St. Louis meeting Al so I met with him. The first thing he says is, 'Do you have a sore knee?' And I go yeah, and, 'You got a rotator cuff problem?' I'm like yeah—he can tell all that by me walking in the room, so I was like, 'This guy's pretty good.' I just learned a lot about fitness and nutrition and training."

That education is what's allowed him to still be a top-level player for this long.

Pronger said his summer workouts address all the things he needs to play his style of game—strength training, cardio, stamina, and quickness. It's a mix he is constantly changing and tinkering with, not only to keep things fresh but to compensate for the long-lasting aches and pains he's picked up over a very physical 16-year career.

"You're always learning new things and you have different injures, different things that you need to work on," he said. "Every year is going to be a little bit different."

During the season his workouts are about maintenance and not backsliding.

"You've got to be committed to working out," he said. "Some days you're tired after three [games] in four nights, I don't feel like doing it, but you get in the gym and get a lift in. Maybe you back it down a set and do two sets instead of three sets, but you've got to continue to stay in the gym and lift and do all the things that will help you maintain during the long grind of a season. You have to really force yourself. You get into a rhythm. You get used to today's my lift day, it's a practice day, I have to go lift and then I go practice, then you do a quick bike ride after. You get used to doing it, your body gets used to it."

It's a remarkable feat and something Pronger is proud of. He won't admit to exactly how long he wants to play, but he did say he expects to finish the seven-year contract he signed when he arrived in Philadelphia, which would take him through his 42nd birthday.

 **Visit Rexy's**

Cheers may have been the bar in Boston where everyone knew your name, and certainly they were glad you came. For the early Flyers, their Cheers was Rexy's in Haddon Township, New Jersey.

Pat Fietto ran the place after his father, Guido "Rexy" Fietto, opened it in 1943. Pat called it a nice, quiet "blue-collar place. The iron workers, the welders, the pipefitters—the average Joe."

Starting in 1967, another set of average Joes moved into the neighborhood—the Philadelphia Flyers. As most of the players settled in South Jersey, Rexy's became a shining beacon in a new world.

"Those 1967 guys were unique," Fietto said in a 2009 interview in *The Retrospect*. "Nobody knew them. They played hockey for six months, lived in Barrington Gardens [apartments], paid $60 a month rent, and went home [in the summer] to their parents and families and other jobs on farms, in the mines, driving trucks.

"They loved Rexy's—the working-man's atmosphere.... They had games Thursdays and Sundays, [and] they would stop after practice for some lunch and after games. I would cash their checks out of my pocket—checks for $150, $160. They had no other place to go. I steered them in the right direction."

As the Flyers became a Delaware Valley institution, so did Rexy's.

"It was just over the bridge, right on the way home for everybody," Bill Barber said. "Pat Fietto owned the place and became real good friends with everybody. Really convenient spot to go to, had a warm feeling, really good food. Ended up being our hangout all the time, which we were fortunate to have on the way home after games. He stayed open long enough for us to eat right. All those little elements pulled us there."

During the championship years, the Flyers made Rexy's their second home.

"If they weren't playing, they were here," Fietto said.

"It was team policy after the game that guys would get together [at Rexy's] after the game, no matter what," Barber recalled. In *The Retrospect*, he added, "We grew as a team at Rexy's."

As Rexy's became more popular with the players, and the team became more popular with the fans, Rexy's became a destination establishment. But to their credit, most fans treated the players right.

"You had your regular fans, but never to a point where guys would turn away because it became a problem," Barber said. "We always had a room shut off for us in the back, so it was always good that way. The bar was good, too. There never were any problems."

Well, that's not always true.

"That day they won the [1974 Stanley] Cup, the people started to accumulate out here in front of Rexy's," Fietto said. "I guess it was around 5:00, I called my brother here, he was all, 'They're going crazy, it's getting wild.' I said don't worry about it, close the place down, but that wasn't enough because it got worse and worse and worse. It built up to the point where we had 8,000 people out there. I wanted to get the boys to come back here because they wanted to celebrate, this is where they always came to party, but I couldn't do that. I couldn't get them here because they would have gotten killed."

As the Broad Street Bullies era came to a close, so did the overwhelming popularity of Rexy's as new players found new places to go. The Fietto family sold Rexy's in 2009, but much of the memorabilia remains, including a blue neon sign marking the Robert E. Clarke Room.

75 A Daily Double at the Draft

Going into the 2003 NHL Draft, the Flyers were one of two teams with two first-round picks in what was considered an extremely deep draft. The Flyers had their own pick, at No. 24, plus the No. 11 pick, which they had acquired from Phoenix in 2001 for Daymond Langkow.

"Bob did a good job getting us all these picks," assistant GM Paul Holmgren told the *Philadelphia Inquirer* prior to the draft. "We have a real opportunity to strengthen our organization in this draft."

How to use those picks was Holmgren's job. He oversaw the amateur scouting department and had the final say on all picks. And with a pair of selections in what some scouts considered the deepest draft in decades, it's safe to say there was a fair bit of pressure on Holmgren and his staff.

With the 11th pick, there were a multitude of options. If it was going to be a forward, there was Dartmouth College giant Hugh Jessiman; Guelph Storm power right wing Dustin Brown; the

Captain Under Contract

It didn't take long for the Flyers to see in Mike Richards what others had before them—captain material.

Richards had been a captain of his junior team and the historic 2005 Canadian World Junior Championship team. He was named an assistant captain with the Flyers during the 2007–08 season, and at the start of the next season, he became the 16th captain in franchise history.

In between, Richards was given the longest contract in club history—a 12-year, $68.4 million deal that binds him to the organization through the 2019–20 season.

Moncton Wildcats' Steve Bernier; and University of North Dakota sniper Zach Parise. If they wanted a defenseman, options included the Lethbridge Hurricanes' Brent Seabrook and Brent Burns of the Brampton Battalion.

Instead, the Flyers opted for a tall, skinny, high-scoring center from the Sault Ste. Marie Greyhounds—Jeff Carter. Playing for a team that won just 26 games in 2002–03, Carter had 35 goals and 71 points. The Flyers also liked his skating and wrist shot.

"Jeff could always skate, and he could always shoot the puck," Holmgren says today. "He glided past players back then without moving his legs. He was a little bit of a projection there, you hope he'd fill out."

At No. 24, the Flyers chose another center. The Kitchener Rangers' Mike Richards was a bit undersized, but the Flyers were sold on the youngster's character and grit—and the 37 goals and 87 points he scored weren't bad, either.

"He does everything," Clarke told the *Inquirer*. "Kills penalties, blocks shots, takes faceoffs. We never felt he would fall that far in the draft to us, so we think we're lucky to get him."

"I think we had Mike 17th on our list, so we were hoping that he was [there]," Holmgren said. He added that it wasn't love at first sight with Richards—more like an appreciation gained over time.

"Players like Mike, when you're watching them at a young age, you have to see them a lot to learn to appreciate what they do. If you go watch his junior team play four or five times, you get the idea that he's in the middle of everything offensively, he's in the middle of everything defensively, he kills penalties, he takes face-offs. We hoped the skating would come along, and it did."

The Flyers also were enamored of his leadership abilities. Many who watched him compared him to Clarke.

"He was like a heart-and-soul player back them," Holmgren said. "You're drafting a kid when he's 18 years old, you're hoping a lot of things go your way. He was even back then a heart-and-soul player."

Now more than seven years after that historic draft, Richards and Carter are the faces of the franchise.

"I think we understand our roles on the team and in the organization," said Richards, who was named captain in 2008. "Say what you will, [but] we understand ourselves and are comfortable with the scenario that we're in."

"They are low-maintenance players," Holmgren said. "You know what you're going to get from both guys. They're going to put up points, and they're going to show up and play their game."

76 Mr. Plus, Mark Howe

When Mark Howe came to the Flyers in 1982, he knew he would give the team something it was missing. "I was something they didn't have," Howe said. "They had a real good defense. They had a big, strong, tough defense, but they didn't have a guy with a lot of mobility."

Howe provided that mobility plus far more, and by the time his 10-year stint with the Flyers was over, Howe left as the best defenseman in club history.

The best seasons of Howe's Philadelphia tenure came from 1984–87. There's no coincidence that two of those three seasons the Flyers went to the Stanley Cup Final.

"He was smart," Rick Tocchet said. "He was the heartbeat of our team. He played hurt; he did everything right. He's a pro. He probably could have scored more and gotten more points if he cheated and played a little more offensive, but he thought of the team first. He played for the crest."

The 1984–85 season marked the first time Howe and Brad McCrimmon were paired together, and it didn't take long for the duo to become arguably the best defensive pairing in the NHL.

That first season Howe had 18 goals, 57 points, and a plus–51 rating. He also helped McCrimmon, who had been an average player in his first five NHL seasons, into a Barry Ashbee Trophy winner with career highs of eight goals, 43 points, and a plus–52 rating.

The following season Howe turned in one of the best stat lines you'll ever see from a blueliner.

Playing through the season-long pain of the death of Pelle Lindbergh, Howe posted career bests of 24 goals and 82 points in just 77 games. Most remarkable, however, was Howe's league-high plus–85 rating—the eighth-best single-season mark in NHL history.

He was a First-Team NHL All-Star, he finished third in voting for the Hart Trophy (won by Edmonton's Wayne Gretzky), and placed second for the Norris (won by Edmonton's Paul Coffey).

And not only did Howe have a stellar season, his partner, McCrimmon, was a plus–83.

In 1986–87, Howe led another charge to the Stanley Cup Final with 15 goals, 57 points, and a plus–57 rating. He again finished second in Norris Trophy voting, this time to Boston's Ray Bourque.

For a three-season span, Howe was an amazing plus–193. And combined with McCrimmon, who had a plus–45 rating in 1986–87, the pair was a total plus–373. The Howe-McCrimmon pairing was the reason the Flyers went to a pair of Stanley Cup Finals and also why goalies Pelle Lindbergh (1985) and Ron Hextall (1987) won Vezina trophies.

"I played with Ray Bourque, had the chance to play with Paul Coffey," Tocchet said, "but that stretch he [Howe], to me, was the best defenseman those years. For me, and I'm being biased, but you're talking Paul Coffey scoring 50 goals Ray Bourque who plays 40 minutes a night—Mark Howe for three years was phenomenal."

77 Eric Desjardins, Mr. Reliable

Chris Therien doesn't hold back when he's asked about his former teammate and defense partner Eric Desjardins.

"He was the best defenseman I ever played with," Therien said, "and maybe in his best years, probably the best player we had here, better and more important than [Eric] Lindros on most nights."

The next mistake found in Desjardins' game during his 11 seasons with the Flyers likely would be his first. In 738 games, he had 396 points—second only to Mark Howe in club history among defensemen—and was a plus–143. In the playoffs, he had 51 points in 97 games. His 14 playoff goals are the most ever by a Flyers blueliner.

He also won a club-record seven Barry Ashbee trophies as the team's best blueliner, including five in a row, and he served as team captain from March 2000—following Lindros' tumultuous removal—until Keith Primeau took over in October 2001.

Eric Desjardins not only was a great player, he also was a role model. "All our young players, they were all told, 'Conduct yourself like Desjardins conducts himself,'" Bob Clarke said. (AP Photo/Tom Mihalek)

"He was the consummate professional," Therien said. "He's a guy you look at and have the ultimate respect for."

More than his on-ice steadiness and reliability was the way Desjardins performed off the ice.

When the Flyers were looking for a top-end defenseman early in the 1994–95 season, GM Bob Clarke looked at a pair of young Canadiens blueliners—Mathieu Schneider and Desjardins. When Montreal wouldn't part with Schneider, the Flyers were fine with taking Desjardins, who came along with a note from Montreal GM Serge Savard.

"He said, 'Clarkie, Eric Desjardins is the finest man you'll ever have,'" Clarke said. "'He's the kind of man you want your daughter to come home with,' and Serge was right. Desjardins is a tremendous man."

Years later, at Desjardins' retirement press conference, Clarke talked more about the character of the person than the skill of the player.

"Desjardins was what everyone believes an athlete should be," he said. "His conduct off the ice was always classy—his dress, his demeanor, his relationship with the fans, the press, with everybody. His play on the ice was at an exceptionally high level every game. You don't find people, or athletes, like that very often.

"All our young players, they were all told—conduct yourself like Desjardins conducts himself."

One of those young players arrived in Philadelphia in 1999 a wide-eyed 19-year-old French-Canadian with little grasp of the English language.

"I realize my first couple years, having a guy on my side such as Rico [Desjardins], it was pretty much a perfect model for me," Simon Gagne said. "Having Eric, especially in my first year, new to the league, not very comfortable speaking English, I was thankful to have Eric on my wing for my first couple of years."

With Desjardins, the Flyers went to the Eastern Conference Finals three times and the Stanley Cup Final in 1997.

Late in his career, however, injuries began to play a major issue. He suffered a broken foot during the 2003 playoffs and missed the final eight games, and then he played just 48 games in 2003–04 thanks to a broken arm suffered on an errant check thrown by teammate Jeremy Roenick. On the eve of the playoffs, he broke the plate that was supposed to be fusing the bones in his arm and missed the postseason.

It first was reported he broke it playing catch with his son, but that's not entirely true. Earlier that day, he felt soreness in the arm after taking a bunch of slap shots during practice. He felt more pain later that day while having that catch with his son. And later, when he reached to put something on a shelf in his home, the pain turned real bad.

"I could feel the bone was moving. I didn't want to believe it at first," Desjardins said in *Orange, Black and Blue*. "I asked my wife to look at it, and she told me to call the doctor and have X-rays. That's how I found out the plate had given. The X-ray showed my bone was completely broken in half." He missed the entire postseason, and after the lockout he played one more season before retiring at age 37. While he had other offers—including one from the Canadiens—he decided it was better to retire as a Flyer.

"It was important to me to retire as a Flyer," he said at his farewell press conference. "You just hope you get to a point where you don't have to move your family too much. I was lucky to be here all these years."

78 A Love Forever Cherished

Bill Barber was a high-scoring 17-year-old forward when he arrived in Kitchener, Ontario, in 1969 to play for the OHA's Kitchener Rangers. He scored lots of goals in his three seasons, but his biggest score came when he met a girl at school named Jenny. After just four dates, love blossomed. They were married May 12, 1973, two weeks after Bill's rookie season with the Flyers.

Jenny Barber took her role as a hockey wife seriously. While Bill was winning Stanley Cups and churning out a Hall of Fame career, she was in the shadows, raising their two children, helping other players and their wives get settled in the community, and serving as one of the most active participants in the Flyers' Wives Fight For Lives Carnival.

That didn't change when Bill began his successful coaching career, first in the minor leagues and later with the Flyers.

As the *Philadelphia Inquirer's* Bill Lyon wrote in a column, "...no linemate was as responsible for setting [Barber] up for success as Jenny."

"Everybody was family for her," Mike Stothers, who served as an assistant to Barber with the Phantoms and Flyers, told the *Inquirer.*

All the hugs Jenny Barber had given out were returned to her ten-fold in the spring of 2001. During Bill's initial playoff run as an NHL coach, he urged her to go for extra testing when she couldn't kick a persistent cough. X-rays revealed a collapsed lung caused by a malignant tumor.

"I knew we were in trouble with the initial diagnosis," Barber said in *Walking Together Forever.* "We had to prepare our family. It was obvious there wasn't a lot of longevity with this type of cancer. Doctors talked about a year, but we didn't even get that."

Just after noon on December 8, 2001, Jenny Barber died at her home, surrounded by her husband of 28 years and their two children. She was just 48 years old.

That afternoon, the Flyers had a home against the Minnesota Wild—and in his usual place stood their coach. The Flyers won that day, and after the game the players presented Barber with the game puck.

"We can't even imagine or fathom the intense stress this caused him," Primeau said that afternoon. "His only release was to come to the rink. Bill Barber has two passions—his family and the Philadelphia Flyers."

"We heard that morning in the press box before the game that she had passed away," *Courier-Post* beat writer Chuck Gormley said. "When I saw him on the bench I couldn't believe it. How you coach in those circumstances is beyond me. Especially when you know he's a good husband and father."

It's for just that reason Barber was on the bench. Long before her passing, Jenny had told Bill to live his life and do the job he loved, no matter what. Coaching that day was his way of fulfilling her final wish.

Barber was urged by numerous people in the organization to take time off, but he refused, and he believes as much today as he did then that it was the right decision.

"It's not like this was a sudden thing," he said. "This was going on for a long, long time. As a family we stood tall for what we believed, and we prepared ourselves right to the very end. We were all mentally stable and understood what really happened here. It's not as if it was happening that day. This was going on for around seven months. The family prepared, I was prepared. I didn't let anything family-wise intrude on the team.

"Time off? Where would it lead? My honest opinion is it would have went worse."

Instead, Barber kept going the same way he always did. The season ended with an open rebellion by the players and his eventual firing, but the fact that the season went sour doesn't change his opinion. And never would he—or could he—blame what happened away from the rink for what happened on the ice.

"There's factors when things don't work out and I'll take some responsibility for that, and I think the players have to take the other part of the responsibility," he said. "We didn't play well enough to win."

Still, not a day goes by where Barber doesn't think about his wife.

"After that [Wild] game, I walked down to the coaches' room, and it's the only time I've ever walked down to the coaches' room, to offer my condolences," Gormley said. "He showed me a ring that his wife had given him and he had it around his neck on a chain, and he said something like, 'I'm never going to take this off.' It was something that you could see, how much he was impacted by this."

79 Last Call at the Spectrum

In a span of just a few years, two of Philadelphia's iconic sporting landmarks were shuttered. Veterans Stadium couldn't be imploded fast enough. The toilet bowl of a stadium now serves a far better purpose as a parking lot for the spectacular Citizens Bank Park.

The Spectrum, however, deserved—and received—a far classier send-off when it enjoyed its final days of use during the 2008–09 hockey season.

The Flyers first considered playing one final regular-season game at the old building, but there was no chance to get all the fans who would demand tickets into the place. Instead, a preseason celebration was held. Prior to an exhibition game against the Carolina Hurricanes—featuring former Flyers fan favorite Rod Brind'Amour—team chairman Ed Snider welcomed back 11 team captains, most of whom wore the "C" while playing at the Spectrum.

"It's a building of history and pride, and anytime I was involved in a game at the Spectrum as a member of the Flyers, I felt extremely fortunate," Bill Barber told NHL.com. "This building is home to a lot of players and great memories."

From winning the club's first Stanley Cup in 1974 to beating the Russians in 1976, from Kate Smith's "God Bless America" to J.J. Daigneault's prayer of a goal in the 1987 Stanley Cup Final, there were numerous unforgettable moments in the little, round, brown-brick building.

"Philadelphia is the No. 1 professional hockey town in this country," Bob Clarke said. "We have sold out our building, and have ever since the beginning of the '70s. No city comes close to Philadelphia fans for professional hockey."

Clarke's Broad Street Bullies set the tone for the decades of Spectrum domination. All-time the Flyers went 696–293 with 140 ties in 1,129 games there—a remarkable .614 winning percentage.

"We never lost at home—hardly ever," Clarke said. "Not to the good teams. There were teams that once in a while you lose at home to because you didn't play your best, but we hardly ever lost to a good team in our building."

Why?

"Most of the teams that came in there for a few years played scared," Clarke said. "People just didn't want to play in that building."

"Even though the Spectrum was a new building in the late 1960s, it was really an old building," Dave Poulin told NHL.com. "It intimidated other teams and was very unique in many ways. I never considered the Flyers an expansion franchise because they established an immediate identity, and the Spectrum was part of the identity. It was an identity that lasted throughout the history of the franchise and that's unusual.... The Spectrum is a unique, tiny little building that somehow enabled the fans to be closer to you physically and as a result were much more closer to you emotionally."

And the opposition certainly felt that emotion.

"Early in my career," Hall of Famer Steve Yzerman said, "they still had the aura of the team from the 1970s. It was quite intimidating for me as a teenager."

The Newest Captain

While the last Flyers game at the Spectrum was a chance to look back, it was also a chance to celebrate the newest captain, Mike Richards. Richards was passed a ceremonial torch by the 11 previous captains who were on hand that afternoon.

"It was really their [the other captains'] day," Richards told the *Bucks County Courier Times*. "I was honored when I found out I was going to be the captain. To see the tradition of the guys who have worn the Flyers' 'C', it sends chills up your spine."

"It was [an intimidating place]," said Sharks GM Doug Wilson, who played many games in the Spectrum during his 16 NHL seasons. "It was exciting. You knew there was not gong to be any easy nights here. You weren't going to sleep through any games."

The Spectrum was as much a part of the Flyers' legacy as any player. It'll be an odd sight to ride down Broad Street, Pattison Avenue, or I–95 and not see the old place, especially for Snider, who sees the building as far more than mortar and bricks.

"It's my baby," he said.

80 Whoa, Bundy!

Chris Therien received as many Norris Trophy votes in his career as your postman, and he never scored more than six goals or 24 points in a season, but he carved out an 11-season NHL career with all but 11 games of it played in Philadelphia.

Some remember Therien as the "Jagr-meister," because of his remarkable—some would say mystifying—ability to shut down scoring star Jaromir Jagr during his heyday with the Penguins. But more refer to Therien as Bundy, as in Al Bundy, the classic character from the show *Married With Children.*

And classic character is exactly how anyone who has spent time with Therien would describe him.

"When I first got to Philly, we had a unique group of characters," Keith Primeau said. "I can't say who led the parade, but Bundy was always one of the conductors."

Playing that role was something Therien aced, so much so that when the Flyers went on their post-lockout spending binge, bringing in Derian Hatcher, Mike Rathje, and Peter Forsberg, Primeau and Jeremy Roenick called GM Bob Clarke and insisted he re-sign Therien.

"The game has to be serious, but at times you need a buffer, you need that icebreaker," Primeau said. "He was a serious guy, but he knew when we needed a good laugh and that's something you can't replace. Team chemistry can never be understated as far as I'm concerned. He was a great presence in the locker room."

Playing that role is as much a learned skill as anything else in the game and often just as important.

"I think before the game, that's the time to be serious," Therien said. "Morning skate, you're getting ready for the day, you don't want to disrupt anybody's preparation.... You never want to set anybody off before a game because you don't want that guy to have a bad game. There's a real fine line how you've got to work that."

When it works, though, it can be brilliant.

Like the time he used rubber cement to glue diminutive Daymond Langkow's shoes to the locker room ceiling in Buffalo.

"When he finally knocked them off with a stick, the whole bottom of the drop ceiling had come off, about an inch thick on the bottom of the soles of his shoes. So I said, 'You're an inch taller with your shoes on.'"

Or the time he made an alteration to defenseman Andy Delmore's new overcoat.

"We were in Chicago and he had this brand new overcoat, and I went up to it and I cut the sleeves off, and I had the trainer put one stitch just to hold them in. The whole team knew what happened, and he went in after practice and the whole team was waiting around and he put his arms through and the sleeves came off and it looked like the guy in *The Matrix*, like he had a coat/vest. He got so mad he almost started crying."

And then there was one frequent target, road roommate John LeClair.

"I would do stuff like turn on the shower and leave in the morning. I already had a shower and would leave it on, and he would be waiting thinking I was still in there. But the best I used to do with him is I would run up to the room really quick, and you know the chocolates they leave on the bed? I would undo the bed, and put it in the sheets, unwrap the chocolate, so he would get into bed and lay there watching a movie and he'd get up two hours later to go to the bathroom and he'd have chocolate all over his body— it had melted from his body heat. He'd look over at me and he'd go, 'Hey Bundy, I think the maid left the chocolates inside the bed,' and I'd go, 'I can't believe she'd do that.'"

Therien's impact in the room was validated when Primeau and Roenick went to bat for him.

"There is room for characters in this league and there always will be," Therien said.

81 The Comcast-Spectacor Merger

Ed Snider's management style always had been to let the people he hired do their job, but he certainly kept a close eye on the operation.

But by 1996, after 30 years of running the team on a day-to-day basis, his fuel tank wasn't as full as it used to be. The stress of dealing with Harold Katz and getting a new building financed and built had taken a lot of the starch out of him.

It was about then that Snider began planning the future of the Flyers for estate-planning purposes, so when Pat Croce—who had parlayed a job as trainer for the Flyers and Sixers into a multi-million dollar fitness empire—partnered with Philadelphia real-estate developer Ron Rubin to try to buy the Sixers, Snider was paying attention. Rubin, a friend of Snider's, said he was going to Comcast to see if they would be interested in financing the deal.

Snider also had something he thought Comcast would be interested in—a start-up all-sports regional television network. Snider, who had launched PRISM in 1976, was unhappy with how Charles Dolan's Rainbow Media—which bought the channel in 1983—was running things, and by 1996 he had aligned with the Phillies' owners to create a channel that would air Flyers and Phillies games, as well as other sports programming.

"Ron Rubin was in the shower one day and came up with the idea that it would be fantastic if Comcast got involved in buying the Sixers and buying me and all the other stuff [the Spectrum and CoreStates Center]," Snider said.

Snider and Rubin met with Comcast founder Ralph Roberts and his son, CEO Brian Roberts, on February 24, 1996. On March 19, a deal was announced that saw Comcast merge with Snider's Spectacor. The joint venture, named Comcast-Spectacor, acquired the Flyers, Sixers, the Spectrum, and the under-construction CoreStates Center. They also announced the formation of a new TV network, Comcast SportsNet, which would start airing Phillies, Flyers, and Sixers games, as well as other sports programming. Comcast owned 66 percent of the venture, Snider 34 percent. Snider was installed as chairman of the new company—a position he retains to this day, despite saying he walked into the deal as a way of finding an "exit strategy."

Snider admits he wasn't sure how the deal would work but said it's been better than he ever could have imagined.

"They [the Robertses] are just wonderful people in the sense that when they have a partner or an executive, they let them run with it," Snider said. "In sports everybody knows better than the owner or the GM. When you think of a two-thirds partner, you'd think you'd have problems because things aren't always done the right way all the time. I've never heard a bad thing from Brian and Ralph Roberts. They're great partners."

82 The Curse of Sarah Palin

The Flyers didn't get into the playoffs until the second-to-last game of the 2008–09 season. Part of that had to do with their terrible start—they lost their first six games.

There were many reasons for that terrible start—poor goaltending, an inability to close out games, bad luck in losing three of the games in overtime. But two things happened that could lead some to believe the Flyers' luck had little to do with any on-ice happening. They involve someone who never put on skates, never wore a hockey jersey—heck, she was just some hockey mom!

Well, not just any hockey mom—Sarah Palin.

Yes, the same Sarah Palin who was the 2008 Republican vice-presidential candidate. During her acceptance speech at the Republican National Convention that summer, she talked about being a hockey mom.

The Flyers, as a take-off to her speech, convened a contest to find the Delaware Valley's Ultimate Hockey Mom, with the winner getting to drop the puck at the team's 2008 home opener. The winner was Cathy O'Connell of Erdenheim, Pennsylvania. Accompanying her to center ice October 11, 2008, was another hockey mom—Palin.

Flyers chairman Ed Snider—who contributed money to the McCain-Palin presidential ticket as well as the Republican National Committee—said the invitation to Palin had nothing to do with politics and everything to do with her being a hockey mom.

"We were so excited when she talked about hockey moms in her acceptance speech," Snider told the *Philadelphia Inquirer*. "She did a great service to our sport.… This is all about having fun with what she said."

Not everyone had fun with it, as Flyers fans greeted her with the kind of boos they generally reserve for players like Sidney Crosby, Martin Brodeur, or anyone on the Rangers—the team they happened to be playing that night.

When Palin dropped the puck, the Flyers' fortunes seemed to go right down with it.

The Rangers scored four times in the first period en route to a 4–3 victory. The pain wouldn't stop there as the Flyers lost two nights later to the Canadiens. Then the Flyers lost four more times—three in overtime.

The Palin Curse was finally snapped October 24 when the Flyers blitzed the Devils 6–3.

That happened to coincide with Palin's arrival in St. Louis—to drop the first puck at a Blues game.

Like a mosquito jumping from person to person on a warm summer night, the Palin Curse landed on the Blues and sucked all the life out of them. In fact, the game didn't even have to start for the Blues to become victims—skating onto the ice for warm-ups, goalie Manny Legace tripped on a piece of carpet that had been laid down for Palin's walk to center ice. He strained a hip flexor muscle, gave up two goals in the first period, and was too hurt to continue in what ended as a 4–0 win for the visiting L.A. Kings.

The Blues lost seven of their next nine games after Palin made her appearance, and after sinking to the bottom of the Western Conference, like the Flyers they needed a miracle rally just to get into the playoffs.

Sarah Palin was on the losing side of the 2008 presidential election, showing that while two hockey teams eventually were strong enough to get past her being around, John McCain wasn't.

83 Slow-Motion Superstar

Dave Poulin never was the most imposing player on the ice, either in size or skill. His heart, though, was nearly too big for his chest, and he showed it every shift of his 467 games for the Flyers.

And there was no better example of that than during the 1985 playoffs.

Captaining the youngest team in the NHL, Poulin guided it to a Patrick Division title and a league-best 113 points. But Poulin, who had 30 goals, 74 points, and a plus–43 rating during the regular season, suffered a slightly torn ligament in his left knee during the Patrick Division semifinal sweep of the Rangers. He missed the division final series against the Islanders, but he returned for the Wales Conference Finals against the Nordiques. He scored in a Game 2 win but suffered cracked ribs when Mario Marois sticked him in the chest.

He missed Games 3 and 4 but returned for Game 5 at Le Colisee wearing a flak jacket. The Flyers won that night and returned to the Spectrum with a chance to make an improbable trip to the Stanley Cup Final.

After a bad day of practice, however, Poulin reminded his teammates that they needed to bring more.

"In order to win, we knew we needed everybody going, and that wasn't happening," he told reporters. "We're a confident, secure group of people, so we could talk over our problems honestly and openly."

Their problems looked to be solved early, as Rick Tocchet scored late in the first period. More problems, however, cropped up in the first minutes of the second, as Joe Patterson was sent off for interference 31 seconds in, and then Brian Propp joined him in the

Dave Poulin persevered through numerous injuries to captain the Flyers to a pair of Stanley Cup Finals. (AP Photo/Charles Krupa)

box 37 seconds later. That left the Flyers two men down for 1:23 against a Quebec team that was third in the conference with 323 goals during the regular season.

Poulin lost the faceoff in the Philadelphia end following the Propp penalty, with the puck going back to Marois, who worked the point with Peter Stastny. Poulin, the point man in the triangle penalty-kill formation, had a plan.

"We talked about how they kept collapsing in to the box," he said. "Human nature, you're pressing toward the net, and those guys had gone across the top so well, Marois and Peter Stastny. Your natural thought is to compress into a triangle and getting deeper and deeper. I just stepped out."

When he did, something magical happened.

"You're on the bench, and it's surreal," Tocchet said. "He's going to read this play, because they were going back and forth. He faked it, and then he stepped in."

As Marois and Stastny played catch, Poulin jumped in, tipping a pass to center ice and breaking out alone.

"I had such a long way to go on the breakaway," Poulin said. "From the top of the circle, it was such a race."

On a bad knee and with busted ribs, Poulin was far from blazing down the ice, but he was in the clear with only goaltender Mario Gosselin to beat. For inspiration, Poulin harkened back to a conversation he had with teammate Murray Craven.

"We had talked a lot about Gosselin, and you had to go over the glove because of the way he played the bottom of the net," Poulin said. "I made the decision around center ice—I was going top shelf."

A Fortuitous Favor

Dave Poulin wasn't expecting to have an NHL career. After four years at Notre Dame, he got married and spent a six-month hockey honeymoon playing for a second-division Swedish team to kill time before he entered the prestigious Proctor & Gamble management program. Instead, Poulin's coach in Sweden, Ted Sator, recommended him to Flyers coach/GM Bob McCammon, who needed an extra player for the Maine farm team.

Poulin lit up the AHL, and then in his first NHL game, he scored on his first two shots against the Maple Leafs in Toronto.

Days later, Poulin received a letter from his boss-to-be at Proctor & Gamble. The letter included a clipping of Poulin's performance in Toronto and a note: "Obviously our paths are going different ways. I'm happy for you. Best of luck."

From about 5 feet out, Poulin snapped a wrister over Gosselin's glove, and even though 38 minutes remained to be played, the series was over.

"When he went in and scored the goal, it was just like, 'Oh my God,'" Tocchet said. "That's a two-goal swing. That never happens."

"It was a killer for them," Poulin said. "It demoralized them and gave us a lift. I think because of the potential it had for them—they were looking at scoring one, maybe two goals and going ahead...it had to be demoralizing."

84 Flyers vs. WIP

Today, the Flyers' relationship with their flagship radio station is good. That wasn't always the case, however. Twice during the 1990s, the Flyers threatened the station with lawsuits, both times over slanderous statements made about Eric Lindros.

The first came in May 1996, when host Mike Missanelli reported that convicted Philadelphia mobster "Skinny Joey" Merlino had been sitting in Lindros' complimentary seats at Flyers home games. Missanelli also reported the story in his short-lived magazine, *The Fan*. The genesis of the story was an item in the *Philadelphia Daily News* that reported Merlino had been sitting in Lindros' seats.

Lindros downplayed any "relationship" with Merlino, saying he had been introduced to Merlino a few times early in his Flyers career. But the fact Merlino was sitting in Lindros' seats—Lindros didn't deny this fact—was pure coincidence, as players routinely return their complimentary tickets to the team, which then sells or distributes them. Lindros had no control over who got his seats.

"That was such [expletive]," Lindros told the *Philadelphia Daily News* in August 1996. "That was just one person [Missanelli], coming up with…they were nothing comments, wanting to publicize his radio show."

Carl Lindros said he and Eric contemplated suing Missanelli, his magazine, and WIP, but let the issue slide.

That changed February 28, 1997, when host Craig Carton reported anonymous sources had told him Lindros had missed a game against the Penguins on February 15 because he had been suspended by the team for being drunk the night before and hung over the following morning.

This time, the club and the Lindros family weren't going to let the issue slide.

First, the Flyers announced Lindros had missed two games—the game in question against Pittsburgh as well as a game the next day—due to a sore back injured when he leaped to avoid a check February 13 against Ottawa and landed hard on his back.

"You know where Lindros was the night before that Pittsburgh game?" GM Bob Clarke fumed at reporters. "He was sitting in a hyperbaric oxygen chamber with our trainer [John Worley]."

When WIP announced it would support Carton and his story—he said he was given the information by four sources, including two inside the Flyers' organization—owner Ed Snider filed a libel suit against Carton, WIP, and Infinity Broadcasting, the station's owner. Snider also said he would consider finding a new radio broadcast outlet for his team's games after the contract with WIP expired.

Why sue now and not when the Merlino issue cropped up? Snider said, "Because this is one step too many. They finally went over the ledge. We were willing to give them the benefit of the doubt last time, but we're not willing to do it any longer. We're not going to sit back and take it."

Carl Lindros also said he was contemplating a suit on Eric's behalf against Carton and the station, saying he had evidence to show Eric's whereabouts February 14–15, including a video rental receipt and phone bills that showed Eric making long-distance phone calls from his South Jersey home.

After initially backing Carton, WIP reversed course. They didn't renew his contract in July of that year, and about a year after the suit was filed, the matter was settled out of court. Lindros was given on-air and written apologies, WIP made a donation to a charity of Lindros' choosing, and the station barred hosts and callers from discussing the settlement or the controversy that spawned it.

The great irony of these problems with WIP is that the station wouldn't exist were it not for Snider. The Flyers' chairman helped launch the all-sports format—making WIP the first all-sports radio station in the U.S.—when Spectacor owned the radio station in the mid–1980s. Spectacor sold the station to Infinity in 1988.

85 The Blackshirt Plague

A great malady overtook the Flyers during the 2003–04 season. It was a plague, however, that spread only through one position on the roster—the defensemen. The malady draws its name from the blueliners' black practice jerseys.

There were the usual bumps and bruises, but the real outbreak can be traced to January 17 in Toronto. That night, the Flyers lost a pair of defensemen—Marcus Ragnarsson strained his left rotator cuff, and Eric Desjardins broke his arm on an errant check thrown by teammate Jeremy Roenick.

While Ragnarsson missed only five games, the injury to Desjardins was devastating—he'd need surgery that would sideline him for the rest of the regular season.

Almost instantly, GM Bob Clarke started making phone calls. One went to Carolina, which resulted in Danny Markov coming over for forward Justin Williams on January 20. Another went to the Islanders and brought in Mattias Timander for a draft pick.

At the trade deadline, Clarke added Vladimir Malakhov, and sent out veterans Chris Therien and Eric Weinrich. With Markov, Malakhov, and a healthy Desjardins, Clarke thought he would be okay for the playoffs.

Fate, however, had other ideas. Desjardins, who had played the final three games of the regular season, broke the plate holding his arm together the night before the postseason began. A second surgery was needed, ending his season. Rookie Joni Pitkanen, who had played 71 games in the regular season but was slated to be an extra player in the postseason, was thrust into the pressure cooker in the first round against the New Jersey Devils.

Then Kim Johnsson, who had played 80 games during the regular season and was one of the Flyers' best players in the first round against the Devils, broke his hand in the series-clinching win. He missed the first three games of the second-round series against the Maple Leafs, forcing forward Sami Kapanen to go back to defense in his place.

Johnsson returned for Game 4, and things were okay until Game 6, when Malakhov suffered a concussion on a first-period cheap shot by Darcy Tucker. That forced Kapanen back to defense and nearly cost him his head. As he tried to hold a puck in at the Leafs' blue line in overtime, Tucker smeared him into the glass. Kapanen struggled to his feet and needed help to get back to the bench.

Kapanen recovered in time to play forward for Game 1 of the conference finals against Tampa Bay, but for Game 2 Pitkanen was removed from the lineup—one of the few healthy scratches for the Flyers in their playoff run—and Kapanen moved back to defense. He was forced to stay back there when Ragnarsson missed the final four games with a broken finger.

To this day, Ken Hitchcock believes that if his team had its full corps of defensemen healthy, the outcome against the Lightning would have been different.

"The one thing you can't control is injuries," Hitchcock said. "You can't control that, especially in playoffs. I think that's one of the biggest disappointments in my life as a coach, losing that series, because I felt that our team poured everything into that season, especially that playoff run. We just ran out of bodies in that series against Tampa."

86 Close the Window!

One of the many nice features of the Spectrum was the big windows that allowed fans inside the building to see the great outdoors—well, the parking lot, but it's better than staring at a concrete wall while waiting to hit the bathroom or buy a drink.

Those giant windows don't open—except for March 13, 1993, when one was opened the hard way.

That day, a blizzard dropped a foot of snow on the Delaware Valley. The storm, which was called by some the Storm of the Century, according to weather models stretched from Canada to Central America. However, the Flyers and L.A. Kings were determined to get their game in that afternoon at the Spectrum. About 2,000 hearty fans made their way to South Philadelphia; with so few fans in the stands, those who had tickets for upper-level seats were invited to sit wherever they wanted.

Flyers GM Russ Farwell made light of the weather before the game, saying, "You call this a storm? I'm from Calgary. I had no problem getting in here."

"It was some kind of snow," Rod Brind'Amour recalled. "We all made it to the game, and the most shocking thing was there were that many people in the building…. What I remember most is that many people managed to get to the game. They love the game and weren't going to give up that ticket. If the game was going to be played, they were going to be there."

Fans were having a good ol' time as the game was tied 1–1 late in the first period.

But that's when things got really ugly.

The driving snow and wind gusts blew one time too hard, and one of the giant windows gave way, sending broken glass like shrapnel through the concourse and even as far as the ice. Thankfully, the only injury was some minor cuts suffered by a concession worker.

With the storm showing no signs of letting up, the decision was made to postpone the game.

"We couldn't be sure the building was safe," said Ron Ryan, then the Flyers' chief operating officer.

Brind'Amour said he had no idea what had happened, and at first he couldn't figure out why the game was being called. "We could have kept playing, had no issue for us. I remember saying, 'We're not going to finish this? We got everybody here.' I remember digging out of my house to get there. The players, we all wanted to finish the game, especially them [the Kings]."

Instead, the decision was made to reschedule the game—a Sixers game that night also was postponed—and on April 1, the Kings returned to replay the game.

The Kings won that night 3–1 in a game best remembered for Mark Recchi scoring his 50th goal in the first period.

Oh, and Farwell, who had made a joke of the weather back in March, had some difficulty leaving the Spectrum that day—his car got stuck in the parking lot, and he needed help from coach Bill Dineen to get out.

R.J. Steps Up

Prior to 2008, R.J. Umberger's biggest playoff moment was one he can't really remember. In overtime of Game 1 of the 2006 playoffs, Umberger was bringing the puck out of the Philadelphia end when Buffalo Sabres defenseman Brian Campbell stepped into him with a monstrous open-ice shoulder hit that separated Umberger from the puck and his senses.

The video of Campbell's hit became a YouTube sensation.

When the 2008 Stanley Cup Playoffs started, Umberger was reminded of the hit when the first-round series against Washington started. "They kept showing it throughout the playoffs that year," Umberger said. "I was kind of sick of it."

He took out his anger on the Montreal Canadiens in the second round. Umberger had just one goal in the first round against Washington, but something changed when he got a look at the *blue, blanc et rouge.*

It started in Game 1 when he opened the scoring 13:15 into the game. The Flyers lost that game 4–3 in overtime, but it would be their only loss in the series.

In Game 2, Umberger again scored the game's first goal, and when the Canadiens pulled to within 3–2 early in the third period,

R.J. Umberger had a series for the ages against Montreal in the second round of the 2008 playoffs. (AP Photo/Alan Diaz)

he iced the game by scoring again, smacking a puck out of the air before goalie Carey Price could glove it.

Umberger was credited with the game-winner in a 3–2 win in Game 3, and in Game 4, he opened the scoring in the second period and then closed it with an empty-net goal.

He saved his best game for the series-clincher. He scored twice in Game 5, with both goals tying the game, and he added an assist. He finished a plus–2 with a team-high six shots in 18:30 of ice time.

Not bad for a player who started the playoffs on the fourth line.

In five games, Umberger finished with eight goals and an assist, and a plus–6 rating. Remarkably, all but one of the goals came at even strength, and only one went into an empty net.

"You dream of playing in the playoffs and having a chance to win the Stanley Cup, but you don't dream of it exactly like this," said Umberger. "It's an unbelievable feeling to be here, and to be a big help in the process is gratifying."

Umberger finished that postseason with a team-high 10 goals, and more importantly for him, he provided a whole new set of playoff highlight videos for people to watch.

88 Mike Knuble, Mr. Lucky

Mike Knuble's big break was literally just that.

Knuble had been a fourth-round pick of the Detroit Red Wings in 1991, and with his 6'3", 223-pound body, nice hands, and good hockey sense, he was a well-regarded prospect. But when he turned pro in 1995, he was stuck behind a Hall of Fame–caliber depth chart of forwards.

"He wasn't that far down [the depth chart]," said Steve Yzerman, Detroit's captain, who watched a young Knuble grow. "He was a good young player; we just had a very deep team. He was a good young player with good size and a good shot. For him at the time, he wasn't getting the opportunity to play. He was behind a few good players."

The Wings traded him to the Rangers in 1998, who then shipped him to the Bruins in 2000. Knuble was just treading water in Boston until his break came—courtesy of a broken arm suffered by top-line forward Sergei Samsonov during the 2002–03 season. Coach Robbie Ftorek put Knuble in Samsonov's spot on a line with center Joe Thornton and winger Glen Murray, and something magical happened. Knuble scored 30 goals that season—double his previous career high—and had 21 the following season.

"You need some people to believe in you, and you need some people not to give up on you and see you a little bit different," Knuble said.

The Flyers signed Knuble in the summer of 2004, and when he came back after the lockout, he was asked if he was worried about finding the same magic in Philadelphia that he did in Boston.

"You never know," he said. "You hope lightning strikes twice like that."

Knuble started with rookie center Mike Richards and winger Jon Sim, and that line was the Flyers' most productive during the preseason. One game into the regular season, though, Coach Ken Hitchcock put Knuble on the top line with center Peter Forsberg and left wing Simon Gagne. And suddenly, as good as Knuble had it in Boston, it became even better with the Flyers.

"That really changed my career, really took me to another level, playing with Peter and Simon," Knuble said. "Peter was a passer, and Simon was a great shooter of the puck. We all complemented each other, we all did something a little different, got along off the ice and enjoyed playing together. We all benefited, we all did well."

Knuble did exceptional. In their first season together, he had a career-best 34 goals. The next season Knuble showed he could play

Knuble's Scary Look

Mike Knuble is a big, tough hockey player, but he certainly isn't a scary guy. Except after his 2007 collision with Brendan Shanahan, he was absolutely terrifying. One side of his face was a swollen, grotesque mess. The white of his eye was three-day-bender red, and the area around it looked like an evil rainbow, with shades of black, blue, and yellow. It was too much for some adult media to deal with. For a 4-year-old girl, well, it was a nightmare.

A friend of his daughter's, a frequent guest at the Knuble home, suddenly refused to come over to play with her friend.

"For a close neighbor that was in and out of the house 12 times a day for a year and half before, all of a sudden she sees me like that…she had never seen anything like that," Knuble said. "My kids are used to me being cut up every once in a while, but this was just really tough for her. She wouldn't come to the house for 3–4 weeks."

with anyone, as he had 24 goals in 64 games despite Forsberg being in and out of the lineup and finally traded in February 2007.

It was during that disastrous season, however, that people saw the real Mike Knuble. First, November 29, while the team was plummeting toward the bottom of the standings, Knuble signed a two-year contract extension.

Then on February 17, Knuble and the Rangers' Brendan Shanahan had a terrifying collision that devastated both men.

"The puck was in the corner," Knuble recalled. "He saw a 2-on-1 developing, I saw a pass heading toward the middle and he's trying to build speed for a 2-on-1, and I'm going to try to head toward the puck, and we literally didn't see each other."

The concussive blast left Shanahan unconscious and Knuble with a broken right orbital bone and right cheekbone. The injury was expected to end Knuble's season, and with the Flyers suffering through a disaster of a campaign, no one would have blamed him for going home to recover.

Instead, he returned after a month.

"It's just the way I think," he said. "I feel like I need to come back faster. I don't want my teammates to wonder what I'm doing. It's not my choice to stay out. I feel like I want to be back faster."

That summed up Knuble's time in Philadelphia.

"He's a good guy to have around," GM Paul Holmgren said. "Not only is he a good player, he's a good guy and a quality person."

89 Special Guest in the Box

Not all the fun memories from Flyers hockey involve a member of the Flyers. In fact, one of the more memorable moments involved a hated opponent—Tie Domi.

Domi was a player who would have looked just right in orange and black. Instead, during the Flyers–Maple Leafs rivalry in the late 1990s and early 2000s, Domi wore the black hat on his square head.

On March 29, 2001, one Philadelphia fan took his hatred of Domi a bit too far. While Domi was sitting in the penalty box early in the third period, fans began heckling Domi and throwing things at him.

"A couple fans were riding him in the front row, so Tie squirted water on himself and he squirted a couple fans," said Tom Capaccio, who was working in the visiting penalty box that night. "He said, 'Here, cool off.' They just laughed about it. Then this fellow about three, four rows behind them, he jumps down over the seats. Now he says something to Tie off the cuff, and he [Domi] said, 'Here, you need to cool off, too,' so he squirts him, too. After he squirts him the first time, he lunges at Tie to curse him out, so

Tie says, 'Here, maybe you need more water,' so he takes the lid off the water bottle and hits him with the whole water bottle, so the guy lunges at him one more time to grab him to take a poke at him."

That's when the real show started. As the fan, a 36-year-old concrete worker from Havertown, Pennsylvania, named Chris Falcone, leaned over the protective glass, the barrier snapped, sending broken pieces of glass—and Falcone—into the penalty box.

"That guy was a pretty heavy-set guy, and he hit me and he fell through the glass and came into my work," Domi told reporters after the game. "If he wants to come in there, he will have to pay the price.... I was not going to let anyone take a swing at me, I don't care who it was."

"I remember Tie saying, 'Welcome to our world now,'" Capaccio said. "He got [Falcone's] jacket over his head and handled it like a regular fight."

With his jacket pulled over his head, Falcone just started swinging, first hitting referee Kevin Collins, who had jumped into the box in an attempt to break things up. Domi pulled Falcone off Collins and got in a few punches before Collins restored order. Meanwhile, Capaccio was stuck in the middle of all the action with no place to go.

"I see Kevin Collins, he's rushing in, I said let me get out of the way," Capaccio said. "I'm trying to open the door, get out of the way, let them get to him."

Falcone suffered a cut to his head and received a police citation but nothing else since no one pressed charges. Domi was fined $1,000 by the league for starting the incident by spraying water on the fans and the glass.

Falcone attempted to sue Domi and later offered to fight him in a celebrity boxing match to settle things, but the suit was dismissed and Domi passed on Falcone's offer.

90 Picking Beezer

The summer of 1998 saw possibly the richest crop of goaltending hit the open market. And dissatisfied with the combination of Sean Burke and Ron Hextall, Flyers GM Bob Clarke planned on some major shopping.

On one aisle was Mike Richter, the Abington, Pennsylvania, native who had led the Rangers to the 1994 Stanley Cup and the U.S. to the 1996 World Cup. On another was Curtis Joseph, who had developed into a consistent performer in St. Louis and Edmonton and had shown he could raise his game in the playoffs.

And there was John Vanbiesbrouck, the oldest of the group, but who had some good seasons on some mediocre Rangers teams and had then guided the miracle Panthers to the 1996 Stanley Cup Final.

Vanbiesbrouck had decent career numbers, but in 1997–98 his 18 wins were fewer than Joseph's 29 and Richter's 21, and his 2.87 goals-against average was higher than Richter's 2.66 and Joseph's 2.63.

When free agency opened, however, Clarke opted for Vanbiesbrouck and signed him to a two-year, $7.25 million contract.

There was more to the deal, however, than numbers—at least stats. Clarke had picked Vanbiesbrouck in the 1993 expansion draft that stocked the Panthers' roster, and Vanbiesbrouck had played his best hockey in Florida under Flyers coach Roger Neilson.

"In our position it's preferable to have John Vanbiesbrouck than the other two goaltenders with Roger Neilson coaching the team," Clarke told reporters. "In Florida, John Vanbiesbrouck was absolutely sensational playing for Roger."

It also didn't hurt that Vanbiesbrouck came a bit cheaper than Richter, who re-signed with the Rangers, and Joseph, who jumped to Toronto.

"The numbers thrown at us and the years involved were really going to handcuff us," Clarke said. "Had we felt it was worth it, we would've done it. We just felt Vanbiesbrouck was the right goaltender for our hockey club."

The fans weren't so sure and called the Flyers cheap. Asked at his first press conference if he considered himself a bargain, Vanbiesbrouck said, "I don't consider myself a coat on a rack.... Whether or not I'm the right fit, I'll let people speculate on that. I'm very proud of the fact they want me here."

Vanbiesbrouck responded to the negativity with one of his best seasons. He won 27 games, the third-most of his 20-season career, and posted a personal-best 2.18 GAA as he helped the Flyers to a second-place finish in the Atlantic Division.

The postseason, however, didn't go so well. The Flyers played the Leafs, and Clarke got to suffer some buyer's remorse. The series was tied 2–2, but a sharp-angle backhand shot in overtime by Yanic Perreault got through Vanbiesbrouck in Game 5, and Sergei Berezin's power-play goal with 59 seconds left in a scoreless Game 6 ended the Flyers' season.

Both goalies played well in the series—Vanbiesbrouck had a better GAA, 1.46–1.47—but Joseph allowed one goal in the final two games, while Vanbiesbrouck was exposed on a few bad-angle backhanders that he should have stopped.

Years later, Clarke admits signing Vanbiesbrouck might not have been the best decision.

"The year we signed John Vanbiesbrouck, we could have gotten Curtis Joseph and we should have," Clarke said in *Orange, Black and Blue*. "Beezer was a lot cheaper, but I think if we had taken Joseph he would have given us a much better chance. He was a better goalie."

91 Trading for Tibbetts

The Flyers have made a lot of trades during their 40-plus years. Some have worked well, others not so much.

But there's never been a trade like the one they pulled off on March 17, 2002.

To Pittsburgh went fourth-line forward Kent Manderville, who had spent two years at Cornell. To the Flyers came fourth-line forward Billy Tibbetts, who had spent nearly four years in a Massachusetts prison.

Tibbetts' four years as a guest of the state came for a variety of crimes. In 1994, he pled guilty to sexually assaulting a 15-year-old girl at a party. Later that same year he received a six-month suspended sentence and 18 months of probation for assault and battery on a police officer, disorderly conduct, and intimidating a witness. In 1995, he was convicted of assault and battery with a BB gun and sentenced to 2½ years in prison. That conviction violated the terms of his probation from the previous year's incidents, which meant he would be locked up for a total of nearly 40 months. And one of the conditions of his release was he would have to register as a sex offender.

After four seasons out of hockey, he split the 2000–01 season between the Pittsburgh Penguins and their AHL affiliate. He was on the same path the following season when the Flyers traded for him.

Fans ripped the organization for acquiring a convicted criminal and registered sex offender who had never shown any significant hockey skill other than being able to fight. Despite a rap sheet nearly as long as Santa's Christmas list, GM Bob Clarke spun the trade thusly, "They all said he was a real good person and that he made a mistake 10 years ago."

Team chairman Ed Snider also signed off on the deal. "I checked this extensively. The kid gets in trouble at 17 years old and soon after that he did some stupid things that tough, young kids do. But he's been clean ever since. Obviously there's a PR consideration there, but we don't make hockey moves based on PR."

On his first day as a Flyer, Tibbetts, then 27, told reporters he had grown up. "I was kind of a wild kid. I've tried to grow out of that. I've tried to mature as a man since being released from prison a good two years ago now."

He proved just how much he had really grown during a Flyers tenure that lasted all of nine games. It was long enough, however, for him rack up one assist, 69 penalty minutes, and one two-game suspension for drawing three instigating penalties—two with the Flyers, plus one he came with from Pittsburgh.

After the season, Tibbetts was allowed to leave as a free agent.

As Flyers coach Bill Barber said when the trade was made, "If the piece doesn't fit, we'll remove the piece."

The Drought is Over

Kent Manderville wasn't exactly a big-time scorer when the Flyers got him from the Carolina Hurricanes on March 14, 2000, for Sandy McCarthy, but he did have some experience putting the puck in the net—he had 17 goals in 28 games his final season at Cornell and 16 goals in 63 games with the Canadian National Team in 1991–92.

While that ability never carried over to the NHL, when he came to the Flyers he was in the Sahara of goal droughts—55 games, dating to October 2, 1999. And like the never-ending desert, Manderville's drought reached a ridiculous 122 games until he scored shorthanded against the Penguins on February 7, 2001.

His post-game reaction? "It's just a relief."

92 Brashear's Journey to the NHL

Donald Brashear follows in the long history of Flyers tough guys. But for him, just getting to the NHL—heck, just surviving childhood—seemed to be tougher than any fight he ever had on the ice.

Born in Bedford, Indiana, on January 7, 1972, Donald was the youngest of three children but was too much to handle for his single mother, who sent him to a foster home in Montreal when he was just 5 years old.

Brashear drifted from one foster family to the next over the ensuing few years, living with all-white, all-French-speaking families. It made for a very tough time for the black, English-speaking Brashear.

"I guess not having my own mom and the love of a mom and not having my own things, I remember at one point I became real jealous," Brashear told the *Courier-Post*'s Chuck Gormley. "I was always looking at the other kids as if they were my real brothers and sisters because I never had the chance to grow up with my brother and sister and become friends with them."

Brashear channeled his emotions in the wrong way, fighting daily at school, mostly because of racial teasing at his nearly all-white schools.

"I was a real aggressive person," Brashear said. "Very, very aggressive every step of the way. Growing up in a white environment and hearing racial slurs all the time got me pretty pissed off. Every time it happened, I would just fight."

Brashear eventually landed with the St. Pierre family and found a fit. The St. Pierres encouraged him to ignore the racial taunts and signed him up for basketball, karate, and hockey as better ways for young Donald to channel his aggression.

He quickly learned hockey was the perfect game for him. When he beat his opponent in his first hockey fight, it was an epiphany.

"When I knocked him out, I was like, 'Oooh, I didn't know I could do that,'" Brashear said. "Just like that I became a fighter. That's not what I really wanted to do. It's not how I perceived hockey. I saw hockey as scoring goals, hitting, and skating."

He grew into a hard-hitting, high-scoring defenseman with Longueuil and Verdun in the Quebec Major Junior Hockey League, and in three seasons he had 42 goals, 106 points, and 647 penalty minutes in 197 games.

During his time in junior hockey, he saw his mother for the first time in 12 years. He had exchanged letters with his older sister over the years, and she helped set up the meeting. It wasn't something Brashear really wanted to do, and he didn't come away from it with any great feelings.

"I always wanted to meet her again," Brashear said, "[so] I went to see her. It was pretty tough. It didn't even feel like my mom. I never grew up with her. It was awkward. You're sitting there and you have so many questions, but at the same time I wasn't asking any because I didn't want to start a process where I'm going to start thinking about what really happened."

He did learn a few things about his mother and his early childhood, including the fact that she had 10 children by three different men, all of whom had abused her. Brashear appreciated seeing her again but had little interest in keeping in touch.

"My life was getting better, and I decided it was not going to be a factor in my life at all," he said.

Instead, Brashear focused on his hockey career. He signed with the Montreal Canadiens in the summer of 1992. After five seasons with that organization, he spent six seasons with the Canucks, then came to the Flyers in a December 2001 trade for Jan Hlavac. He quickly became one of the team's most popular players, and in 270 games during four seasons, he had 22 goals, 66 points, and 648 penalty minutes.

None of the 59 fights he had with the Flyers, though, was as impressive as the one that got him to the NHL in the first place.

93 Step Up or Step Out

Simon Gagne always has been regarded as a nice player. A first-round draft pick, he seemed to be a player on the rise with three straight 20-goal seasons to start his career, plus a spot on the gold medal–winning 2002 Canadian Olympic team.

After an injury-plagued 2002–03 season that saw him score just nine goals in 46 games, he returned to form in 2003–04 with 24 goals in 80 games.

The playoffs, though, were a different story. Gagne had just 12 goals in 41 career playoff games heading into the 2004 postseason, and things didn't seem like they would change as Gagne entered the Eastern Conference Finals with just three goals in 11 games.

Gagne was a consistent top-line presence, but he wasn't producing like one offensively. He had a goal in Game 1 of the first-round series against the Devils and a goal in Game 1 of the conference semifinal against the Maple Leafs. He had another goal in Game 4, but on the morning of May 20, 2004, it had been seven games since Gagne had put the puck in the net.

That night, the Flyers had a win-or-go-home Game 6 against the Tampa Bay Lightning. Over breakfast, Gagne was greeted with this headline in the *Philadelphia Inquirer*: "GM Clarke watching and waiting for Gagne to be great."

*Simon Gagne had been an underwhelming playoff performer, but in Game 6
of the 2004 Eastern Conference Finals, he showed just how good he could be.*
(AP Photo/Matt Slocum)

And inside were some choice quotes from GM Bob Clarke:
"We've talked to him—it's all you can do," Clarke told the newspaper's Tim Panaccio. "Simon doesn't play many bad games. He's so smart, and he's got speed. He can either be a player that, when the game is over, you say, 'He didn't help us, he didn't hurt us, he was just good.' Or you can say, 'That damn Gagne was great, wasn't he?' He has to do it on his own. I can only point out to him what his options are."

He then added, "I think Simon hasn't demanded enough out of himself. He never plays poorly. He always plays good. But I think he could play great."

Could Gagne step up and be the player his GM was hoping he could become?

"[Clarke] tells me I am a good player right now, and I have all the tools to be a great player and he wants me to take the next step," Gagne said in the story. "That is something I have to work on. Every night I show up and I try to think that I will be the difference in the game."

That night, he lived up to his words.

After Vincent Lecavalier gave the Lightning an early lead, Gagne answered with a nifty backhand goal midway through the period.

Tampa led into the game's final minutes, but Keith Primeau memorably scored to force overtime. That's when Gagne showed just what kind of player he could be.

"He had a very determined effort that night," Primeau remembered. "The message we delivered to him was, it's the time of year that great players rise to the occasion. It's not so much calling you on the carpet, it's [that] you have this ability to be a difference-maker. Embrace that challenge because we need you to."

As the first overtime period was winding down, Kim Johnsson skated the puck into the Tampa end and pushed it deep, where Jeremy Roenick controlled it. Roenick, Gagne, and Primeau cycled the puck down low, with Roenick taking a pass from Primeau and walking in front. His wraparound attempt on the left post was deflected through the slot to an open Gagne, who scored the game-winner from the right post.

Clarke claims today that no message was being sent. "I would never send a message through the paper," he said. "Not that way. If I have something to talk to Simon about, I would have talked to him."

Regardless of Clarke's intentions, the message got through. "Usually I don't read the papers, but I got calls from back home and read it," Gagne told reporters that night. "It was a message he was trying to tell me. I had to find a way to put the puck in."

94 Rebuilding Effort

There was a lot to dig out from when the Flyers' 2006–07 season ended. GM Paul Holmgren had started the effort months earlier when he traded away Peter Forsberg, Kyle Calder, Alexei Zhitnik, and a second-round draft pick, and got back Scottie Upshall, Ryan Parent, Lasse Kukkonen, Braydon Coburn, and Martin Biron.

Those moves cleared cap space and put the Flyers in good position to shop heavily in what looked to be a rich crop of unrestricted free agents.

"We talked a lot about turning things around quickly," Holmgren said. "We knew we were going to have some money to spend in the summertime, and we knew there would be free agents. On the outside it looked like it would be a pretty good market and there would be players [who] could plug holes in the areas we needed—goaltending and puck-moving, mobile defensemen were on the horizon from all of last year."

Prior to the market opening, however, Holmgren laid the groundwork for what became a masterstroke. Holmgren had good discussions with Nashville GM David Poile in putting together the Forsberg deal that netted Upshall, Parent, and first- and third-round draft picks. Holmgren reached out to Poile again after the Preds were knocked out of the playoffs with another offer. Knowing the club's dire financial straits would make it tough for them to re-sign their top players headed for unrestricted free agency, Holmgren discussed the opportunity for Poile to at least get something for two players in particular—Scott Hartnell and Kimmo Timonen—before they left.

In late June, Holmgren and Poile agreed on a deal that would give the Flyers 48 hours to talk with the two players and try to negotiate new contracts with them.

"We agreed to a timeframe where I could talk to the players themselves, and if we came to an agreement with those players, there would be a return for Nashville," Holmgren said. "If we could only sign Timonen it was a certain price, if we could only sign Hartnell it was a certain price, and if we could sign both it was the first-round pick." The pick was the same one Nashville had given the Flyers for Forsberg months earlier.

Hartnell quickly agreed to a six-year deal, but Timonen was a bit tougher fish to snare.

"As the time was ticking down, I had to call [Poile] for a half-hour extra," Holmgren recalled. "We just had to finalize a few things with Timonen."

It was done, and with that the Flyers had solved two major issues—a scoring winger and a puck-moving defenseman.

That issue settled, Holmgren went into July 1 feeling good. When the free-agent market opened, he immediately made offers to four big-time forwards—Danny Briere, Chris Drury, Scott Gomez, and Ryan Smyth. The hooks were in the water, and Holmgren could only sit back and wait.

"To me, that was more nerve wracking than the trade deadline," Holmgren said. "It was the first time I ever went through that as a manager. You're just waiting. There's nothing you can do but wait."

Holmgren worked off his nervous energy by talking with Edmonton GM Kevin Lowe. The Oilers had been asking about enigmatic defenseman Joni Pitkanen for months and had been offering winger Joffrey Lupul in exchange. Holmgren wasn't interested—until the Oilers increased their offer.

"I had a hard time even talking about moving Joni," Holmgren said, "but when Jason Smith's name came up that morning, I think something just said, 'I better think about that one.'"

He didn't need long to think. Out went Pitkanen along with forward Geoff Sanderson, and in came Smith and Lupul. The Flyers gained a dependable leader with snarl in Smith—who was named captain before the season started—as well as another young scorer in Lupul.

A few hours later, Briere agreed to an eight-year, $52 million contract. The productive day landed the Flyers a top-line center, two young wingers who could score, some snarl for the defense, and locker-room leadership—Smith, Timonen, and Briere all had served as captains of their previous teams.

"That was the first time in our 40 years that we ended with the worst record in the league, and not only was it embarrassing, it was unacceptable, and I certainly hope that the moves that we've made will fix that problem," team chairman Ed Snider told reporters that day.

Playing Through Pain

There's playing through pain, and then there's playing through disabling injuries. Defensemen Jason Smith and Derian Hatcher did the latter during the 2008 playoffs.

Smith played through two separated shoulders while leading the team in the playoffs with 56 hits and 45 blocked shots, while Hatcher blocked out the pain of a broken leg and the need for fluid to be drained from his knee every other day—all while playing more than 21 minutes per game.

"I get shivers thinking about it," GM Paul Holmgren said. "It was almost like we'd have to shoot him [Smith] for him not to play. That was his attitude. I've been around hockey a long time, and I don't know that I've ever seen anything like that."

They certainly did, as the Flyers went from worst in the league to one step from the Stanley Cup Final, powered by their off-season acquisitions.

95 Silent Bob Lets His Play Speak for Him

Goalies generally are a finicky lot—well, there's got to be something a little messed up to volunteer to be the duck in the shooting gallery. And Robert Esche was no exception to that rule.

The Flyers' netminder had all of 30 minutes of postseason experience prior to the 2004 playoffs, so it was only natural to look at Esche as a weak link for the Flyers, especially considering who would be opposing him at the other end of the ice—three-time Stanley Cup champion and future Hall of Famer Martin Brodeur.

It also didn't help that Esche struggled down the stretch; Flyers fans didn't see Esche as a championship-worthy netminder, and the local media was fueling that opinion.

In the days leading to the postseason opener, Esche began to take things personally. Among the passages penned in the local newspapers that he found offensive was this one from the *Philadelphia Inquirer*'s Tim Panaccio: "After looking fit and seaworthy through a strong January and February, Esche has begun to list perilously to the port side over the last week or so. Not coincidentally, the good ship Eschie began taking on water just as it approached the rocky shoals of the postseason."

Also likely bothering Esche was the fact that his coach didn't really have confidence in him.

"The interesting part was we weren't sure what we were doing, but our decision was made easy when Sean [Burke] got hurt one of the last two games," Hitchcock said. "That's why Esche started. Robert went in because Sean gut hurt."

With all that weighing on him, Esche went into shut-down mode, and the usually garrulous goaltender turned into Silent Bob, hiding from the media and ignoring them at every opportunity.

Players and coaches didn't care who Esche did or didn't talk to, however—they only cared about how he played. After preserving a one-goal lead over the final 15-1/2 minutes of Game 1, thereby shutting up all his critics, Esche still refused to speak. Even after his Game 4 shutout, he gave simple, blasé answers after waiting for most reporters to run for their deadlines.

The quieter Esche got, the better he performed. He outplayed Brodeur and the Leafs' Ed Belfour in the second round.

"He was the best goalie in the first two series," Hitchcock said, "and that's what you need to win. Your goalie has to outplay them if you expect to win. You need great goaltending to get you to that next level."

And that's just what Esche gave them. That strong play carried over to the conference finals against the Lightning, and if the Flyers had a few extra healthy bodies, especially on defense, he would have gotten the Flyers to the Stanley Cup Final.

Esche finished the playoffs 11–7 with a 2.32 GAA and .918 save percentage.

Later, Esche admitted that while his Silent Bob act had been necessary for him to focus, it was an act of immaturity.

Prior to the 2006 playoffs, he talked about how he handled things. "With '04, that was a long time ago," he told the *Philadelphia Inquirer*. "I took something to heart that I probably shouldn't have right prior to the playoffs. That was stupid. You can't worry about that stuff."

96 The Next Generation Right Next Door

When the Flyers moved into their new home for the 1996–97 season, it left the Spectrum barren. Tractor pulls, figure skating, concerts, and pro wrestling wasn't enough, so the Flyers searched for an alternative.

They purchased an American Hockey League expansion franchise in December 1995, named it the Phantoms, and housed them at the Spectrum. All the amenities were first-rate, NHL quality, and the minor-league operation was geared toward a Flyers fan base that had grown up watching the Broad Street Bullies maul teams in the Spectrum in the 1970s.

With such characters as Frank "The Animal" Bialowas, team captain John Stevens, and goalie Neil Little, and coached by Bill Barber, the first team finished with a league-best 111 points. And with low prices that appealed to hockey families who couldn't afford Flyers tickets, the Phantoms became an instant hit on and off the ice. The next season, the Phantoms won the AHL title before a sell-out crowd at the Spectrum.

"It was the highlight of my hockey life," Stevens said. "It was a unique situation where we piggybacked on the tradition the Flyers established. You're playing in the old Spectrum, we had a rugged team put together in the old image of the Flyers. We were a tough team, Bill Barber was coaching, Gene Hart was announcing. Our following was unbelievable. We had six or seven sellouts, the building was full. It was as close to being in the big leagues without being there."

"As far as the American League was concerned," Little said, "it was the place to play."

Stevens replaced Barber as coach when Barber moved up to the Flyers, and the Phantoms' success continued. They won another

Calder Cup in 2005, a team that featured future Flyers stars Mike Richards, Jeff Carter, R.J. Umberger, Joni Pitkanen, and Antero Niittymaki. The final game drew an AHL playoff record 20,103 to the Wachovia Center.

Not only did the Phantoms share a sports complex with the Flyers, they also shared the Skate Zone practice site in suburban Voohees, New Jersey. Anytime the Flyers needed a player from the minors, all he had to do was grab his bag, walk through a set of double doors, and he was in the NHL.

"It was definitely a unique situation," Little said. "It worked great for the Flyers organization. It was ideal."

"If you get called up in other places, you're away from your family," Stevens said. "Here if you get called up you never had to leave your home or your day-to-day routine. There was a lot of continuity in your domestic life outside playing hockey."

With the Spectrum marked for demolition, the Phantoms were sold and moved to upstate New York after the 2008–09 season, ending an era of tremendous success on and off the ice.

"The Phantoms organization was so great," Stevens said. "So many young people who loved working there.... It was great hockey, affordable, and a high level of play."

"It was a first-class organization," Little said. "They treated us like gold, really."

It's Not the Stanley Cup, But...

While the Flyers were shut down during the 2004–05 season, their minor-leaguers enjoyed tremendous success that season. The AHL Philadelphia Phantoms won the Calder Cup with a number of future NHL stars, including Mike Richards and Jeff Carter.

The team's ECHL affiliate, the Trenton Titans, also won their first league title.

It marked the first time in hockey history that a club's top minor-league affiliates both won league titles in the same season.

97 Fire It Like Carter

Dial up Jeff Carter highlights on NHL.com or YouTube. Watch his goals. Watch how he shoots the puck. Watch where his stick goes on his backswing, and it's barely past his right skate. It's all hands and wrists.

And it travels harder and faster than many players' slap shots. About the only time Carter lifts his stick above his knee is when he puts it in the stick rack.

"He makes it look easy," said Flyers GM Paul Holmgren, who played 10 NHL seasons.

"You have it or you don't," teammate Mike Richards said. "I've been working on my snapshot since I was young. Some people have it; some people don't."

Carter certainly has it, no question there. He isn't sure—or wouldn't say—just how he came upon his rocket wrist shot. "Just comes naturally," is all he'll reveal.

Like most kids growing up, he fired hundreds of thousands of pucks during summers to develop his shot. So while most folks—NHL players or otherwise—won't ever be able to fire the puck like Carter, we at least can look back at how he grew to have such a tremendous weapon.

Craig Hartsburg coached Carter at the beginning and end of his junior hockey career with the Sault Ste. Marie Greyhounds. When he had the 16-year-old Carter during the 2001–02 season, he could see the foundation of something special.

"He had the same release [he has now]," Hartsburg said. "He's always had that great release. Even as a 16-year-old, he had the great release, but he had the mindset that he was going to shoot the puck. Knowing he could shoot the puck and he was going to do it as

Jeff Carter isn't telling how he developed a wrist shot that's as hard as some slap shots. (AP Photo/H. Rumph Jr.)

much as he could, that's something a lot of young players don't do."

Selflessness is the hallmark of most junior players, but Carter never had that problem. No, Carter's problem back then was that he didn't weigh much more than his hockey stick.

"When you're 16, the biggest thing you have to do is get stronger," Hartsburg said.

As Carter's off-ice work grew, so did the power of his simple shot. It wasn't what it is now, but when Hartsburg returned to the Greyhounds for the 2004–05 season, he saw a marked difference in Carter.

"When he was 16 he was a long, lanky kid with a good release," Hartsburg said. "As a 19-year-old, he became this fast, smart player who had a great release with some velocity."

As Carter has continued to get bigger and stronger—he's now packed 200 pounds on his 6'3" frame—the shot has gotten harder and faster. At the same time, the natural ability remains.

"You can't shoot the puck unless you've got good, strong hands," Hartsburg said. "You can have a good release, but if you don't have strong hands and balance, you're not going to have a good shot. It's a combination of a lot of things, its not just one thing."

So how do you shoot it like Jeff Carter? Shoot thousands of pucks, be big and strong, and be genetically blessed—his father, Jim, was picked in the first round of the 1976 OHL draft.

Okay, so maybe we can't all shoot it like Carter. But we can certainly appreciate how he does it.

98 Dmitri Tertyshny, Gone Far Too Soon

During the summer of 1999, it seemed like Dmitri Tertyshny had everything in the world going for him. He was just 22, and coming off a season in which he had made his NHL debut. He had a young wife, and the couple was expecting their first child. And he was being sent on a retreat with other Flyers prospects to Kelowna, British Columbia, for a skating and conditioning camp.

Tertyshny, a 6'2", 180-pound defenseman, had played 62 games with the Flyers in the 1998–99 season, and it stands to reason that if they're paying to ship him to the other side of North America, the team must view him pretty highly.

On the final day of the camp, however, tragedy struck. Tertyshny and teammates Francis Belanger and Mikhail Chernov rented a boat for a cruise around Okanagan Lake. Belanger hit a wake and Tertyshny, who was sitting at the front of the boat, got tossed overboard, and the boat ran right over top of him. Tertyshny was mangled by the motor's propeller blades; he made it back to the boat, but the blades had, among other horrific damage, sliced both his carotid artery and jugular vein. He bled to death on the boat before it could return to the dock.

Speaking to the *Philadelphia Daily News*, GM Bob Clarke recalled Tertyshny as "a nice, quiet kid who worked hard all the time and always had a grin on his face." He felt Tertyshny had "lots of potential, because he had skill and brains."

Flyers captain Eric Lindros, like several teammates, didn't learn of the accident until they got back from John LeClair's charity golf tournament in Vermont. Lindros told the *Daily News* he was "just shocked," and praised Tertyshny as "a real gamer. Consistent. A terrific person. Kind of quiet, with a great sense of humor. He was outgoing; his wife was just wonderful. He'll certainly be missed.... He always put the team first, always worked extra hard. He was going to be an All-Star one day."

Assistant GM Paul Holmgren had a similar view of Tertyshny, a 1995 sixth-round pick.

"What stood out, right from the start of training camp, was his ability to play defense," Holmgren told reporters. "It's very rare for a young guy to be so smart in his own zone. What we saw last season [62 games, two goals, eight assists, minus–1] was just the tip of the iceberg. He needed to get a little bigger, a little stronger. We thought that would come."

The Flyers paid Polina Tertyshny, Dmitri's widow, his full $350,000 salary for the 1999–2000 season, and a charity game between the Flyers and Phantoms raised more money to take care of any financial burden Polina or her unborn child might have to deal with.

"He was just so young, so full of life," trainer Jim McCrossin told the *Daily News*. "He loved being in Philadelphia. I know a lot of people didn't get a chance to know him. I really wish they had."

Bad Vacation

Bob McCammon didn't coach the Flyers long, but he certainly made an impact—just not in the way you want to make one.

During the 1983–84 season, McCammon devised a plan to keep some of his veteran players—Bobby Clarke and Bill Barber among them—fresh going into the playoffs by sending them on five-day mini-vacations late in the season.

The players weren't particularly fond of being taken out of the lineup, nor did they enjoy the fact that they'd be given precise workout schedules while they were gone.

But like good soldiers, they went along with them.

"We logged a lot of hockey over the years," Barber says today. "Guys were banged up a little bit. At that time he thought it would be best to give the older guys the time-off period before playoffs started."

Barber, though, had been in and out with a knee injury, and was just starting to get comfortable when his vacation orders came. His five days in the Poconos came with a workout aimed to further strengthen his knee.

Part of that workout entailed modified squat thrusts—which generally don't help a player with chronic knee problems.

"I had a little workout problem they got me on, didn't help my cause any," Barber said. That problem involved a sickening crack in his leg that sounded like a gunshot. It was the femur snapping in the knee joint.

Barber missed the rest of the 1983–84 season, and after spending all of the next season rehabbing, he was forced to retire in 1985.

"At the time it was probably a really good idea," Barber said of the vacation plan. "Didn't pay off."

It's little wonder McCammon was let go as coach and GM following the season. But going out the way he did doesn't change Barber's stellar place in the game.

Barber spent his entire 12-year career in orange and black and carved his name into the top of the franchise record books. His 420 goals is the club standard, and he ranks second all-time in points (883), games played (903), power-play goals (104), and short-handed goals (31). His 463 assists ranks third.

The playoff record book reads the same—Barber is tied with Rick MacLeish for the most goals (53), and he's third in assists (55) and points (108). And his 129 playoff games ranks second.

Barber was inducted into the Flyers Hall of Fame in 1989 and the Hockey Hall of Fame in 1990. The club retired the seven-time All-Star's No. 7 on October 11, 1990.

100 Nobody Bakes a Cake as Tasty as...John Stevens?

After the Flyers' miserable 2006–07 season, just reaching the playoffs the following season was icing on the cake.

And the Flyers kept eating their cake during the postseason.

Coaches are renowned for finding whatever they can to motivate their players through word or deed. But turning the locker room into a bakery? Well, that one took the cake—literally.

Prior to the start of the postseason, Stevens convened his players and with him were eggs, milk, and cake mix. Separately, there's not much there; put together the right way, however, it's a pretty tasty treat.

Stevens said the idea developed during the 2004–05 season when he was coaching the Phantoms. The team had won 17

John Stevens came up with a pretty unique and tasty way to motivate his players in the 2008 playoffs. (AP Photo/Gene J. Puskar)

straight games and was cruising along at the top of the AHL, but they didn't have a single scorer in the top 25.

"We were a lot stronger collectively than as individual parts," Stevens said. "We went into the playoffs and used that analogy." To highlight his point, Stevens brought in a dozen eggs, milk, and some cake mix. "Alone," he said, "you don't have much. But if you mix it all together and if you add heat—don't overcook it, just the right amount—it's a symbol of all the ingredients working together more than anything working by itself."

It must have worked, because the Phantoms won the Calder Cup that season.

When Stevens got the Flyers back into the playoffs in 2007–08, he reopened his bakery, starting before the first-round series against the Washington Capitals. "They were really into it," Stevens said of his players.

Once they figured out just what was going on, of course. "Not right away," Danny Briere said, "but we got the picture as he was explaining it."

"I have a friend who's a baker, and he scanned a photo of the team on [the cake], and it almost became a superstition," Stevens said. "Every round we had a new cake."

"Every round it was nice to see our cake," Briere said.

There was worry that there wouldn't be a cake after the first-round win against the Capitals. They won Game 7 in overtime in Washington, and after returning home that night, they were scheduled to jump on a plane the next day for Montreal.

"When we won they were joking with me, they didn't think I could get the cake on the plane to Montreal in time and I did," Stevens said.

They had another cake after beating the Canadiens, but dessert time ended when they lost to the Penguins in the conference finals. Still, for a time the Flyers' private bakery was the best one around.

"Hockey players are very superstitious," Stevens said. "The guys understood the meaning behind it. Plus they got a piece of cake, so they were happy."

Postscript

2009–10: A Season No One Will Forget

The Philadelphia Flyers' 2009–10 season was lots of things, but boring wasn't one of them.

Let's see—they dressed seven goalies, fired the coach, bottomed out in 14th place at Christmas, survived rumors of a divided locker room, watched a waiver-wire pickup backstop a miracle comeback to contention, made the playoffs on a last-day shootout, became the first team in 35 years to win a series they trailed 3–0, and made the Stanley Cup Final.

"It was a real roller-coaster ride this season," GM Paul Holmgren said.

The ups and downs of the regular season came to a head April 11, the last game of the season, against the New York Rangers. It was do-or-die for both teams—the winner played on; the loser went to the golf course.

After 65 minutes, the game went to a shootout. Danny Briere scored on the Flyers' first shot, and then P.A. Parenteau scored on the Rangers' second. The Flyers' third shooter was Claude Giroux, who found a gap between Henrik Lundqvist's pads wide enough to fit a puck through to put the Flyers ahead.

That left it to Brian Boucher to stop the Rangers' Olli Jokinen.

"I was almost sick," said Scott Hartnell, watching from the bench. "It was just incredible. I literally was almost sick."

"You're just like, you can't believe it's April 11 and this might be the end of your season," Simon Gagne said.

"I was just telling myself to be patient and that's it," Boucher said. "I didn't think about the repercussions if I didn't stop it. I knew if I stopped it we won. I didn't think about what happens if I don't stop it."

Jokinen tried to deke Boucher to open his pads, but the goalie stayed up and easily stopped a backhand attempt, igniting the crowd at the sold-out Wachovia Center and sending Boucher into a fist-pumping, one-legged victory jig.

"You're taught as a hockey player not to get like that, especially the goaltender," he said. "You have to play the next night, you have the next game ahead of you. You don't celebrate the victories as much as you might think. You have to get ready for the next shot, the next game. But the enormity of the situation, I think it was called for to have that type of celebration, especially at home."

All the energy built up from the last-day win was like spinach for Popeye, and the Devils, the Flyers' first-round foe, didn't stand a chance. Boucher was astounding, allowing just eight goals in five games, and the Flyers, the last team into the playoffs, was the first to advance to the second round.

However, the victory came at a price. In Game 4, Gagne broke his right big toe blocking a shot, and Jeff Carter, who had missed two weeks just before the end of the regular season with a broken left foot, broke his right foot when he was hit by a Chris Pronger shot. And in Game 5, inspirational forward Ian Laperriere was hit in the face blocking a shot. The gruesome toll was 70 stitches above his right eye, a broken orbital bone, and a brain contusion that likely was season-ending.

Rust from a nine-day layoff before the start of the second round showed early, as the Flyers dropped the first three games of the semifinals to the Boston Bruins. With their season on the line, they got a bonus prior to Game 4—Gagne's return.

The Flyers led late in the third period, but ex-Flyer Mark Recchi tied it with 31.5 seconds left. Rather than starting to pack for the summer, the mood in the locker room during the intermission was surprisingly positive.

"It was pretty good," Gagne said. "It's almost like we said we've got nothing to lose. Nobody expected us to get back. It was positive. We had the feeling it was going to happen."

And it was Gagne who made it happen, scoring from in close at 14:40 to give the Flyers another breath.

The good feelings didn't last long in Game 5. With a 1–0 lead halfway through the game, a pileup in front of the Philadelphia net saw Boucher get bent over backward with his skates caught under the weight of his body as well as that of two other players. The result was a pair of sprained knee ligaments.

Michael Leighton, the waiver-wire savior who had backstopped the Flyers from the cellar to playoff contention, just happened to be dressed for his first game since spraining his ankle in Nashville two months ago. With no warm-up time, he was tossed right into the fire. Moments after entering he stopped Patrice Bergeron on the doorstep, and he held the fort for a 4–0 victory that got the Flyers to 3–2 in the series.

A 4–0 Leighton shutout in Game 6 set the stage for a historic Game 7.

"It's nice, but we haven't done anything yet," Mike Richards said the day before the game. "We've fought all the way back to tie it, but we still need one more win. Obviously, it's a Game 7, and it's going to be tough. We have to be prepared for it."

They certainly didn't look prepared early, as Boston bolted to a 3–0 lead just 14 minutes into the game. After the third goal, Coach Peter Laviolette called time out, gathered his team at the bench, and delivered a Rockne-esque speech.

"The message was, 'Just score one goal,'" Laviolette said. "Get on the board, get in the game. That first goal, for me, was huge."

Moments later, James van Riemsdyk scored his first of the playoffs, and in the second, Scott Hartnell and Briere added goals to tie the game. Gagne put the Flyers ahead in the third, and from there

Leighton did the rest as the Flyers became a most improbable Eastern Conference finalist.

"I was thinking about it all last night, just staring up at the ceiling, just thinking about different plays in different games," Hartnell said the day after. "How we came back—10 minutes into the first period we're down 3-cob. Van Riemsdyk did a great job getting that first goal, gave us a little confidence, only a two-goal deficit going into the second period. I don't know what the play was, but we just kept on building and building and going after them and going after them. It led to a couple goals in the second period. We felt we were going to come out on top of this thing and make history."

The next step in their attempt at history was the Montreal Canadiens, and Leighton never gave them a chance. He shut out the Habs in Games 1 and 2, and after allowing five goals in Game 3, came back with another shutout in Game 4. That game also featured a courageous return by Laperriere, who took a roughing penalty five minutes into the game, had one hit, and blocked a shot.

Montreal scored 59 seconds into Game 5, but Richards scored shorthanded, Arron Asham netted a pretty goal early in the second, and Carter, in his second game back from injury, scored twice as the Flyers cruised to a 4–2 victory and a berth in the Stanley Cup Final for the first time since 1997.

"It's been great so far," Richards said after the game. "Obviously the journey hasn't ended, hopefully we have a little of a Cinderella story here at the end. We have to prepare for Chicago now. It feels good."

The Blackhawks were the clear favorite. The Flyers had the advantage in Game 1, however, taking three one-goal leads, but they blew them all in a 6–5 defeat. Game 2 turned in a 28-second span in the second period, as Marian Hossa and Ben Eager scored in quick form, and all the Flyers could get past Antti Niemi was Gagne's third-period power-play goal.

That game nearly ended in a melee as Pronger scooped up the puck at the end for the second game in a row. When Eager yapped at him, Pronger flipped a towel a fan had thrown onto the ice at Eager, which enraged the Chicago fourth-liner.

Pronger's antics dominated the off-day chatter, allowing his teammates to relax and focus on Games 3 and 4 in Philadelphia.

The Flyers scored first in Game 3; as Hartnell was falling to the ice, he slipped a perfect pass to Briere for a 1–0 lead. Chicago tied the game early in the second, but Hartnell deflected a Pronger shot that crossed the goal line for a split second and needed replay approval.

Chicago scored two straight goals to go ahead, but 20 seconds after Patrick Kane's breakaway goal gave the Hawks a 3–2 third-period lead, Ville Leino scored off a sweet Giroux pass to tie the game and force overtime.

With 5:59 left in extra time, the Flyers caught Chicago on a line change, and Giroux cut through the crease to tip Matt Carle's shot behind Niemi.

"I just had a feeling we were going to win tonight," Briere said. "I remember driving to the rink earlier this afternoon, and I just had this good feeling we're going to win; there was absolutely no way we were going to lose this game."

There was the same kind of feeling in Game 4 as the Flyers stormed to a 4–1 lead in the third period and held on for a 5–3 victory.

Game 5 back in Chicago was a one-sided affair won 7–4 by the Blackhawks. Leighton was pulled after 20 minutes, and Pronger had the worst game of his professional life, being on the ice for six of the goals and in the penalty box for the seventh. However, the big defenseman answered the postgame media deluge with his usual aplomb: "I'm day-to-day with hurt feelings."

Facing the end of their season, Laviolette indignantly responded to a goaltending question for Game 6 by asking who Chicago was going to start. He then added, "Our goaltender has the best numbers in the playoffs. I didn't think I had to announce it."

He meant Leighton, and the numbers certainly backed up Laviolette's choice. At the time Leighton had a playoff-leading 2.34 GAA, three shutouts, and a second-best .918 save percentage—and in home playoff games, he was 6–0 with a 1.48 GAA, .949 save percentage, and two shutouts.

"I'm very confident in Michael," Laviolette said. "He's played excellent in the playoffs. His home numbers are terrific. I'm very confident in Michael."

The players were confident in themselves. All year long, every time they needed to drink from their well of resolve, they found enough to climb off the deck one more time. Being down actually felt like a natural position.

"It's kind of where our season has been," Carle said. "We've been faced with some tough times. If we're going to win this series, this is how we'd do it."

They faced even more adversity when Dustin Byfuglien scored from in front with 3:11 left in the first, but moments later, Hartnell—playing possibly the best game of his NHL career— banged in a puck in the crease to tie the game.

In the second, Hartnell got away with a pick on Duncan Keith, which allowed Leino to pick up a puck floated in by Pronger and send a pass across to Briere, who scored to give the Flyers the lead. It didn't last long as Chicago scored twice to go up 3–2.

One more time, however, the Flyers pulled themselves off the deck. As the final minutes of the game ticked down, Leino split a pair of Chicago players to enter the attacking zone. He cut wide down the right side around Keith and then threw the puck in front, hoping. The wild pass hit Brent Seabrook's skate, bounced off Marian Hossa's shin pad, off Hartnell's stick—nothing but net, and a tie game with 3:59 to play.

Moments later, Jeff Carter had a sensational chance in the slot after a great pass by Richards, but Niemi lunged forward and swatted it away with his blocker with just 1:29 left.

"We had the feeling we were going to win the game and go win Game 7," Gagne said. "That's the way we believed this year. We felt it was made for us to make history. We thought it was going to happen right to the end."

The end nearly came 20 seconds into the extra session. Richards tipped a lazy Keith pass that Niemi pushed into the corner. Richards got to it first and threw it into traffic in front. The bouncing puck got to Giroux, but he couldn't get enough on the shot and Niemi was able to stop it.

That was their last best chance. Moments later, a final blow was landed that not even this most resilient of hockey teams could overcome. Kane carried the puck down the left side and sent a low shot on net from the bottom of the left circle. Leighton couldn't get his pad down in time, and the puck zipped under him and got caught in the padding that runs along the bottom of the net. The Flyers didn't know what to do as the Blackhawks started celebrating, but that's how the losing fighter feels after the knockout punch is landed—dazed and confused.

The Flyers had lost, but they certainly weren't losers. They set a number of records—Leino's 21 points tied an NHL rookie scoring record. Briere's 30 playoff points led the League and set a club record; his 12 points in the Cup Final was one shy of Wayne Gretzky's league standard.

"I'm proud of the guys for giving themselves an opportunity to compete for the Cup," Laviolette said. "It's going to sting for a while. It hurts right now, but they never quit. They are a resilient group. I think we grew through adversity.... And I'm proud of the way they competed and the way they fought."

Did You Know?

Have You Seen My Teeth?

In a November game against the Buffalo Sabres, Ian Laperriere went down to block a Jason Pominville slap shot, only he blocked it with his face, losing four teeth in the process.

Laperriere had a mold taken for seven replacement teeth. The mold was shipped to Los Angeles, and the teeth were returning to New Jersey when the package made a stopover in Louisiana. That's when trouble struck in the form of a criminal Tooth Fairy.

"Jimmy [McCrossin, trainer] tells me, 'I got good and bad news for you. The box is in, but your teeth aren't there. They stole them,'" Laperriere said. "Are you kidding me? A tooth thief. They took seven teeth."

The company that made the teeth shipped Laperriere a new set the next day.

What's Your Number?

What's the most popular number in Flyers history? Without a doubt, it's No. 15, which has been worn by 33 different players, starting with Andre Lacroix in the Flyers first season straight through to Andreas Nodl in 2009–10. Second is No. 21, worn by 29 different Flyers and currently by James van Riemsdyk.

Only three players have worn numbers in the 90s. Rick Tocchet wore No. 92 from 1999–2002, Petr Nedved was No. 93 in 2006–07, and from 2001–04 No. 97 was worn by Jeremy Roenick.

And 13 may be an unlucky number, but not to these Flyers—Dave Michayluk, Claude Lapointe, Glen Metropolit, and Daniel Carcillo.

That's The Wrong Net!

Garry Galley had a nice four-season stint with the Flyers, posting 28 goals and 172 points in 236 games. It could have been 29 goals except for one thing—he scored into his own net.

In a game against the Chicago Blackhawks on December 18, 1993, a delayed penalty was called on the Blackhawks, and as goalie Tommy Soderstrom left his net for an extra attacker, Galley, deep in the Chicago end, tried to pass back to Kevin Dineen at the point. The puck had other ideas, however, as it made a beeline for the Flyers' net.

Soderstrom tried in vain to race back for the puck, but he had no chance.

"As soon as I saw Kevin miss it, I knew it was going in," Galley said. "I was hoping it would hit a snowman or something."

A Rat With Guts

Ken Linseman was known as the Rat because players thought he resembled a hairy rodent, and he was a nasty rat to play against.

But Linseman didn't back down on or off the ice. A case in point was his rookie season in 1978, when the 20-year-old forward began dating a young woman who worked at the Philadelphia Art Museum—Lindy Snider, the 19-year-old daughter of team owner Ed Snider.

It wasn't the most popular move he could have made, but Linseman didn't care.

"We went out one night and her curfew was 11:00 PM," Linseman said in *Orange Black and Blue*. "I brought her home at midnight and the first thing he said to me was 'I'm her father first—not the owner.'"

Linseman was traded to Hartford in 1982 in the Mark Howe deal, and Linseman claims his relationship with the owner's daughter had nothing to do with the trade.

Two Cups, Please

Patrick Thoresen didn't make much of an impact on the Flyers during his short stay in 2007–08, but that time certainly left an impact on him.

Thoresen, a fourth-line forward picked up on waivers from the Edmonton Oilers late in the season, turned into an effective penalty-killer. He was killing a penalty during Game 1 of the Flyers' first-round playoff series against the Washington Capitals when he went down to block a Mike Green shot. Only the puck found the most sensitive part of a male's body. Thoresen was helped off the ice in great pain and taken to a hospital, where it was feared he would need surgery to repair a ruptured testicle.

Thankfully, Thoresen didn't need surgery, and remarkably only missed one game. He was walking a bit bow-legged the next day in the locker room.

Where's That Ref From?

Terry Gregson was one of the most respected referees during his 25 years as an on-ice official. That didn't' stop Ed Snider from calling him out during the 1999 playoffs.

The Maple Leafs led the first round series against the Flyers 3–2 when the series returned to Philadelphia for Game 6. The game was scoreless late in regulation when John LeClair was called for a questionable elbowing penalty by Gregson with 2:54 left. Toronto's Sergei Berezin scored with 59 seconds left, and the Leafs won the series.

An irate Snider lambasted Gregson. "When the official decides a game it's a disgrace," the owner ranted. "Everybody in the stands knows what that guy did. Where's he from, anyway?"

Gregson was from Erie, Ontario, about an hour west of Toronto.

Acknowledgments

There's a scene in the third Indiana Jones movie where Harrison Ford has to close his eyes and believe there's a bridge at the end of a cliff, even though he can't see it. He has to take that leap of faith. I thought of that scene a lot while I was writing my first book on the Philadelphia Flyers, *The Good, The Bad, & The Ugly*, and I had those same visions again as I wrote this book.

Having been a Flyers fan for nearly half the life of the franchise, and having a pretty good handle on its history and important moments, I thought it would be a fairly interesting attempt to come up with a list of things that every Flyers fan should know and do.

But to cap that list at 100? Well, that took some serious work. But I hope you'll find *100 Things Every Flyers Fan Should Know & Do Before They Die* interesting, entertaining, and informative.

I consider myself blessed to be able to work with and around so many smart, giving people who were extremely generous with their time. If you enjoy this book, it's mostly because of these people— Al Hill, Bill Barber, Brian Boucher, Danny Briere, Rod Brind'Amour, Jeff Carter, Bob Clarke, Braydon Coburn, Dave Brown, Dave Leonardi, Don and Mary Ann Saleski, Doug Wilson, Simon Gagne, Scott Hartnell, Holly Cote, Paul Holmgren, Jim Montgomery, Mike Knuble, Ian Laperriere, Peter Laviolette, Neil Little, Lou Nolan, Peter Luukko, Cam Neely, Peter Anson, Peter Stastny (who interrupted a trip to Europe to speak to me), Keith Primeau (who put up with Detroit airport announcements while we spoke), Chris Pronger, Mike Richards, Dave Schultz, John Stevens, Leon Stickle, Chris Therien, Kimmo Timonen, Rick Tocchet, and Steve Yzerman (who took time out from scouting for the Canadian Olympic team to talk).

Also major kudos go to Zack Hill and Joe Siville from the Flyers' always-great public-relations staff; Erik Heasley, communications coordinator for the Pittsburgh Penguins; Mike Sundheim, director of media relations for the Carolina Hurricanes; and Brian Breseman, manager of media relations for the Tampa Bay Lightning.

There also are a number of tremendous resources I used to put this book together, among them *Full Spectrum* by Jay Greenberg; *Walking Together Forever* by Jim Jackson; *Orange, Black and Blue* by Chuck Gormley; *The Broad Street Bullies: The Incredible Story of the Philadelphia Flyers* by Jack Chevalier; *Pelle Lindbergh—Behind The White Mask* by Bill Meltzer and Thomas Tynander. Oh, and one other very special book I take a great deal of pride in: *The Good, The Bad, & The Ugly—The Philadelphia Flyers*.

Also, a tremendous assist goes to one of my favorite websites, and one I am certain all Flyers fans will like once they surf there (feel free to jump to No. 55 to find out).

I also have to send a thanks to my colleagues at NHL.com who allowed me to work on this book, as well as my very understanding wife, Sheryl, and two fabulous kids, Breanna and Logan, who were kind enough to allow Daddy some quiet time over the last few months to get this project finished.

I hope you enjoy reading it as much as I enjoyed writing it.

Sources

1. Bob Clarke

"Bob Clarke, more than any other person…is responsible for the success the Flyers have had through the years," "A Shakeup with Flyers," by Adam Kimelman, *Trenton Times*, 10/23/06, pg. C1.

"As long as I looked after myself, the diabetes wouldn't affect my game…," *The Good, The Bad, & The Ugly*, by Adam Kimelman, pg. 263.

"Through most of it, we were always competitive…," *The Good, The Bad, & The Ugly*, by Adam Kimelman, pg. 267.

"(Poile) said we already have a center, I don't need another center," *The Good, The Bad, & The Ugly*, by Adam Kimelman, pg. 23.

2. Walking Together Forever

"Freddy Shero was the perfect guy for this bunch of characters…," *Walking Together Forever*, by Jim Jackson, pg. 30.

3. Please Hurt 'Em, Hammer

"Davey is the player who gave the Broad Street Bullies their personality…," "Tales of The Hammer," by Bill Fleischmann, November 11, 2009, http://flyers.nhl.com/club/news.htm?id=505674.

"That took something out of New York…," *Full Spectrum*, by Jay Greenburg, pg. 81.

"Dave Schultz helped define Philadelphia Flyers hockey…," "Schultz to Join Flyers Hall of Fame," by Philadelphiaflyers.com, October 13, 2009, http://flyers.nhl.com/club/news.htm?id=502004.

4. Eric Lindros—The Good, the Bad, and the Ugly

"I always got along great with Eric…," *The Good, The Bad, & The Ugly*, by Adam Kimelman, pg. 195.

"The big interference came from his mom and dad…," *The Good, The Bad, & The Ugly*, by Adam Kimelman, pg. 189–90.

"I sat there in the press box…," *The Good, The Bad, & The Ugly*, by Adam Kimelman, pg. 199.

"Once that happened…," *The Good, The Bad, & The Ugly*, by Adam Kimelman, pg. 200.

"Through most of all the messes that went on,…" *The Good, The Bad, & The Ugly*, by Adam Kimelman, pg. 202.

5. Cup-Winning Goal by MacLeish

"Only Rick could have done what he did…," *The Good, The Bad, & The Ugly*, by Adam Kimelman, pg. 37.

"Rick is a victim of his own good success in juniors…," *The Broad Street Bullies*, by Jack Chevalier, pg. 153.

"He was the best player we had in every one of our playoff series…," *Walking Together Forever*, by Jim Jackson, pg. 191.

"It was a simple play, really…," *Walking Together Forever*, by Jim Jackson, pg. 192.

"I never in a million years…," *Walking Together Forever*, by Jim Jackson, pg. 192.

6. Somerdale Elementary School and the Wall of Sorrow

"He scared me…" *Full Spectrum*, by Jay Greenberg, pg. 198.

"The news has shaken all of Philadelphia…," *Behind the White Mask*, by Bill Meltzer and Thomas Tynander, pg. 181.

"It just takes one time to ruin a life," *Behind the White Mask*, by Bill Meltzer and Thomas Tynander, pg. 205.

7. Only the Lord Saved More Than Bernie Parent

"I cried when he left…," *The Good, The Bad, & The Ugly*, by Adam Kimelman, pg. 25.

8. Eric Lindros and How a Trade Is Made

"They would always talk whatever the cash was going to be…," *The Good, The Bad, & The Ugly*, by Adam Kimelman, pg. 173.

"It was the natural thought that the NHL is going to take care of the Rangers…," *The Good, The Bad, & The Ugly*, by Adam Kimelman, pg. 176.

"The Lindros deal changed how deals were made…," *The Good, The Bad, & The Ugly*, by Adam Kimelman, pg. 181.

10. Building the Bullies

"We played St. Louis…," *The Good, The Bad, & The Ugly*, by Adam Kimelman, pg. 22.

"Teams had in those days…," *The Good, The Bad, & The Ugly*, by Adam Kimelman, pg. 22.

"We might not be able to skate with these guys…," *The Good, The Bad, & The Ugly*, by Adam Kimelman, pg. 23.

"He was the strongest guy mentally that I've ever seen," *Walking Together Forever*, by Jim Jackson, pg. 65.

"I didn't know Freddie well…," *Full Spectrum*, by Jay Greenberg, pg. 52.

"That was the great move…," *The Good, The Bad, & The Ugly*, by Adam Kimelman, pg. 30.

11. Ron Hextall, Hockey Pioneer

"Who the hell are you?… Who the hell are you?" *Full Spectrum*, by Jay Greenberg, pg. 213.

"Sitting in between periods…," *The Good, The Bad, & The Ugly*, by Adam Kimelman, pg. 239.

"For a full 80-game schedule…," *The Good, The Bad, & The Ugly*, by Adam Kimelman, pg. 240.

"He was not a lunatic…" *The Good, The Bad, & The Ugly*, by Adam Kimelman, pg. 242.

"His son and my son are the same age…," "Fourth generation of Hextalls on the way?" by John Kreiser, NHL.com, http://www.nhl.com/ice/news.htm?id=372082.

12. They Just Couldn't Lose

"You beat the best team in the league…," *Full Spectrum*, by Jay Greenberg, pg. 143.

"I was brought in to be a little rough on them…," *The Good, The Bad, & The Ugly*, by Adam Kimelman, pg. 227.

"It was around 18 or 19 games…," *The Good, The Bad, & The Ugly*, by Adam Kimelman, pg. 229.

"They can put on the tap when they want to," *Full Spectrum*, by Jay Greenberg, pg. 145.

"There's a tremendous feeling of relief…," *Full Spectrum*, by Jay Greenberg, pg. 147.

"It was a magical ride…," *Full Spectrum*, by Jay Greenberg, pg. 148.

13. Keith the Thief

"We could have gone ahead and kept trying…," *Full Spectrum*, by Jay Greenberg, pg. 50.

"(Leach) has never played with a good team…," *Full Spectrum*, by Jay Greenberg, pg. 87.

14. Listen to the Greatest Duet in Hockey History

"I thought I'd do something to shake things up…," *Full Spectrum*, by Jay Greenberg, pg. 45.

"The cheers went right through me…," *Full Spectrum*, by Jay Greenberg, pg. 74.

15. Trading for Doom

"[Teams] kept throwing their biggest people out there against Eric…," *Full Spectrum*, by Jay Greenberg, pg. 346.

"We thought we could try him with Lindros," *Full Spectrum*, by Jay Greenberg, pg. 347.

"Serge didn't want to trade Schneider…," *Full Spectrum*, by Jay Greenberg, pg. 346.

"Clarkie called and at that point…," Backchecking With Bob Clarke," by Zack Hill, Philadelphiaflyers.com, November 5, 2004, http://flyers.nhl.com/club/news.htm?id=434605.

"Nobody could get the puck off them…," *The Good, The Bad, & The Ugly*, by Adam Kimelman, pg. 183.

16. The Flyers Family

"They've always said the Flyers are like family…," *The Good, The Bad, & The Ugly*, by Adam Kimelman, pg. 272.

"I have a special affection for most players…," *The Good, The Bad, & The Ugly*, by Adam Kimelman, pg. 271.

"These guys earn their living…," *The Good, The Bad, & The Ugly*, by Adam Kimelman, pg. 273.

"Organization-wise, the way the Sniders run the Flyers…," *The Good, The Bad, & The Ugly*, by Adam Kimelman, pg. 273.

"I'm grateful for what he did for me…," *The Good, The Bad, & The Ugly*, by Adam Kimelman, pg. 275.

"We had older players in the minors…," *The Good, The Bad, & The Ugly*, by Adam Kimelman, pg. 276.

17. Classic Memories

"Thornton and I were kind of laughing and smiling…," "Bruins walk off Fenway field a Classic winner," by Shawn P. Roarke, NHL.com, January 1, 2010, http://www.nhl.com/ice/news.htm?id=511978.

18. Barry Ashbee—The Definition of Tough

"I have always said that he taught…," *Walking Together Forever*, by Jim Jackson, pg. 65.

"I sat next to him in the (locker) room...," *Walking Together Forever*, by Jim Jackson, pg. 65.

"It was like a softball was stuck in my eye...," *Full Spectrum*, by Jay Greenberg, pg. 80.

"It took an incurable blood disorder...," *Full Spectrum*, by Jay Greenberg, pg. 119.

"Barry Ashbee's retired number hangs in the rafters...," "Bill Meltzer's Heros Of The Past—Barry Ashbee," by Bill Meltzer, Flyershistory.net, http://www.flyershistory.com/cgi-bin/hero.cgi?hero_2_.

19. Leave Leon Alone

"I pull the picture of that team out...," "*Full Spectrum*, by Jay Greenberg, pg. 148.

"Udvari said the officials felt the puck...," *The Good, The Bad, & The Ugly*, by Adam Kimelman, pg. 110.

"I guess I blew it...," *Full Spectrum*, by Jay Greenberg, pg. 154.

"We got screwed out of two goals...," *The Good, The Bad, & The Ugly*, by Adam Kimelman, pg. 110.

20. Founding the Franchise

"With his reputation as a developer...," *Full Spectrum*, by Jay Greenberg, pg. 3.

"I had never wanted to own...," *Full Spectrum*, by Jay Greenberg, pg. 13.

"There was a blackout in Philadelphia...," *The Good, The Bad, & The Ugly*, by Adam Kimelman, pg. 10.

"How could something like that happen...," *The Good, The Bad, & The Ugly*, by Adam Kimelman, pg. 10.

21. Suprimeau

"He stepped up in the meeting...," "Captain Primeau rises to the occasion," by Adam Kimelman, *Trenton Times*, 5/3/04, pg. C1.

"I kind of directed it with my skate…," *The Good, The Bad, & The Ugly*, by Adam Kimelman, pg. 81.

"I know how many people remember…," *The Good, The Bad, & The Ugly*, by Adam Kimelman, pg. 82.

"Probably the best individual performance…," *The Good, The Bad, & The Ugly*, by Adam Kimelman, pg. 82.

22. Watch the Game That Would Never End

"After the second overtime…," *The Good, The Bad, & The Ugly*, by Adam Kimelman, pg. 257–58.

"Two other times earlier in the game…," *History of the Philadelphia Flyers*, Warner Home Video.

23. The Spectrum

"I'm thinking about how this building…," *Full Spectrum*, by Jay Greenberg, pg. 12.

"The Spectrum—it's dark, the music is intimidating…", "Physical play defines rivalry between Rangers, Flyers," by Adam Kimelman, NHL.com, 2/12/09, http://www.nhl.com/ice/news.htm?id=408951.

24. A Choking Situation

"I saw this team really struggling to break though…," *The Good, The Bad, & The Ugly*, by Adam Kimelman, pg. 113–14.

"I remember very clearly…," *The Good, The Bad, & The Ugly*, by Adam Kimelman, pg. 114–15.

"All of us couldn't believe…," *The Good, The Bad, & The Ugly*, by Adam Kimelman, pg. 115.

"Nobody likes to be called that…," "Murray's Words Stick in Flyers' Throats," by Helene Elliott, *Los Angeles Times*, 6/7/97.

"I don't think anybody liked it…," *The Good, The Bad, & The Ugly*, by Adam Kimelman, pg. 116.

"It was the wrong thing to say…," *The Good, The Bad, & The Ugly*, by Adam Kimelman, pg. 119.

25. Vengeance!
"One or two things can happen, even three…," "Flyers put on notice after Cote suspended 3 games," ESPN.com, 12/3/07, http://sports.espn.go.com/nhl/news/story?id=3139926.

"I think five incidents in the first quarter…," "Flyers put on notice after Cote suspended 3 games," ESPN.com, 12/3/07, http://sports.espn.go.com/nhl/news/story?id=3139926.

26. Flyers Fall to the Fog
"It was dive-bombing the crowd…," "Greatest HockeyLegends. com—Jim Lorentz," http://sabreslegends.blogspot.com/2006/12/jim-lorentz.html.

"It's almost impossible to score from that angle…," Sabres win first Stanley Cup game in fog," by George Walters, 6/13/99, http://www.angelfire.com/nv/Sabresword/bluegold3.html.

"I didn't see Perreault's pass…," Sabres win first Stanley Cup game in fog," by George Walters, 6/13/99, http://www.angelfire.com/nv/Sabresword/bluegold3.html.

27. The Winner from the Kennel
"If I was going to war…," *Walking Together Forever*, by Jim Jackson, pg. 105.

I told Freddy he owed…," *The Good, The Bad, & The Ugly*, by Adam Kimelman, pg. 45.

"You have to be there in the end…," *Full Spectrum*, by Jay Greenberg, pg. 96.

28. Hextall Shoots…He Scores!
"The media kept asking me…," *The Good, The Bad, & The Ugly*, by Adam Kimelman, pg. 240.

"I remember when I scored…," *The Good, The Bad, & The Ugly*, by Adam Kimelman, pg. 241.

"Somebody told me the other day…," *Full Spectrum*, by Jay Greenberg, pg. 248–49.

29. Firing Bob Clarke

"Bob's philosophy is that…," *Full Spectrum*, by Jay Greenberg, pg. 267.

"It was like having two sons…," *The Good, The Bad, & The Ugly*, by Adam Kimelman, pg. 268.

30. Who Named the Legion?

"That was the game where things…," *The Good, The Bad, & The Ugly*, by Adam Kimelman, pg. 182.

31. Jonesy the Lifesaver

"I don't think much of it…," *Jonesy: Put Your Head Down and Skate*, by Keith Jones, pg. 146.

"I come back up and…," *Jonesy: Put Your Head Down and Skate*, by Keith Jones, pg. 146.

"We did everything right…," *The Good, The Bad, & The Ugly*, by Adam Kimelman, pg. 192.

"Did I save his life?" *Jonesy: Put Your Head Down and Skate*, by Keith Jones, pg. 147.

32. Foppa Goes Floppa

"I think starting this year…," "Cup favorite Flyers strong in the right spots," by Adam Kimelman, *Trenton Times*, 8/6/05, pg. C7.

"It can be a burden…," *The Good, The Bad, & The Ugly*, by Adam Kimelman, pg. 129.

"It was literally five, seven…," "Sudden news 'was tough to take,' Gagne said," by Phil Sheridan, *Philadelphia Inquirer*, 2/16/07.

34. Crosby the Flyer Killer
"I don't really know anything different…," "Penguins win in shootout, sweep Flyers," by Adam Kimelman, NHL.com, 12/17/09, http://www.nhl.com/ice/recap.htm?id=2009020504.

35. Chelios' Dirty Hit
"It's too important just to go…," "Montreal thrust into disfavor," by Francis Rosa, *Boston Globe*, 5/3/89.
"You never know what to expect with Hextall," *Full Spectrum*, by Jay Greenberg, pg. 257.
"Did you see what he did to Brian Propp?" *Full Spectrum*, by Jay Greenberg, pg. 257.
"It was just a dirty hit…," *The Good, The Bad, & The Ugly*, by Adam Kimelman, pg. 151.
"Chelios never got anything…," *The Good, The Bad, & The Ugly*, by Adam Kimelman, pg. 152.
"I know it was…," *The Good, The Bad, & The Ugly*, by Adam Kimelman, pg. 149.

36. From the Locker Room to the Board Room
"I still intended to play…," *The Good, The Bad, & The Ugly*, by Adam Kimelman, pg. 265.
"Had I kept playing…," *The Good, The Bad, & The Ugly*, by Adam Kimelman, pg. 266.
"Losing a game tore me apart…," *The Good, The Bad, & The Ugly*, by Adam Kimelman, pg. 268.

37. The Saddest Streak
"I still have a picture of Pelle…," *The Good, The Bad, & The Ugly*, by Adam Kimelman, pg. 148.
"We were poised to go to the Final…," *The Good, The Bad, & The Ugly*, by Adam Kimelman, pg. 145–46.

"There was nothing else to do…," *The Good, The Bad, & The Ugly*, by Adam Kimelman, pg. 146.

"I came back to the bench…," *The Good, The Bad, & The Ugly*, by Adam Kimelman, pg. 147.

"Winning or losing was not a factor…," *Full Spectrum*, by Jay Greenberg, pg. 205.

38. Because Freddy's Philistines Doesn't Have the Same Ring

"We have no Rocket Richards on this team…," *The Broad Street Bullies*, by Jack Chevalier, pg. 7.

"So many clubs are tough only in their own rinks…," *The Broad Street Bullies*, by Jack Chevalier, pg. 7.

40. Big Fish, Small Island

"They had already put him…," *The Good, The Bad, & The Ugly*, by Adam Kimelman, pg. 176.

41. The Passion of the Fans

"About halfway down to the Spectrum…," *Full Spectrum*, by Jay Greenberg, pg. 22.

"One thing we realized is…," *The Good, The Bad, & The Ugly*, by Adam Kimelman, pg. 90.

42. Flyers 4, Communism 1

"We were hated…," *The Good, The Bad, & The Ugly*, by Adam Kimelman, pg. 49.

"It was their all-star team…," *The Good, The Bad, & The Ugly*, by Adam Kimelman, pg. 48–49.

"Once you had the patience…," *The Good, The Bad, & The Ugly*, by Adam Kimelman, pg. 51.

"He basically ran into my elbow…," *The Good, The Bad, & The Ugly*, by Adam Kimelman, pg. 50.

"We went down, and they said…," *The Good, The Bad, & The Ugly*, by Adam Kimelman, pg. 52.

"Probably the only time…," The Good, The Bad, & The Ugly, by Adam Kimelman, pg. 54.

43. J.J. Daigneault's One Shining Moment

"Mark Howe was coming off…," "Flyers get even, 3–2," by Francis Rosa, *Boston Globe*, 5/29/87.

"I looked at the net…," "Flyers get even, 3–2," by Francis Rosa, *Boston Globe*, 5/29/87.

44. When Animals Attack

"I couldn't let him do that to Donny…," *The Broad Street Bullies*, by Jack Chevalier, pg. 48.

"We don't go to jail…," *Walking Together Forever*, by Jim Jackson, pg. 73.

46. The Seven-Year Five-Day Deal

"We were in the best location…," *Full Spectrum*, by Jay Greenberg, pg. 258.

"From the time I had the idea…," *The Good, The Bad, & The Ugly*, by Adam Kimelman, pg. 225.

47. Gene Hart—The Cheap Alternative

"I'd like to think the Flyers…," "Gene Hart, longtime voice of Flyers, dies," by Tim Panaccio, *Philadelphia Inquirer*, 7/15/99, pg. A1.

"Gene was a fabulous…," "Gene Hart, longtime voice of Flyers, dies," by Tim Panaccio, *Philadelphia Inquirer*, 7/15/99, pg. A1.

"A lot of people don't realize…," "Gene Hart, longtime voice of Flyers, dies," by Tim Panaccio, *Philadelphia Inquirer*, 7/15/99, pg. A1.

"I would fall asleep with Flyers games…," *The Good, The Bad, & The Ugly*, by Adam Kimelman, pg. 167.

"Gene Hart taught us the game,"… "Gene Hart remembered by his fans," by Tim Panaccio, *Philadelphia Inquirer*, 7/19/99, pg. D1.

"When you think of Gene Hart…," "Gene Hart remembered by his fans," by Tim Panaccio, *Philadelphia Inquirer*, 7/19/99, pg. D1.

48. The Rifle Shoots 5

"We stayed at a hotel down in Valley Forge…," *Walking Together Forever*, by Jim Jackson, pg. 232.

"I had a couple of beers…," *Walking Together Forever*, by Jim Jackson, pg. 232.

"When we got to the Spectrum…," *Walking Together Forever*, by Jim Jackson, pg. 232.

49. From the Checking Line to the Front Line

"He could play on your fourth line…," "Stafford feels the call to do more," by Adam Kimelman, NHL.com, 11/12/07, http://www.nhl.com/ice/news.htm?id=369729.

"I wanted to play hockey for as long as I could…," "Ben Stafford: From hockey player to Marine," by Sam Carchidi, *Philadelphia Inquirer*, 4/10/09, pg. D5.

"It was something he'd been thinking about…," "Stafford feels the call to do more," by Adam Kimelman, NHL.com, 11/12/07, http://www.nhl.com/ice/news.htm?id=369729.

"A lot of people ask me why…," "Ben Stafford: From hockey player to Marine," by Sam Carchidi, *Philadelphia Inquirer*, 4/10/09, pg. D5.

"He feels strongly about it…," "Stafford feels the call to do more," by Adam Kimelman, NHL.com, 11/12/07, http://www.nhl.com/ice/news.htm?id=369729.

"He's got real strong beliefs…," "Stafford feels the call to do more," by Adam Kimelman, NHL.com, 11/12/07, http://www.nhl.com/ice/news.htm?id=369729.

"He said he was in Iraq…," "Stafford remains an active-duty Marine," by Adam Kimelman, NHL.com, 11/11/09, http://www.nhl.com/ice/news.htm?id=505591.

52. JR Style
"I was standing up against the glass…," "A fun four years," by Chuck Gormley, *Courier-Post*, 10/22/08.

54. Do the Guffaw
"I had the usual crowd of players…," "Guffaw," by Brian Propp, http://www.brianpropp.com/ssp/bio.

"I thought Turk…," "Guffaw," by Brian Propp, http://www.brianpropp.com/ssp/bio.

"I have been very proud…," "Guffaw," by Brian Propp, http://www.brianpropp.com/ssp/bio.

56. More Than a Nice Head of Hair
"You can't have hair like that…," "Hartnell: Big hair, big play," by Adam Kimelman, NHL.com, 3/13/09, http://www.nhl.com/ice/news.htm?id=413690.

57. Bibs, Bonnets, and Soothers
"It was the craziest thing I've ever seen…," *Orange, Black & Blue*, by Chuck Gormley, pg. 143.

"I guess I'll have plenty…," *Orange, Black & Blue*, by Chuck Gormley, pg. 144.

"I probably had as much…," *Orange, Black & Blue*, by Chuck Gormley, pg. 144.

"Those people in Quebec…," *Orange, Black & Blue*, by Chuck Gormley, pg. 143.

58. The Icemen Cometh

"We come to Philadelphia...," *The Good, The Bad, & The Ugly*, by Adam Kimelman, pg. 15.

"It's understandable because...," *The Good, The Bad, & The Ugly*, by Adam Kimelman, pg. 16.

59. King Kong Keenan

"Everybody I talked to said...," *Full Spectrum*, by Jay Greenberg, pg. 182.

"He was magnificent...," *The Good, The Bad, & The Ugly*, by Adam Kimelman, pg. 146.

"Mike did an excellent job," *The Good, The Bad, & The Ugly*, by Adam Kimelman, pg. 146.

60. Know Your Philadelphia Hockey History

"I was young and full of enthusiasm...," *The Philadelphia Flyers— 25 Years of Pride and Tradition*, 1992.

"The attendance this season...," "A Brief History of The American Hockey League & Minor League Pro Hockey in Philadelphia: 1927–2006," by Bruce Cooper, http://www.hockeyscoop.net/ahlphl/.

"The hot colors are always more...," *Full Spectrum*, by Jay Greenberg, pg. 6.

61. Four 50s for Kerr

"My first two years...," *The Good, The Bad, & The Ugly*, by Adam Kimelman, pg. 243.

"It was one of those games...," *The Good, The Bad, & The Ugly*, by Adam Kimelman, pg. 245.

"It's an easy game...," *The Good, The Bad, & The Ugly*, by Adam Kimelman, pg. 243.

"There was no secret...," *The Good, The Bad, & The Ugly*, by Adam Kimelman, pg. 248.

62. Good-Time Roger Comes to Philly

"He was standing right...," *Orange, Black & Blue*, by Chuck
 Gormley, pg. 187

"'We put together this great video...," "Courage under Flyer," by
 Les Bowen, *Philadelphia Daily News*, 12/11/99, pg. 46.

"The character on this team...," "Sabres cut the Flyers to pieces,"
 by Rob Parent, *Philadelphia Inquirer*, 10/18/06.

65. Black Sunday

"A performance like that...," "Snider does some housecleaning in
 Flyers uproar," by Anthony SanFilippo, *Delaware County Daily
 Times*, 10/19/06.

"Homer called me into his office...," *The Good, The Bad, & The
 Ugly*, by Adam Kimelman, pg. 128.

67. Sami Kapanen—Eight Feet of Heart in Five Feet of Body

"He's the toughest little guy in the league...," "Kapanen's guile-
 and-grit move sets up Roenick for game-winner," by Phil
 Sheridan, *Philadelphia Inquirer*, 5/4/04.

68. Nearly Neely

"You're looking at having...," "In another time, Neely may have
 been a Flyer," by Adam Kimelman, NHL.com, 12/2/09,
 http://www.nhl.com/ice/news.htm?id=508286.

"Arthur Griffiths, who was...," "In another time, Neely may have
 been a Flyer," by Adam Kimelman, NHL.com, 12/2/09,
 http://www.nhl.com/ice/news.htm?id=508286.

"It was obviously an extremely...," "In another time, Neely may
 have been a Flyer," by Adam Kimelman, NHL.com, 12/2/09,
 http://www.nhl.com/ice/news.htm?id=508286.

"I was out to dinner...," "In another time, Neely may have been a
 Flyer," by Adam Kimelman, NHL.com, 12/2/09,
 http://www.nhl.com/ice/news.htm?id=508286.

"(It was) that close...," "In another time, Neely may have been a Flyer," by Adam Kimelman, NHL.com, 12/2/09, http://www.nhl.com/ice/news.htm?id=508286.

69. The Forgotten GM
"We just felt he may have...," The Good, The Bad, & The Ugly, by Adam Kimelman, pg. 185.

74. Visit Rexy's
"Those 1967 guys were unique...," "Landmark Rexy's Restaurant Passes the Torch," by Julie Dengler, *The Retrospect*, 7/3/09.

"We grew as a team at Rexy's," "Landmark Rexy's Restaurant Passes the Torch," by Julie Dengler, *The Retrospect*, 7/3/09.

"That day they won...," "Rexy's Bar and Restaurant," NHL.com Productions, http://video.nhl.com/videocenter/console?catid=0&id=18233.

75. A Daily Double at the Draft
"Bob did a good job getting...," "Heading into draft, Flyers have a wealth of choices," by Tim Panaccio, *Philadelphia Inquirer*, 6/19/03.

"He does everything...," "Flyers opt for a Primeau clone," by Tim Panaccio, *Philadelphia Inquirer*, 6/21/03.

77. Eric Desjardins, Mr. Reliable
"Desjardins was what everyone believes...," "Desjardins a class act to the end," by Adam Kimelman, *Trenton Times*, 8/11/06, pg. C4.

"I realize my first couple years...," "Desjardins a class act to the end," by Adam Kimelman, *Trenton Times*, 8/11/06, pg. C4.

"I could feel the bone was moving," *Orange, Black & Blue*, by Chuck Gormley, pg. 283.

"It was important to me to retire as a Flyer…," "Steely demeanor melts away as Desjardins says goodbye," by Ray Parillo, *Philadelphia Inquirer*, 8/11/06.

78. A Love Forever Cherished
"Everybody was family for her…," "Bill Barber honors late wife's last wish," by Bill Lyon, *Philadelphia Inquirer*, 12/10/01.
"I knew we were in trouble…," *Walking Together Forever*, by Jim Jackson, pg. 89.
"We can't even imagine…," "Philadelphia Wins One for Barber," *Washington Post*, 12/9/01.
"We heard that morning…," *The Good, The Bad, & The Ugly*, by Adam Kimelman, pg. 157.
"It's not like this was a sudden thing…," *The Good, The Bad, & The Ugly*, by Adam Kimelman, pg. 158.
"After that (Wild) game…," *The Good, The Bad, & The Ugly*, by Adam Kimelman, pg. 157.

79. Last Call at the Spectrum
"It's a building of history…," "Spectrum memories flood back for Flyers, fans," by Mike G. Morreale, NHL.com, 9/27/08, http://www.nhl.com/ice/news.htm?id=383747.
"Philadelphia is the No. 1…," "Spectrum memories flood back for Flyers, fans," by Mike G. Morreale, NHL.com, 9/27/08, http://www.nhl.com/ice/news.htm?id=383747.
"Even though the Spectrum…," "Spectrum memories flood back for Flyers, fans," by Mike G. Morreale, NHL.com, 9/27/08, http://www.nhl.com/ice/news.htm?id=383747.
"It was really their…," "Flyers say goodbye in style to Spectrum," by Wayne Fish, *Bucks County Courier Times*, 9/28/08.

81. The Comcast-Spectacor Merger

"Ron Rubin was in the shower…," *The Good, The Bad, & The Ugly*, by Adam Kimelman, pg. 205.

"They (the Robertses) are just wonderful…," *The Good, The Bad, & The Ugly*, by Adam Kimelman, pg. 206.

82. The Curse of Sarah Palin

"We were so excited when she talked…," "Sbisa, Palin (Palin!) are in," by Sam Carchidi, Philly.com, 10/8/08, http://www.philly.com/philly/blogs/inqflyersreport/Sbisa_Palin_Palin_are_in.html.

83. Slow-Motion Superstar

"In order to win…," *The Good, The Bad, & The Ugly*, by Adam Kimelman, pg. 253–54.

"We talked about how…," *The Good, The Bad, & The Ugly*, by Adam Kimelman, pg. 254.

"I had such a long way…," *The Good, The Bad, & The Ugly*, by Adam Kimelman, pg. 254.

"It was a killer for them…," *The Good, The Bad, & The Ugly*, by Adam Kimelman, pg. 255.

"Obviously our paths…," *Full Spectrum*, by Jay Greenberg, pg. S21.

84. Flyers vs. WIP

"That was such…," "Fall guy—Lindros beats the heat," by Les Bowen, *Philadelphia Daily News*, 8/20/96, pg. 78.

"You know where Lindros…," "Flyers, WIP host clash on Lindros story," by Tim Panaccio, *Philadelphia Inquirer*, 3/4/97.

"Because this is one step too many…," "WIP-LASH—Fighting back Flyers drop gloves on station," by Les Bowen, *Philadelphia Daily News*, 3/6/97.

86. Close the Window!

"We couldn't be sure the building was safe...," "Storm cripples sports schedule," by Fred Lief, Associated Press, 3/14/93.

89. Special Guest in the Box

"That guy was a pretty...," "Flyers lose; Domi creates ugly scene," by Tim Panaccio, *Philadelphia Inquirer*, 3/29/01.

90. Picking Beezer

"In our position...," "Ex-Ranger, Panther reunited with former coach Neilson," Associated Press, 7/7/98.

"The numbers thrown...," "Ex-Ranger, Panther reunited with former coach Neilson," Associated Press, 7/7/98.

"I don't consider...," *Orange, Black & Blue*, by Chuck Gormley, pg. 194.

91. Trading for Tibbetts

"I checked this extensively...," *Orange, Black & Blue*, by Chuck Gormley, pg. 250.

"I was kind of...," *Orange, Black & Blue*, by Chuck Gormley, pg. 250.

"If the piece...," *Orange, Black & Blue*, by Chuck Gormley, pg. 250.

92. Brashear's Journey to the NHL

"I guess not having...," *Orange, Black & Blue*, by Chuck Gormley, pg. 248.

"I was a real aggressive person...," *Orange, Black & Blue*, by Chuck Gormley, pg. 248.

"When I knocked him out...," *Orange, Black & Blue*, by Chuck Gormley, pg. 249.

"I always wanted...," *Orange, Black & Blue*, by Chuck Gormley, pg. 249.

"My life was getting...," *Orange, Black & Blue*, by Chuck Gormley, pg. 249.

93. Step Up or Step Out

"We've talked to him...," "GM Clarke watching and waiting for Gagne to be great," by Tim Panaccio, *Philadelphia Inquirer*, 5/19/04, pg. D6.

"I think Simon hasn't...," "GM Clarke watching and waiting for Gagne to be great," by Tim Panaccio, *Philadelphia Inquirer*, 5/19/04, pg. D6.

"[Clarke] tells me...," "GM Clarke watching and waiting for Gagne to be great," by Tim Panaccio, *Philadelphia Inquirer*, 5/19/04, pg. D6.

"Usually I don't read...," "Flyers win a thriller to force Game 7," by Tim Panaccio, *Philadelphia Inquirer*, 5/20/04.

94. Rebuilding Effort

"We knew we were going to have...," *The Good, The Bad, & The Ugly*, by Adam Kimelman, pg. 211.

"We agreed to a timeframe...," *The Good, The Bad, & The Ugly*, by Adam Kimelman, pg. 212.

"As the time was...," *The Good, The Bad, & The Ugly*, by Adam Kimelman, pg. 212.

"To me, that was more nerve...," *The Good, The Bad, & The Ugly*, by Adam Kimelman, pg. 213.

"I had a hard time...," *The Good, The Bad, & The Ugly*, by Adam Kimelman, pg. 214.

"That was the first time...," *The Good, The Bad, & The Ugly*, by Adam Kimelman, pg. 214.

"I get shivers thinking...," *The Good, The Bad, & The Ugly*, by Adam Kimelman, pg. 95.

95. Silent Bob Let His Play Speak for Him
"With '04, that was a long time ago...," "Experienced Esche to start in playoffs," by Rob Parent, *Philadelphia Inquirer*, 4/20/06.

98. Dmitri Tertyshny, Gone Far Too Soon
"a nice, quiet kid...," "Tragedy strikes Flyers—Promising young defenseman is killed in boating accident," by Les Bowen, *Philadelphia Daily News*, 7/26/99, pg. 110.

"a real gamer. Consistent," "Tragedy strikes Flyers—Promising young defenseman is killed in boating accident," by Les Bowen, *Philadelphia Daily News*, 7/26/99, pg. 110.

"What stood out...," "Tragedy strikes Flyers—Promising young defenseman is killed in boating accident," by Les Bowen, *Philadelphia Daily News*, 7/26/99, pg. 110.

"He was just so young...," "Tragedy strikes Flyers—Promising young defenseman is killed in boating accident," by Les Bowen, *Philadelphia Daily News*, 7/26/99, pg. 110.